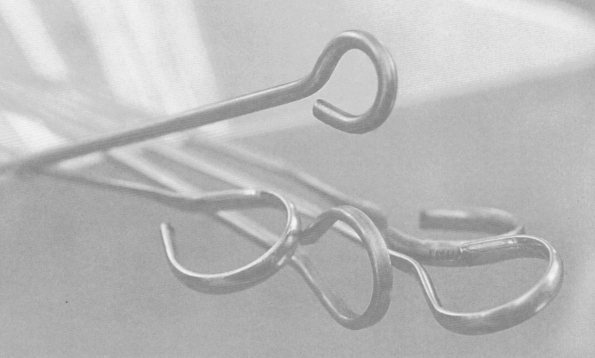

180 BARBECUES

180 BARBECUES

One for every day of the summer: the complete guide to barbecuing and grilling with meal ideas for every occasion shown step-by-step in over 675 photographs

Get the most out of your barbecue with expert tips, techniques and sizzling recipes for grilled and griddled meat, fish, vegetables, sweets and every kind of sauce and accompaniment

LINDA TUBBY
Contributing Editor: JAN CUTLER

LORENZ BOOKS

This edition is published by Lorenz Books

Lorenz Books is an imprint of Anness Publishing Ltd
Hermes House, 88–89 Blackfriars Road, London SE1 8HA
tel. 020 7401 2077; fax 020 7633 9499
www.lorenzbooks.com; www.annesspublishing.com

If you like the images in this book and would like to investigate using
them for publishing, promotions or advertising, please visit our website
www.practicalpictures.com for more information.

© Anness Publishing Ltd 2006

UK agent: The Manning Partnership Ltd, 6 The Old Dairy,
Melcombe Road, Bath BA2 3LR; tel. 01225 478444; fax 01225
478440; sales@manning-partnership.co.uk

UK distributor: Grantham Book Services Ltd, Isaac Newton Way,
Alma Park Industrial Estate, Grantham, Lincs NG31 9SD; tel. 01476
541080; fax 01476 541061; orders@gbs.tbs-ltd.co.uk

North American agent/distributor: National Book Network,
4501 Forbes Boulevard, Suite 200, Lanham, MD 20706;
tel. 301 459 3366; fax 301 429 5746; www.nbnbooks.com

Australian agent/distributor: Pan Macmillan Australia, Level 18, St
Martins Tower, 31 Market St, Sydney, NSW 2000; tel. 1300 135 113;
fax 1300 135 103; customer.service@macmillan.com.au

New Zealand agent/distributor: David Bateman Ltd, 30 Tarndale Grove,
Off Bush Road, Albany, Auckland; tel. (09) 415 7664;
fax (09) 415 8892

A CIP catalogue record for this book is available from the British Library.
Publisher: Joanna Lorenz
Editorial Director: Helen Sudell
Contributing Editor: Jan Cutler
Project Editor: Catherine Stuart
Production Manager: Steve Lang
Cover Design: Lisa Tai
Page Design: Adelle Morris and Diane Pullen

Parts of this edition previously appeared in *Grill: Stylish Food to Sizzle*

10 9 8 7 6 5 4 3 2 1

NOTES
Bracketed terms are intended for American readers.
For all recipes, quantities are given in both metric and imperial measures
and, where appropriate, in standard cups and spoons. Follow one set, but
not a mixture, because they are not interchangeable.
Standard spoon and cup measures are level. 1 tsp = 5ml, 1 tbsp = 15ml,
1 cup = 250ml/8fl oz.
Australian standard tablespoons are 20ml. Australian readers should use
3 tsp in place of 1 tbsp for measuring small quantities of gelatine, flour,
salt, etc.
American pints are 16fl oz/2 cups. American readers should use 20fl oz/
2.5 cups in place of 1 pint when measuring liquids.
The nutritional analysis given for each recipe is calculated per portion (i.e.
serving or item), unless otherwise stated. If the recipe gives a range, such as
Serves 4–6, then the nutritional analysis will be for the smaller portion size,
i.e. 6 servings. Measurements for sodium do not include salt added to taste.
Medium (US large) eggs are used unless otherwise stated.

Main front cover image shows Steak Ciabatta – for recipe, see pages 142–3.

CONTENTS

INTRODUCTION

The sun is shining, the weather is warm and you feel like eating outside – it's got to be a barbecue! There's nothing quite like *al fresco* eating, especially if the food is cooked over an open fire. A barbecue is a comfortable and sociable affair, loved by children and adults alike, and can be just as delightful at home in the garden, in the countryside or on the beach.

TRACING ITS ROOTS

No one is certain where the term "barbecue" actually began, but it probably derived from the Spanish word *barbacoa* in the mid-17th century, which originally meant "a wooden frame on posts". This might have been equipment for smoking meat, and it is believed that the Caribbean Arawak Indians taught the Spanish sailors the art of smoking meat in this way.

Barbecuing has certainly been popular in America for a long time. Even before the Civil War, people in the South were roasting pigs outdoors at social gatherings. In the 1800s the cowboys on the cattle ranches cooked tougher cuts of meat for several hours over an open fire, and during the 19th century churches, political rallies and parties were using the barbecue as a great way to get people together. But, over the years, even in cooler climes,

Above: For tasty little snacks, combine minced meat with herbs and nuts, shape into balls and grill on sticks.

the barbecue has become one of the exciting things about summer – eating outside in the warm air, getting together with other people and being sociable. If you are eating with your family, this is a time when everyone feels involved, even if the kids are playing and running outside while the adults cook and enjoy a long, relaxing drink.

Also, because barbecues come in all sizes and to suit all pockets, there's one for every situation, so you can cook outside even if you have a fairly small space, as long as you are careful not to site the barbecue unsafely, such as under a garage door or a carport or within 3m/10ft of the house.

Of course, cooking over an open fire goes back to our ancestors' distant past and is still an essential part of the culinary cultures of countries all over the world. In hotter climes daily cooking takes place outdoors for a variety of reasons, especially because the heat (as well as the smoke) makes it unbearable to cook inside. Once cooking is transferred outside it takes on a completely different appeal; it becomes sociable and that's probably the most important aspect of the

barbecue today: sitting together and chatting, surrounded by the aroma of food cooking over open coals. And because the juices of barbecued food drip on to the coals and form aromatic smoke, it has that special, taste-bud-tingling smell. Indeed, the smell is so delicious and outdoor eating so enjoyable that it really stimulates the appetite, so when catering for a barbecue, cook plenty!

MODERN BARBECUES

Barbecuing techniques have changed over the years and modern barbecues, too, have made cooking more efficient. The kettle barbecue, for example, has a lid and this helps to create an even temperature for cooking small items of food as well as whole joints. Barbecues can also have spits, and these days if you don't want to get messy with the charcoal you can use a gas or electric barbecue, which are available in a variety of sizes.

DISCOVERING BARBECUE STYLE

A barbecue can be a wonderfully spontaneous affair with food quickly prepared and cooked. Choose straightforward recipes, perhaps using the griddle, for that fast, fun and no-

Below: Use aromatic wood to add a smoky flavour to barbecued foods.

fuss barbecue. Griddles are also ideal for the spontaneous barbecue, and for a first course or for nibbles, so that the main course can be cooked when the heat is less fierce. Tips and techniques like these are explained in the book.

If you are catering for larger numbers of people, careful planning will ensure everything runs smoothly. Have all the preparation completed in advance, and if you are cooking away from home everything will need to be easily transportable to the picnic site. Make sure you have plenty of equipment for carrying raw food (as well as keeping it cool) and clean equipment for the food once cooked. Keep a griddle on hand if possible: it is not just a rainy weather substitute, but an ideal platform for cooking foods when coals are very hot.

BE ADVENTUROUS

Once you learn how versatile your barbecue can be, you can enjoy a world of different flavours and textures. Not only can you cook up your favourite burgers and other quick, simple but nevertheless delicious meals, but you can also create tasty kebabs, steaks, parcels of fish wrapped in leaves or foil, whole chickens and also griddled main courses or side dishes of meat, fish and

Below: Sprigs of herbs can be smoked over coals to add extra flavour.

vegetables – flavoured in all kinds of different ways! And if you want to stay healthy and keep trim for the summer, barbecued food can be made healthy and low in fat simply by replacing oily marinades with low-fat ones and misting with oil, and by using lean meat or fish.

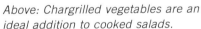

Above: Chargrilled vegetables are an ideal addition to cooked salads.

The other great thing about all the barbecue recipes in this book is that they can be cooked indoors under a grill (broiler), in the oven, or over the hob, so you can try some of the hearty barbecued dishes in the winter too. Of course, you must never cook with a barbecue indoors unless it is specially designed for this purpose, as are some electric barbecues.

Use this book to help you choose the right barbecue for the right occasion, and to understand the basics of setting up and cooking. By trying out the many preparation and cooking techniques given in the following pages, you will become a truly versastile cook, able to experiment with new flavours and to present the food beautifully. Recipes from all over the world are included, and many have helpful tips, ensuring that you have as much information at your fingertips as possible to ensure that your barbecue is a success.

BARBECUE WITH SUCCESS

Barbecue cooking should always be a relaxed affair if possible — in fact, one of its advantages is that you can use the simplest type of equipment to achieve a tasty meal in the garden or on outings to the beach or the country. Even a disposable barbecue or an old grill rack over coals on the beach will do the trick, but if you want to barbecue more often or cook larger cuts of meat or whole birds, it's worth finding out about all the different kinds of barbecues available. This section introduces gas, electric and charcoal barbecues with tips on how best to use them, as well as the additional equipment you will need for easy and safe cooking outdoors. Hints on what food to buy and how to prepare it are also included, as well as techniques and recipes for giving food extra flavour by marinating or adding savoury butters, and how to cut down on fat while keeping food flavoursome. With a useful Basic Timing Guide to help you judge the correct cooking time, you will be ready to try your hand at the fabulous selection of recipes in this book.

CHOOSING YOUR BARBECUE

Barbecuing food gives it a delicious smoky taste, but it is not the charcoal that flavours the food. When the food cooks, melted fat is released and drips on to the heat source. This then gives off smoke, which permeates the food. If you marinate the food first in herbs, or in spice-and-oil combinations, they will contribute to the taste, as will aromatic wood chips or herbs strewn over the charcoals or used in a smoking box in a gas barbecue. So, whether you choose a charcoal or a gas barbecue, you will still achieve fantastic flavours.

The main thing to consider when choosing your barbecue is how often you intend to use it. If you enjoy regular family meals *al fresco* or party barbecues in the garden, a larger one might be the best for you. If, however, you like to act spontaneously and light up a barbecue on the beach or in the countryside you will need something portable – and this smaller kind of barbecue would also be perfect if you plan to use a barbecue at home only occasionally. Remember that the larger barbecues will need to be stored somewhere dry when not in use, so you will most likely need a shed or a corner of the garage to tuck them away into.

CHARCOAL BARBECUES

Among the plethora of barbecues you will find in any showroom are the three basic types of charcoal barbecue. In the first category is the original small and compact Japanese hibachi, which is basically a firebox on short legs with a tray in the base to hold the coals. There are several rungs for the grill rack so that the height can be adjusted over the heat source. On some models, the lid opens to create a windshield at the back; and when closed the unit is easily transported.

Above: You can use an old grill rack to improvize a beach-style barbecue.

Also in this category are small disposable barbecues that contain their own coals set beneath a grill rack. The heat cannot be controlled so you must keep the food moving all the time, and it's best to choose food that cooks quickly for these easily portable all-in-one barbecues that are used just once.

The second category is the brazier type, which normally has an open firebox on a stand with a windshield at the back. The pedestal barbecue, made from stainless steel, comes into this category. It comprises a pillar that is packed with newspaper beneath a rounded bowl containing the coals and grill rack. When the paper is lit the coals soon ignite. Although pedestal barbecues look stylish, beware that the pillar gets very hot indeed and needs to be positioned on a stable and level flameproof surface.

The pot-bellied or barrel type of barbecue also comes into this second category. It is made from cast iron and has air vents to speed up the

Left: The Japanese-style hibachi barbecue is small, inexpensive and ideal for impromptu meals at home, or when planning an outing in the country.

burning process. The coals will be ready to use in 30 minutes. The grill rack can be adjusted to several heights.

The third category of barbecue is the kettle barbecue, which is made from steel and is usually round. It has a lid that can be lifted off and there are air vents in the firebox and the lid. Kettle barbecues come in a range of sizes and the smaller ones are portable. Because this has a lid it is probably the most efficient barbecue, as it enables you to cook either directly over the coals or indirectly (when the coals are pushed to either side of a drip tray) so that larger cuts of meat, such as whole chickens, can be cooked. With the lid on, the food cooks evenly in the all-round heat and this is beneficial for indirect and direct cooking.

GAS AND ELECTRIC BARBECUES

If you are not keen on the hands-on, getting-mucky-with-the-coals type of barbecuing, a gas or electric one will probably be a wise choice, as they are easy to use and efficient. You will still achieve the authentic barbecue aroma and taste with a gas barbecue because

Above: Brazier barbecues are popular with those seeking portable, fold-away barbecues, and their tall legs make them very accessible to the cook.

the juices from the food will drop on to the ceramic rocks, hot lava rocks, or vitreous enamelled steel bars, and once connected up to the gas bottle it is lit by the flick of a switch. You will find small portable ones as well as table-height versions that are easily moved around on their trolley units.

The heat from an electric barbecue comes from heated elements beneath the grill rack. Electric barbecues are probably the easiest to use and heat up almost immediately. The lack of smoke means that they are the only kind of barbecue viable for use inside. Quick and clean, they are, however, usually smaller than gas grills. If you decide on one, you will probably need to use an extension lead for cooking outside.

EQUIPMENT

For ease of cooking and safety, always use long-handled tools. Here are some of the most useful items of equipment.

Brushes

As well as using a long-handled basting brush, you can make herb brushes by tying together twigs of thyme, bay, rosemary or sage to give flavour to foods when basting. Soak them in oil for a few hours beforehand to flavour the oil.

Dishes

Use shallow, non-corrosive dishes and bowls for marinating that are large enough to hold the food in a single layer (do not use aluminium or metal).

Drip trays

When cooking by indirect heat, place a metal drip tray beneath the food to catch the juices. You can use disposable foil trays or make your own from heavy-duty foil.

Foil

Heavy-duty foil is useful for making a lid if your barbecue does not have one. Use regular foil for wrapping food in parcels for cooking. Tented parcels can be used to gently steam many meat, fish and vegetable dishes – and are particularly useful for holding fragile foods, such as those with a filling.

Above: Make tented foil parcels to cook delicate foods such as stuffed vegetables.

Fork

Use a long-handled fork for lifting large pieces of meat from the barbecue.

Gloves or mitts

For the best protection choose oven gloves or mitts with a long sleeve.

Griddle

A cast-iron ridged griddle makes cooking small items of food on the barbecue easier. As it needs high heat, it is best to use it when the coals are first alight (or you can increase the heat if using a gas or electric barbecue).

Grills

Hinged wire grills are available to hold burgers, fish and small items. They come in a range of shapes and make turning easy and keep foods intact that might otherwise easily disintegrate.

Skewers

Keep a range of skewers in different thicknesses and lengths. Choose flat

Below: A large spatula made of wood or metal will help when turning hot foods.

Above: Metal skewers can be used to hold food in place during cooking.

metal skewers, as they will stop food from spinning round as you turn them. Try cocktail sticks (toothpicks) and wooden and bamboo skewers as well, but always soak them in water for 30 minutes before use.

Spatula

A wide spatula or pizza server with a long handle will make turning flat foods, such as steaks, easier.

Tongs

Use one pair of tongs for the coals, another pair for handling raw food and another for cooked food.

Trays

Metal trays are ideal for carrying raw food to the barbecue; keep others handy to hold the cooked food.

Wire brush

Use a stiff wire brush to clean the grill rack after cooking. Scrub clean with lots of hot soapy water.

Below: Use long-handled tongs for arranging hot coals.

SETTING UP YOUR BARBECUE

Have everything ready to hand before you set up the barbecue, including anything you need in case of accidents – see the Safety Tips opposite.

GETTING STARTED

Whichever type of barbecue you are using, always ensure it is stable before lighting it. For a gas barbecue check that you have enough fuel in the gas bottle before lighting up and follow the manufacturer's instructions carefully. Once switched on, the barbecue will be ready to use within about 15 minutes. Ensure that an electric barbecue is safely connected away from any patches of water before switching it on.

Charcoal barbecues are a little more involved to get started; understanding the properties of different types of fuel will help to ensure success. Lumpwood charcoal and charcoal briquettes are the most frequently used types of fuel and are ideal for all uses; wood, however, is less easy to use.

Lumpwood charcoal is usually made from softwood and comes in lumps of varying sizes, although the larger sizes are best. It is easier to ignite than briquettes but tends to burn up faster.

Charcoal briquettes will burn for a long time with the minimum of smell and smoke, although they can take a

Below: If using a fire chimney to light a barbecue, fill it with newspaper first.

little while to ignite. Use charcoal from sustainable managed forests; these will carry the FSC (Forest Stewardship Council) logo.

Self-igniting charcoal is simply lumpwood or briquettes that have been treated with a flammable substance. Always wait until the ignition agent has burnt off before cooking, or the smell may taint the food.

Wood

Hardwoods such as oak, apple, olive and cherry are best for barbecues, as they burn slowly with a pleasant aroma – which should keep everyone in the vicinity happy too. Softwoods, however, burn too fast and give off sparks and smoke. Wood can be used as kindling or to add aroma while cooking, but as it requires more care than charcoal it is best to use for impromptu beach barbecues than garden parties.

Firelighters

Use only odourless barbecue firelighters and push two between the pieces of fuel. Use a long match to light them. If using firelighter fluid or gel, spray or squeeze on to the cold fuel, leave for a few minutes, then light with a long match, following the manufacturer's instructions carefully.

Below: Light the newspaper using a long match and it will soon ignite the charcoal.

Above: Always use a long match or taper to light a barbecue.

Aromatics

Woodchips or herbs can be added to the coals to give a pleasant aroma to the food. Scatter them straight on to the coals during cooking, or place them in the drip tray under the grill rack. Try hickory or oak chips (soaked for 30 minutes before use), which are easily available from barbecue stockists, or scatter twigs of juniper, rosemary, thyme, sage or fennel over the fire. They can also be added to a smoke box for use with a gas barbecue. Put the aromatics into the smoke box and position it to one side on the grill rack.

LIGHTING A CHARCOAL BARBECUE

1 Spread a layer of wood, charcoal or briquettes on the fire grate, about 5cm/2in deep. Pile the fuel into a small pyramid in the centre of the grate. Use newspaper or kindling beneath the pile, if you wish, or push two firelighter sticks into the centre of the pyramid. Alternatively, add barbecue firelighter liquid or gel over the fuel, according to the manufacturer's instructions, then leave for 1 minute.

2 Light with a long match or taper and leave until the coals are covered with a grey ash – this will take about 25 minutes. (While the coals glow red with a light dusting of white or grey ash, thin foods can be seared quickly, and it is ideal for cooking rare steaks, but most other foods require a grey ash.)

3 Use tongs to arrange the coals. For cooking by direct heat spread them evenly over the surface of the fire grate;

for indirect heat either push them all to one side or part them in the centre so that a drip tray will fit into the space.

4 Place the grill rack over the heated coals and leave for about 10 minutes to heat up before adding the food.

USING A FIRE CHIMNEY

A metal, tube-shaped fire chimney is an easy way to get the fire going. Place the chimney on the fire grate and fill with newspaper. Pile coals on to the paper. Light the paper with a long-handled match and leave it to ignite the coals. When the top coals are dusted with ash, lift off the fire chimney. The coals will then spread evenly over the fire grate.

CLEANING

Brush the grill rack with a wire brush after use while still hot – you can turn on a gas barbecue to reheat the rack if necessary. For charcoal barbecues brush the grill rack after use while the coals are still warm. Brush again thoroughly before use when heating up.

Make sure gas and electric barbecues are turned off at the gas tank or power switch. If your barbecue has a lid, close this and close the air vents. If on the beach, make sure that the coals are fully extinguished before leaving.

Below: You can check large joints of meat are cooked by gently piercing them.

STORAGE

You can buy plastic covers to protect charcoal and gas barbecues for short periods when they are not in use. However, note that these covers will provide limited protection if a barbecue is left outside for several months. When storing for winter, make sure that the equipment is thoroughly cleaned and dried before putting away in a dry utility space, such as an attic or cellar.

Controlling the heat

All you need to control the heat on a gas or electric barbecue is to turn the control knob to high, medium-high, medium or low heat – so nothing could be simpler. For charcoal barbecues, however, there are three basic ways to control the heat during cooking:

1 Raise the grill rack for slow cooking; or use the lowest level for searing foods.

2 Push the burning coals apart for a lower heat; or pile them closer together to increase the heat.

3 Open the air vents to make the fire hotter; or close them to lower the temperature.

Safety Tips
• Ensure the barbecue is firmly sited on a level surface before lighting it. Never move a lit barbecue. Position the barbecue away from trees and shrubs, and shelter from the wind.
• Read the manufacturer's instructions for your barbecue, as there are some types that use only one type of fuel.
• Never pour flammable liquid, such as firelighter fluid, on to the lit barbecue.
• Extinguish a flare-up by closing the lid and all vents and turning off a gas barbecue. Use a fire extinguisher or bucket of sand if it gets out of control. Do not use water.
• Keep children and pets away from the fire.
• Keep a first-aid kit handy. Hold burnt skin under cold water immediately.
• Always use long-handled tools and oven gloves or mitts.
• If using a frying pan or griddle over the barbecue, opt for one with a metal hand if possible. If the handle is plastic, it may melt upon prolonged contact with the heat, so wrap it in thick foil before using and reserve use for quick cooking only.
• Keep raw foods cold until ready to cook. A cool bag is useful if you are barbecuing away from home. Keep raw and cooked foods apart.
• Make sure meats are thoroughly cooked with no traces of pink in the juices. Test by piercing the thickest part of the flesh; the juices should run clear.
• Wash your hands after handling raw meats and before touching other foods. Use different utensils for raw and cook foods, and never return cooked food to a plate where raw has been.
• Trim excess fat from meat and avoid using too much oil in marinades as fatty foods can cause dangerous flare-ups.

INGREDIENTS AND FLAVOURINGS

For the tastiest barbecues always buy the freshest ingredients. Most of the food will have to be freshly bought although there are several store cupboard (pantry) essentials and some items can also be frozen.

FRESH FOOD

Although supermarkets now stock most of the fresh foods you need for your main ingredients, remember that quality fishmongers and butchers can provide food of excellent quality. Fish from the fishmonger should be super-fresh and the fishmonger will clean, gut and fillet fish for you. Try to buy organic meat, poultry and vegetables if possible for the best flavour. You might be able to subscribe to a weekly organic vegetable box where you live, and some organic suppliers also provide fruit, dairy produce, meat and poultry.

Barbecued food is an adventure in flavour combinations and so fresh herbs are a must. Supermarkets now stock many different types and you can also

Below: Use pitta bread to serve tasty morsels of cooked food. Pittas can also be grilled over the barbecue.

Above: Choose the freshest ingredients for the best possible flavour.

buy large bunches from greengrocers and market stalls. You could also try growing your own; even a few plants in pots or a window box will be useful and always available to make a fresh and flavoursome difference to your cooking. Some of the more unusual flavours are also suitable for barbecuing. Lavender,

Try something new
Look round ethnic markets to source other rare flavourings such as Australian aniseed myrtle, Mexican oregano, ground sumac and dried pink rose petals. While you're at a market, look out for banana and pandanus leaves, as these make good parcels for cooking food and keeping it moist.

for example, is delightful with chicken and lamb, and combines wonderfully well with summer fruits such as berries.

Salads are ideal and refreshing accompaniments to barbecued food and can be made with a variety of leaves including mizuna and rocket. Look out for bags of mixed leaves from your local organic greengrocer or supermarket. Choose tomatoes ripened on the vine for the fullest flavour; summer is the best time to buy these sumptuous vegetable fruits. Cherry tomatoes are perfect in salads, and a combination of yellow and red will add a dash of colour. Experiment with flavour combinations and textures: crunchy radishes, red

Below: Pandanus and banana leaves make great packets for barbecuing, ensuring the food inside stays moist and succulent.

onions and bright (bell) peppers, crisp beansprouts, succulent cucumbers, peppery watercress, bitter chicory.

To accompany your barbecued food think about using flat breads, such as pitta bread. This book includes some useful bread recipes, but if you are short of time you can buy them fresh. You can warm them quickly on the grill rack and they make great pockets for holding food such as kebabs, and children love them. Corn and wheat tortilla wraps are also useful and can be stored in the freezer, as can ciabatta bread. You could serve a quick starter of slices of ciabatta bread toasted on the grill rack and then topped with warm chopped or cherry tomatoes and olives in oil – cooked using the griddle.

IN THE STORE CUPBOARD

Many barbecued foods are marinated before cooking and usually oil is one of the ingredients, so keep a good quality olive oil in the store cupboard. Chilli oil and other flavoured oils are also handy for flavouring foods and can be made at home: half-fill a jar with washed and dried fresh herbs such as rosemary or basil, or a chilli. Pour over olive oil to cover, then seal the jar and place in a cool, dark place for 3 days. Strain the oil into a clean jar or bottle and discard the herbs or chilli.

Stock a few different types of vinegar as well – wine, cider, balsamic, rice and raspberry are some of the most useful kinds – because these, too, are used in marinades as well as salad dressings. Strong flavourings such as tamari and shoyu are available from health food shops and ethnic stores, which will also sell spice mixes such as ras al hanout.

ADDING FLAVOUR

Herbs, spices and aromatics such as garlic and lemon grass transform food when it is barbecued. The flavourings can be used in stuffings, rubs or glazes during cooking, and there is a stunning variety of flavourful combinations. Unlike marinades, which foods are left to absorb, rubs are added just before cooking and glazes are brushed on towards the end.

Above: Combinations of crushed spices can be applied to meats as a dry rub.

FISH AND SHELLFISH

Whole fish are wonderful filled with flavourings. Try lemon and lime slices combined with one or more of the following – sprigs of parsley, dill or fennel, or bay leaves – packed inside the cleaned fish, as these flavourings will complement the delicate taste of the fish without overpowering it.

Once filled, the fish can be wrapped in foil before barbecuing. If you do this, you could add more flavourings inside the packet. The stronger flavour of basil is particularly suitable for oily fish such as trout or mackerel and goes very well with the lemon slices. Remember to season the cavity after filling it.

MEAT AND POULTRY

As with fish, small birds such as quail or poussins are excellent when stuffed and cooked over the barbecue. Spatchcocking will keep the stuffing in place, or you can wrap them in foil. Another popular method of giving a flavour boost to all meats is to add a dry rub or sticky glaze. The stronger flavours of the food go well with robust aromatics such as crushed cumin seeds or peppercorns, as well as more delicate flavourings. Try the following combinations for meaty main dishes:

Cajun spice rub for steaks and chicken

Mix together 5ml/1 tsp each dried thyme, oregano, finely crushed black peppercorns, salt, crushed cumin seeds and hot paprika. Rub the spice mix into the raw meat or poultry then barbecue until cooked.

Above: Apply the mixture to raw meats using your fingertips, then cook to taste.

Chilli rub for meat and poultry

Mix together 10ml/2 tsp each of chilli flakes, paprika, caster (superfine) sugar, soft light brown sugar, salt and ground black pepper. Add 5ml/1 tsp each of ground cumin and cayenne pepper. Mix well and rub in.

Mildly spiced sticky mustard glaze for chicken, pork and red meat

Mix 45ml/3 tbsp each of Dijon mustard, clear honey and demerara (raw) sugar with 2.5ml/1/2 tsp chilli powder and 1.5ml/1/4 tsp ground cloves. Add salt and ground black pepper. Brush the glaze over the meat about 10 minutes before the end of the cooking time.

Ginger and honey glaze for chicken and pork

Put 2.5cm/1in fresh root ginger (peeled and grated) into a pan with 90ml/6 tbsp clear honey, 30ml/2 tbsp dry sherry and the grated rind and juice of 1 lime. Season, bring to the boil and allow to simmer for 3 minutes. Apply as above.

Below: Herb and chilli oils are easily prepared at home.

MAGICAL MARINADES

Meat, poultry and fish are so often marinated before barbecuing as this gives them a beautiful flavour and succulent moistness. Generally, use oily marinades for dry foods, such as lean meat or white fish, and use wine- or vinegar-based marinades for rich foods with a higher fat content. Many of the lemon and herb combinations used for fish work equally well with chicken. For the best results, marinate overnight.

Fillets of fish can be marinated in olive oil with crushed garlic and the grated rind and juice of a lime. One of the quickest marinades for salmon fillets can be made from a little light olive oil and a split vanilla pod (bean).

How much will you need?
The amount of marinade you will need to prepare depends on the quantity and type of food, but, as a guide, use about 150ml/¼ pint/ ²/₃ cup for about 500g/1¼lb food.

Above: Wherever possible, marinate foods the night before to allow maximum time for flavour to permeate.

Herb marinade to salmon

Roughly chop the leaves of a large handful of fresh herb sprigs, such as chervil, thyme, parsley, sage, chives, rosemary and oregano. Combine with 45ml/3 tbsp olive oil and 30ml/2 tbsp tarragon vinegar. Add 1 crushed garlic clove, 2 chopped spring onions (scallions) or shallots and some ground black pepper. Mix well.

Orange and green peppercorn marinade for fish

Mix together 1 sliced red onion, 2 small oranges (peeled, pith removed and sliced), 90ml/6 tbsp light olive oil and 30ml/2 tbsp each of cider vinegar and drained green peppercorns in brine. Add 30ml/2 tbsp chopped fresh parsley and a pinch of sugar. Mix well. (If you like, you can make the fish into a parcel with foil and lay the orange slices over the top before cooking.)

Ginger and lime marinade for prawns

Mix together 15ml/1 tbsp each of clear honey, light soy sauce and dry sherry. Add 2 crushed garlic cloves, a small piece of fresh root ginger (peeled and finely chopped) and the juice of 1 lime.

Red wine marinade for red meats

Mix 150ml/¼ pint/²/₃ cup red wine, 15ml/1 tbsp olive oil, 15ml/1 tbsp red wine vinegar, 2 crushed garlic cloves, 2 crumbled dried bay leaves and ground black pepper.

How to marinate
Many barbecue recipes include a marinade so it is important to plan ahead to allow for the correct length of marinating time. Not only do marinades flavour foods in all kinds of different ways but they also tenderize meat and keep food moist during cooking. However, be careful of salting food that is marinating, as salt will draw out the natural juices if left to marinate for too long. If you are marinating for longer than 30 minutes, follow this guide:

Adding salt
Meat salt 30 minutes before cooking
Fish and vegetables salt 15 minutes before cooking

1 Place the food for marinating in a wide dish or bowl, preferably large enough to allow it to lie in a single layer. (Always use a non-corrosive dish if the marinade contains wine, vinegar or citrus juices.)

2 Mix together the ingredients for the marinade thoroughly.

3 Pour the marinade over the food and turn the food to coat it evenly.

4 Cover the dish and refrigerate for 30 minutes or up to several hours depending on the recipe. As a rough guide, marinate red meat, poultry and game for 2 hours at room temperature or 24 hours in the refrigerator. Fish, seafood and vegetables should be marinated for between 30 minutes and 2 hours in the refrigerator.

5 Turn the food over occasionally and spoon the marinade over it. If marinating for long periods, add salt as above.

6 Remove the food with a slotted spoon or lift it out using tongs, and drain off and reserve the marinade. Allow the food to come to room temperature before cooking.

7 If basting or brushing the food during cooking, make sure the last coat is added in time for it to be well cooked before the food is served.

Lavender balsamic marinade for lamb

Mix 1 finely chopped shallot with 45ml/3 tbsp chopped fresh lavender and 15ml/1 tbsp balsamic vinegar. Add 30ml/2 tbsp olive oil and 15ml/1 tbsp lemon juice. Mix well. Scatter a few lavender sprigs over the grill rack before cooking the lamb.

Lemon grass and lime marinade for chicken

Finely chop 1 lemon grass stalk. Whisk the grated rind and juice of 1 lime with 45ml/3 tbsp olive oil, black pepper and the lemon grass. This also works well with fish.

Honey citrus marinade for chicken

Mix together the finely grated rind and juice of 1/2 lime, 1/2 lemon and a small orange. Add 45ml/3 tbsp sunflower oil, 30 ml/2 tbsp clear honey, 15ml/1 tbsp soy sauce and 5ml/1 tsp Dijon mustard. Season with pepper. This marinade also works well with fish.

Lemon grass and ginger marinade for chicken or pork

Chop the bulb end of two lemon grass stalks and put them in the bowl of a food processor with 30ml/2 tbsp sliced fresh root ginger, 6 chopped garlic cloves and 4 chopped shallots. Add a bunch chopped coriander (cilantro) roots, 30ml/2 tbsp each Thai fish sauce and light soy sauce, 120ml/4 fl oz/1/2 cup coconut milk and 15ml/1 tbsp palm sugar. Process until smooth.

Using it as a sauce?

Remember: if a marinade is also intended as a sauce, you can either divide the mixture into two and retain one half to marinate or brush over the food while it cooks, or heat up the marinade in a pan until bubbling for at least 1 minute before serving with the cooked food.

Right: Herb butters make an excellent impromptu sauce for baked fish. Simply prepare and chill, and then slice as needed. They will keep for several days.

Above: Black olives combine very well with butter when finely chopped.

BUTTERS

Herb butters are easy to make and, because they are made in advance, are useful for entertaining. Add a knob (pat) of cold herb butter to top cooked fish, meat, poultry or vegetables; as it melts over the surface it creates a delicious sauce. Fresh aromatic herbs such as tarragon and chives combine well with the butter, but other ingredients can be used too – try chopping up a few pitted olives, or some anchovy fillets from the store-cupboard. Then transfer to a piece of clear film (plastic wrap) and form into a roll. Refrigerate until hard. Slice the chilled butter and use to top the hot food. The following combinations should be mixed with 115g/4oz softened butter.

Anchovy butter for white fish

Rinse 6 canned anchovy fillets in cold water and dry on kitchen paper. Rub through a sieve and mix with the butter.

Lemon butter for fish, chicken and vegetables

Mix the grated rind of 1 lemon, and salt and pepper with the butter.

Herb or garlic butter for fish, meat or vegetables

Finely chop 50g/2oz fresh herbs, such as chives, tarragon, parsley, chervil or thyme or crush 3 garlic cloves. Mix with the butter, adding salt and pepper.

Horseradish butter for beef

Pound 60ml/4 tbsp grated horseradish in a pestle and mortar and mix with the butter for a sharp-tasting melt-in-the-mouth sauce.

Mustard butter for meat and fish

Mix 15m/1 tbsp dry English mustard or made Dijon mustard (for a milder flavour) with the butter.

Olive butter for fish, meat, poultry and vegetables

Finely chop 50g/2oz pitted black or green olives and mix with the butter and the grated rind of 1/2 lemon.

BARBECUE TECHNIQUES

Above: By learning a few simple techniques, you can use the barbecue to prepare all kinds of dishes.

A successful impromptu barbecued meal can be put together at the last minute with very little planning. If you are cooking for a crowd or planning something special, however, think through your menu carefully and organize yourself so that everything will run smoothly when you begin cooking. It's worth getting to know some basic preparation techniques and cooking procedures before you start.

GETTING READY

For smooth barbecuing, have everything prepared in advance so that as soon as the coals reach the correct temperature cooking can begin. This means that all chopping, marinating, stuffing and skewering should be done beforehand. Plan your menu thoughtfully; for example, if you are using a griddle it's best to take advantage of the fierce early heat for this, so perhaps your first course could be griddled. During preparation, remember to trim all excess fat away from meat as this can drip on to the coals, causing flare-ups.

Remember to take any foods out of the freezer in good time, but if you are using frozen seafood try to cook it when it has just thawed and before the juices start to flow.

HOW TO GRILL

The key to successful grilling is to give the food just enough time to allow the heat to penetrate fully to the centre without overcooking the outside. To

Preparing whole fish for grilling
Small whole fish are ideal for barbecuing especially oily fish such as mackerel or trout. You can ask your fishmonger to prepare them but it is also very easy to do yourself. A hinged wire basket is ideal for barbecuing fish.

1 Cut off the fins and strip out the gills with scissors.

2 Hold the fish firmly at the tail end and use the back of a small knife blade to remove the scales, scraping towards the head end. Rinse under cold water.

3 Cut a long slit under the fish, from just under the tail to just behind the gills, to open up the belly. Use the knife to push out the entrails and discard them. Rinse the fish in cold water.

4 Rub the inside cavity of the fish with salt and rinse again; then dry with kitchen paper.

achieve that lovely caramelized and smoky taste, sear the food for just a short period first, then continue to cook over a lower heat.

Cooking in foil parcels

Delicate foods or food that are best cooked slowly in their own steam can be cooked in foil parcels and either placed directly into the coals or on the grill rack. You can wrap all kinds of flavourings in the foil parcels, too.

1 Use heavy-duty foil and cut two equal pieces to make a double thickness large enough to wrap each fish or portion of food. Lightly brush the centre of the foil with melted butter or oil.

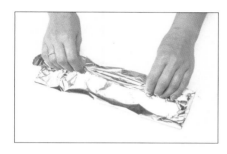

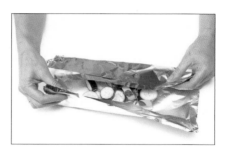

2 Place the food in the centre of the foil and add any flavourings and seasonings. Pull up the edges of the foil on opposite sides, over the food.

3 Make a double fold in the top of the foil so that fish will cook gently in its own steam.

4 Fold over the ends of the foil or twist them together, making sure the parcel is sealed completely, so that the juices cannot escape.

Be careful not leave a large piece of meat over a high heat for too long or all the juices will bubble up to the surface and a thick crust will form and blacken, but the insides will be cold; or if the food is cooked over a longer period it will become tough. Once it is seared and golden, move the food frequently between the cooler and hotter areas of the barbecue for the remainder of the cooking time. A kettle barbecue is useful here, as when you close the lid you will have an all-round heat.

Before serving, rest meat and fish away from the heat. They will continue to cook for a little while and meat needs to rest to allow the juices to settle.

Try to avoid turning food more often if the recipe tells you to turn only once. Also avoid the temptation to prod or cut meat while it is cooking to test if it is done, as this will allow the juices to escape. You can check for doneness by piercing cooked meat with a skewer – the juices should run clear if it is ready. Similarly, avoid pressing down with a spatula while food is cooking as this will also cause moisture to be lost.

COOKING FOOD WITH DIRECT AND INDIRECT HEAT

Although we usually associate barbecued food with individual portions of food such as steaks, burgers, small fish and chicken portions, larger cuts can also be cooked using a barbecue. Some barbecues have a spit attached, which is useful for cooking whole chickens and joints of meat directly over the coals at high heat; otherwise cook them over indirect heat. For charcoal, this is when the coals are moved either to one side of the fire grate or parted in the centre and a drip tray placed in the space. The meat is then positioned over the drip tray. You will need a lid or tented foil for this method. Most small portions of food will be cooked directly over the coals (direct heat). If you are cooking a large joint of food as well as smaller foods, move the coals to one side so that the joint can be positioned to one side and smaller foods can be cooked over the coals. Gas barbecues can be set to cook using indirect heat.

HOW LONG WILL FOOD TAKE TO COOK?

You might prefer beef or lamb to be slightly pink inside but poultry or pork must always be well done until all the juices run clear with no trace of pink. Most foods need to be turned only once but small items such as kebabs or sausages may need to be turned more frequently to ensure even cooking. Foods cooked in foil will take a little longer to cook.

If your barbecue allows you to adjust the height of the grill rack, this is the easiest way to adjust the heat of the coals during cooking. For a medium heat the grill rack should be about 10cm/4in from the coals. Raise the rack to obtain a lower heat or lower it for a higher heat. If you wish to sear food, such as steaks, over a very high heat,

Below: This ornamental barbecue has slats for grilling kebabs on skewers.

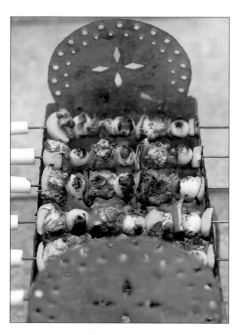

Above: Meat can be cooked on a spit over a high heat and brushed regularly to keep it moist.

move the rack to 4-5cm/1½-2in from the coals and then finish cooking over a lower heat. If the barbecue has air vents you can also use these to control the heat.

The chart to the right gives you a rough guide to the lengths of time that different types of meat, poultry and fish take to cook.

HOW TO KNOW WHEN IT'S DONE

In addition to piercing the thickest part of the meat as advised, you can also test for doneness by pressing it with your finger:
• Rare meat will be soft to the touch.
• Medium meat will be springy.
• Well-cooked meat will be very firm to the touch.

For large joints of meat use a meat thermometer to check the temperature inside: chicken 85°C/185°F; beef 65°C/150°F; lamb 60°C/140°F; pork 75°C/170°F.

USING A GRIDDLE

A ridged, cast-iron griddle is a useful piece of equipment to use on a hot barbecue. It is important that it is searing hot and very dry when the food is first put on it. Test by splashing a few drops of water on to the surface; they should evaporate instantly. Oil the food rather than the pan and, to help reduce the amount of smoke, pat any excess

marinade off with kitchen paper. You need only a very small amount of oil. A good time to use the griddle is while the coals glow red with a light dusting of white or grey ash; this is just before they are ready. Use this time to sear thin foods, remembering to lower the heat when they are done.

LOW-FAT BARBECUES

Although barbecuing is often associated with rich foods – meats in particular – there are many ways to cook healthy foods over hot coals. You just need to give a little thought to preparation, and to substitute one or two of the more indulgent ingredients in a dish.

BASIC TIMING GUIDE

type of food	weight or thickness	heat	cooking time (total)
beef			
steaks	2.5cm/1in	hot	rare: 5 minutes; medium: 8 minutes; well done: 12 minutes
burgers	2cm/³⁄₄in	hot	6–8 minutes
kebabs	2.5cm/1in	hot	5–8 minutes
joints, such as rump or sirloin	1.6kg/3½lb	spit or indirect heat medium	2–3 hours
lamb			
leg steaks	2cm/³⁄₄in	medium	10–15 minutes
chops	2.5cm/1in	medium	10–15 minutes
kebabs	2.5cm/1in	medium	6–15 minutes
butterflied leg	7.5cm/3in	low	rare: 40–45 minutes well done: 1 hour
rolled shoulder	1.6kg/3½lb	spit or indirect heat medium	1¼–1½ hours
pork			
chops	2.5cm/1in	medium	15–18 minutes
kebabs	2.5cm/1in	medium	12–15 minutes
spare ribs		medium	30–40 minutes
sausages	thick	medium	8–10 minutes
joints, such as shoulder or loin	1.6kg/3½lb	spit or indirect heat medium	2–3 hours
chicken			
whole	1.6kg/3½lb	spit or indirect heat medium	1–1¼ hours
quarters, leg or breast		medium	30–35 minutes
breast fillets, boneless		medium	10–15 minutes
drumsticks		medium	25–30 minutes
kebabs		medium	6–10 minutes
poussin, whole	450kg/1lb	spit or indirect heat medium	25–30 minutes
poussin, spatchcocked	450kg/1lb	medium	25–30 minutes
duck			
whole	2.25kg/5lb	spit or indirect heat high	1–1½ hours
half		medium	35–45 minutes
breast fillets, boneless		medium	15–20 minutes
fish			
large, whole	2.25–4.5kg/5–10lb	low/medium	allow 10 minutes per 2.5cm/1in thickness
small, whole	500–900kg/1¼–2lb	hot/medium	12–20 minutes
sardines		hot/medium	4–6 minutes
fish steaks or fillets	2.5cm/1in	medium	6–10 minutes
kebabs	2.5cm/1in	medium	5–8 minutes
large prawns, in shell		medium	6–8 minutes
scallops/mussels, in shell		medium	until open
large prawns, shelled		medium	4–6 minutes
scallops/mussels, shelled or skewered		medium	5–8 minutes
half lobster		low/medium	15–20 minutes

Above: An upside-down wok will fit snugly over a small grill rack as a lid, and helps to seal in moisture.

Which foods?

Red meats such as lamb and beef are particularly high in saturated fats and should either be avoided or kept to a minimum if you are following a low-fat diet or want to reduce the unhealthy fats (saturated fats) in your diet. Chicken and turkey, however, are good low-fat meats, although it is best to remove the skin. This can be done after cooking, if you like.

When choosing fish, look out for white fish such as cod or monkfish for a low-fat diet (although oily fish contains the healthy omega-3 fatty acids so can be included in most healthy diets). Be creative with the vegetable dishes that you barbecue – adding marinated tofu to vegetable kebabs, for example.

Avoiding too much fat

Keep oil to a minimum and use olive oil in preference during marinating and cooking. You can always adjust a recipe to use the minimum amount of olive oil supplemented with citrus juices or fat-free yogurt mixed with spices. Baste the food with the marinade to keep it moist but do this sparingly so that you are not replacing oil that has already dripped away. Brush once just before you turn the food during cooking, and if the food becomes dry, squeeze on a little citrus juice. You can also buy oil misters, which can be useful for adding a fine haze of oil before cooking.

Barbecue fish in its skin to keep it moist; it is easy to skin once cooked.

Above: Stuffing meat and fish with citrus is a great way of adding flavour without fat.

Cook small vegetables, baked potatoes or fish in foil parcels to seal in the moisture and avoid using too much oil.

Use wine, cider, vinegar, lemon or lime juice to provide liquid in place of large amounts of oil. Avoid using large amounts of wine, however, as the alcohol may not burn off sufficiently from quickly cooked foods.

Adding flavour without fat

It's not necessary to use lots of fat to add flavour into your food. Try rubbing herbs, spices and crushed garlic into

skinless chicken before cooking, or pierce the skin and tuck herbs and garlic underneath to trap in their flavour during cooking. Remove the skin before eating. Try prepared mustard marinades to spread over skinless chicken breasts to trap in moisture and add piquancy. Use finely chopped shallots, onions or spring onions for a pronounced flavour in marinades.

Brighten up the taste buds by accompanying your barbecued food with a refreshing salsa or relish made from finely chopped fruit or vegetables, spring onions and chopped fresh herbs. These are also delicious tucked into pitta bread kebabs. Salads with light dressings and fat-free dips also taste great with barbecued food, and a pile of wholemeal rolls or pitta breads make a healthy, substantial accompaniment, and are, of course, useful for soaking up juices. Remember to choose low-fat yogurt, fromage frais or crème fraîche for your marinades or dips – they will taste just as delicioius as their full-fat counterparts and are guilt-free!

Below: Use the timing guide opposite to cook lean cuts of meat according to your preference.

APPETIZERS AND LIGHT BITES

As soon as the barbecue is set alight, appetites awaken and everyone gets ready to enjoy some exceptionally flavourful food. So don't keep those hungry people waiting — whip up some exciting and adventurous nibbles and appetizers. Many of the recipes in this chapter use the griddle, which can be placed over coals that are too hot for cooking most foods direct on the grill rack, and is therefore ideal for use during the first flush of heat from the barbecue. You will be surprised at the variety of foods that you can cook on the barbecue, from mini pizzas and griddled corn cakes to hot avocado halves and tender morsels of meat mounted on sticks, plus quickly cooked shellfish that needs hardly any preparation. And remember that many of these light bites can also be included on the side as part of a main course, or are simply perfect as party food.

CORN TOSTADITAS WITH SALSA

THIS IS JUST THE RIGHT SNACK OR APPETIZER TO COOK WHEN THE COALS ARE VERY HOT, AS IT USES A GRIDDLE. THE SALSA AND GUACAMOLE ARE QUICK TO PREPARE AND TASTE WONDERFUL WITH THE STRIPY TOSTADITAS. MAKE SURE THE GRIDDLE HAS HEATED UP WELL BEFORE YOU ADD THE TOSTADITAS.

SERVES SIX

INGREDIENTS
   30ml/2 tbsp chipotle or
      other chilli oil
   15ml/1 tbsp sunflower oil
   8 yellow corn tortillas, about
      300g/11oz total weight
For the salsa
   4 tomatoes
   30ml/2 tbsp chopped fresh basil
   juice of ½ lime
   20ml/4 tsp good quality sweet
      chilli sauce
   1 small red onion, finely chopped
      (optional)
   salt and ground black pepper
For the guacamole
   4 avocados
   juice of ½ lime
   1 fresh fat mild chilli, seeded and
      finely chopped
   salt and ground black pepper

1 Make the salsa 1 or 2 hours ahead if possible, to allow the flavours to blend. Cut the tomatoes in half, remove the cores and scoop out most of the seeds. Dice the flesh. Add the chopped basil, lime juice and sweet chilli sauce. Stir in the onion, if using, then add salt and pepper to taste.

2 To make the guacamole, cut the avocados in half, prize out the stones (pits), then scoop the flesh into a bowl. Add the lime juice, chopped chilli and seasoning. Mash with a fork to a fairly rough texture. Prepare the barbecue.

3 Mix the chilli and sunflower oils together. Stack the tortillas on a board. Lift the first tortilla off the stack and brush it lightly with the oil mixture. Turn it over and place it on the board, then brush the top with oil. Repeat with the other tortillas to produce a new stack.

4 Slice this stack of tortillas diagonally to produce six fat triangles. Heat the griddle on the grill rack over hot coals. Peel off a few tostaditas to griddle for 30 seconds on each side, pressing each one down lightly into the ridges.

5 Transfer the tostaditas to a bowl, so that they are supported by its sides. As they cool, they will shape themselves to the curve of the bowl. Serve with the salsa and guacamole.

Energy 334kcal/1396kJ; Protein 5.6g; Carbohydrate 36.8g, of which sugars 6.3g; Fat 19.1g, of which saturates 3.6g; Cholesterol 0mg; Calcium 71mg; Fibre 4.4g; Sodium 313mg.

CROSTINI

THIS IS A GREAT WAY TO KEEP HUNGER PANGS AT BAY WHILE YOU WAIT FOR THE MAIN COURSE. AS SOON AS THE BARBECUE IS READY, SIMPLY GRILL THE SLICED BREAD, HEAP ON THE SAUCE AND DRIZZLE OVER PLENTY OF GOOD EXTRA VIRGIN OLIVE OIL.

SERVES SIX

INGREDIENTS
  2 sfilatino (Italian bread sticks),
    sliced lengthways into 3 pieces
  1 garlic clove, cut in half
  leaves from 4 fresh oregano sprigs
  18 Kalamata olives, slivered off
    their pits
  extra virgin olive oil, for drizzling
  ground black pepper
For the aromatic tomatoes
  800g/1¾lb ripe plum tomatoes
  30ml/2 tbsp extra virgin olive oil
  2 garlic cloves, crushed to a paste
    with a pinch of salt
  1 small piece of dried chilli, seeds
    removed, finely chopped

VARIATION
Baguettes or ciabatta bread, cut diagonally to give long slices, will work just as well as sfilatino.

1 Prepare the barbecue. To make the aromatic tomatoes, plunge the tomatoes into boiling water for 30 seconds, then refresh in cold water. Peel away the skins, remove the seeds and core and roughly chop the flesh. Mix the oil and crushed garlic in a large frying pan.

2 Place on the stove over a high heat. Once the garlic starts to sizzle, add the tomatoes and the chilli; do not let the garlic burn. Cook for 2 minutes. The aim is to evaporate the liquid rather than pulp the tomatoes, which should keep their shape.

3 Toast the bread on both sides either by laying it on the grill rack or by using a griddle. If you use the griddle, press the bread down with a spatula to produce the attractive stripes. Generously rub each slice with the cut side of a piece of garlic.

4 Roughly chop all but a few of the oregano leaves and mix them into the tomato sauce. Pile the mixture on to the toasted sfilatino. Scatter over the whole oregano leaves and the olive slivers. Sprinkle with plenty of pepper, drizzle with lots of olive oil and serve at once.

Energy 261kcal/1103kJ; Protein 7.8g; Carbohydrate 38.8g, of which sugars 6.2g; Fat 9.4g, of which saturates 1.4g; Cholesterol 0mg; Calcium 95mg; Fibre 3.1g; Sodium 558mg.

CORN GRIDDLE CAKES

KNOWN AS AREPAS, THESE GRIDDLE CAKES ARE A STAPLE BREAD IN SEVERAL LATIN AMERICAN COUNTRIES. THEY ARE DELICIOUS FILLED WITH SOFT WHITE CHEESE, AS IN THIS RECIPE, OR SIMPLY EATEN PLAIN AS AN ACCOMPANIMENT. WITH THEIR CRISP CRUST AND CHEWY INTERIOR, AREPAS MAKE AN UNUSUAL AND TASTY SNACK OR ACCOMPANIMENT TO A BARBECUE MEAL.

MAKES FIFTEEN

INGREDIENTS
- 200g/7oz/1¾ cups *masarepa* (or *masa harina*) (see Cook's Tip)
- 2.5ml/½ tsp salt
- 300ml/½ pint/1¼ cups water
- 15ml/1 tbsp oil
- 200g/7oz fresh white cheese, such as queso fresco or mozzarella, roughly chopped

1 Combine the *masarepa* or *masa harina* and salt in a bowl. Gradually stir in the measured water to make a soft dough, then set aside for about 20 minutes.

2 Divide the dough into 15 equal-sized balls, then, using your fingers, flatten each ball into a circle, approximately 1cm/½in thick. Prepare the barbecue.

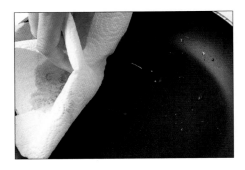

3 Heat a large, heavy frying pan or flat griddle over a medium heat and add 5ml/1 tsp oil. Using a piece of kitchen paper, gently wipe the surface of the frying pan, leaving it just lightly greased.

4 Place five of the *arepas* in the frying pan or on the griddle. Cook for about 4 minutes, then flip over and cook for a further 4 minutes. The *arepas* should be lightly blistered on both sides.

5 Open the *arepas* and fill each with a few small pieces of fresh white cheese. Return to the pan to cook until the cheese begins to melt. Remove from the heat and keep warm.

6 Cook the remaining ten *arepas* in the same way, oiling the pan and wiping with kitchen paper in between batches, to ensure it is always lightly greased. Serve the arepas while still warm so that the melted cheese is soft and runny.

COOK'S TIP
Masarepa is a flour made with the white corn grown in the Andes. Look for it in Latin American food stores. If it is not available, replace it with *masa harina*, the flour used to make tamales. The result will not be quite as delicate, but the *arepas* will be equally delicious.

VARIATION
Instead of cheese, try a delicious beef filling. Simply fry some minced (ground) beef in oil in a frying pan with ½ chopped onion, 1 small red chilli, finely chopped, 1 crushed garlic clove, ground black pepper and fresh thyme. When thoroughly cooked, stuff the mixture inside the *arepas*.

Energy 86kcal/363kJ; Protein 3.7g; Carbohydrate 10.4g, of which sugars 0.2g; Fat 3.6g, of which saturates 2g; Cholesterol 8mg; Calcium 67mg; Fibre 0.4g; Sodium 53mg.

Smoky Aubergine on Ciabatta

Cooking the aubergines whole, over an open flame, gives them a distinctive smoky flavour and aroma, as well as tender, creamy flesh. Cook them when the heat is fierce. They then need to cool for about 20 minutes before they are chopped and served.

SERVES FOUR TO SIX

INGREDIENTS

2 aubergines (eggplants)
2 red (bell) peppers
3–5 garlic cloves, chopped, or more
    to taste
2.5ml/½ tsp ground cumin
juice of ½–1 lemon, to taste
2.5ml/½ tsp sherry or wine vinegar
45–60ml/3–4 tbsp extra virgin
    olive oil
1–2 shakes of cayenne pepper,
    Tabasco or other hot pepper sauce
coarse sea salt
chopped fresh coriander (cilantro),
    to garnish
pitta bread wedges or thinly sliced
    French bread or ciabatta bread,
    sesame seed crackers and cucumber
    slices, to serve

1 Prepare the barbecue. Place the aubergines and peppers over a medium-low heat on the grill rack (they can also be cooked inside). Turn the vegetables frequently until deflated and the skins are evenly charred.

2 Put the aubergines and peppers in a plastic bag and seal tightly or under an upturned bowl. Cool over 20 minutes.

3 Peel the vegetables, reserving the juices, and roughly chop the flesh. Put the flesh in a bowl and add the juices, garlic, cumin, lemon juice, vinegar, olive oil, hot pepper seasoning and salt. Mix well to combine. Turn the mixture into a serving bowl and garnish with coriander. Serve with bread, toasted on the barbecue, sesame seed crackers and cucumber slices.

Energy 95kcal/391kJ; Protein 1.3g; Carbohydrate 5g, of which sugars 4.7g; Fat 7.9g, of which saturates 1.2g; Cholesterol 0mg; Calcium 12mg; Fibre 2.5g; Sodium 4mg.

WALNUT BREAD WITH MASHED AUBERGINE

THIS TURKISH DISH CONSISTS OF GRILLED MASHED AUBERGINE WITH CHEESE SERVED WITH OLIVES AND TOASTED BREAD. YOU CAN BUY MARINATED OLIVES INSTEAD OF MAKING YOUR OWN, BUT IT'S FUN TO DO IT YOURSELF, BY STEEPING THE OLIVES WITH VARIOUS FLAVOURINGS IN A GOOD QUALITY OIL.

SERVES EIGHT

INGREDIENTS
    3 aubergines (eggplants), about
      675g/1½lb total weight, cut
      widthways into 5mm/¼in slices
    60ml/4 tbsp finely grated Kefalotiri
      or Kasseri cheese
    juice of ½ lemon
    1 loaf walnut bread, sliced as thinly
      as possible
    extra virgin olive oil, for brushing
    salt and ground black pepper
For the marinated olives
    175g/6oz/1 cup olives of
      various colours
    fennel seeds or dried fennel seed
      heads and ground black pepper
    fresh hot chillies and rosemary sprigs
    lemon slices and fresh
      thyme branches
    120ml/4fl oz/½ cup extra virgin
      olive oil

1 To make the marinated olives, divide them among three bowls and add a different flavouring combination to each: try the fennel seeds and pepper with mixed olives, the chillies and rosemary with black olives, and the lemon and thyme with green olives. Divide the oil among the bowls and leave to stand for several hours.

2 Prepare the barbecue. Heat the griddle on the grill rack over hot coals. Brush the aubergine slices with some of the oil from the olives and griddle for 5 minutes, or until soft and branded with griddle marks on both sides. Tip the slices into a small bowl and mash to a rough pulp.

3 While the mixture is still hot, add the finely grated cheese and lemon juice, and stir well to mix these ingredients in thoroughly. Add salt and pepper to taste. Drain most of the oil from the olives and mix it into the pulp. Cover the aubergine mixture and put in a cool place until needed.

4 Brush the bread slices sparingly with oil on one side and toast on the griddle or on an oiled grill rack over the barbecue. Keep an eye on the toast because it just needs to become crisp, not blacken, and the coals are hot at this stage.

5 Serve the toast with small bowls of the aubergine and cheese mixture and the marinated olives.

COOK'S TIP
This dish can also be cooked next to a slow-cooking main course. Get the main course food going, then cook the aubergines beside it directly on the grill rack.

Energy 240kcal/1004kJ; Protein 7.5g; Carbohydrate 23.2g, of which sugars 2.5g; Fat 13.5g, of which saturates 3.1g; Cholesterol 7mg; Calcium 94mg; Fibre 5.2g; Sodium 823mg.

CLASSIC QUESADILLAS

THESE CHEESE-FILLED TORTILLAS ARE THE MEXICAN EQUIVALENT OF TOASTED SANDWICHES. SERVE THEM HOT OR THEY WILL BECOME CHEWY. IF YOU ARE MAKING THEM FOR A CROWD, YOU COULD FILL AND FOLD THE TORTILLAS IN ADVANCE THEN ADD THE CHILLI AND COOK THEM TO ORDER.

SERVES EIGHT

INGREDIENTS
400g/14oz mozzarella,
  Monterey Jack or mild
  Cheddar cheese
2 fresh Fresno chillies (optional)
16 wheat flour tortillas, about
  15cm/6in across
onion relish or tomato salsa,
  to serve

COOK'S TIP
It is best to put on protective gloves before peeling the skin from the roasted chillies. It is actually the membrane attached to the seeds, rather than the flesh, that emits the stinging toxins.

1 If using mozzarella cheese, it must be drained thoroughly and then patted dry and sliced into thin strips. Monterey Jack and Cheddar cheese should both be coarsely grated, as finely grated cheese will melt and ooze away when cooking. Set the cheese aside in a bowl.

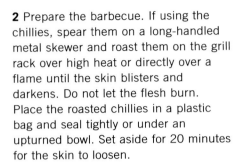

2 Prepare the barbecue. If using the chillies, spear them on a long-handled metal skewer and roast them on the grill rack over high heat or directly over a flame until the skin blisters and darkens. Do not let the flesh burn. Place the roasted chillies in a plastic bag and seal tightly or under an upturned bowl. Set aside for 20 minutes for the skin to loosen.

3 Remove the roasted chillies from the bag and carefully peel off the skin. Cut off the stalk, then slit the chillies and scrape out all the seeds. Cut the flesh into 16 even-sized thin strips.

4 Heat the griddle or a frying pan on the grill rack over hot coals. Place one tortilla on the griddle or pan at a time, sprinkle about one sixteenth of the cheese on to one half and add a strip of chilli, if using. Fold the tortilla over the cheese and press the edges together gently to seal. Cook the filled tortilla for 1 minute, then turn over and cook the other side for 1 minute.

5 Remove the filled tortilla from the griddle or pan, cut it into three triangles or four strips and serve immediately while it is still hot, with the onion relish or tomato salsa.

VARIATIONS
Try spreading a thin layer of your favourite salsa on the tortillas before adding the cheese, or add some cooked chicken or prawns (shrimp) before folding the tortillas.

Energy 392kcal/1645kJ; Protein 18.2g; Carbohydrate 44.8g, of which sugars 0.8g; Fat 16.8g, of which saturates 10.4g; Cholesterol 53mg; Calcium 428mg; Fibre 1.8g; Sodium 545mg.

TOMATO AND MOZZARELLA SALAD

GRIDDLING THE TOMATOES ADDS A NEW DIMENSION TO THIS DELICIOUS DISH AND A SUPERB SWEETNESS TO THE TOMATOES. AVOID MAKING THE BASIL OIL TOO FAR IN ADVANCE SO THAT ITS FRESH FLAVOUR AND VIVID EMERALD-GREEN COLOUR WILL BE RETAINED.

SERVES FOUR

INGREDIENTS
    6 large plum tomatoes
    350g/12oz fresh mozzarella, cut into
        8–12 slices
    fresh basil leaves, to garnish
For the basil oil
    25 fresh basil leaves
    60ml/4 tbsp extra virgin olive oil
    1 garlic clove, crushed
For the salad
    90g/3½oz salad leaves
    50g/2oz/2 cups mixed herbs, such
        as coriander (cilantro), basil and
        rocket (arugula)
    25g/1oz/3 tbsp pumpkin seeds
    25g/1oz/3 tbsp sunflower seeds
For the salad dressing
    60ml/4 tbsp extra virgin olive oil
    15ml/1 tbsp balsamic vinegar
    2.5ml/½ tsp Dijon mustard

1 To make the basil oil, place the basil leaves, olive oil and garlic in a blender and whizz until smooth. Transfer to a bowl and chill.

2 Start to prepare the salad. Put the salad leaves in a large bowl. Add the mixed herbs and toss lightly with your hands to mix. To make the salad dressing, combine the ingredients in a screw-top jar or bowl. Shake or mix with a small whisk or fork until combined. Set aside.

3 Cut the tomatoes in half lengthwise and remove the seeds. Prepare the barbecue. Heat a griddle on a grill rack over hot coals. Place the tomatoes skin-side down on the griddle and cook for 12–15 minutes or until the tomatoes are tender.

4 Meanwhile, toast the pumpkin and sunflower seeds in a dry frying pan on the grill rack for 2 minutes, or until golden, tossing frequently. Cool then sprinkle them over the salad. Stir the dressing then pour over the salad and toss to mix.

5 For each serving, place the tomato halves on top of 2 or 3 slices of mozzarella and drizzle over the basil oil. Season well. Garnish with basil leaves. Serve with the salad.

COOK'S TIP
Try to keep an eye on the toasting seeds even if griddling tomatoes at the same time – they will burn quickly if left.

GRIDDLED CHEESE BITES

THESE GRIDDLED CHEESE CUBES WRAPPED IN AROMATIC LEAVES ARE DELICIOUS WITH A COLD RESINOUS WINE, PLENTY OF EXCELLENT OLIVES, FRUITY OLIVE OIL AND RUSTIC BREAD. THEY TAKE ONLY MINUTES TO COOK AND MAKE THE PERFECT PRE-DINNER SNACK FOR A CROWD.

SERVES SIX

INGREDIENTS

18 large bay leaves or mixed bay and
    lemon leaves
275g/10oz Kefalotiri or Kasseri
    cheese, cut into 18 cubes
20ml/4 tsp extra virgin olive oil
ground black pepper

1 Soak 18 short wooden skewers in cold water for 30 minutes. Add the bay and/or lemon leaves to the water to prevent them from burning when cooked in the griddle.

2 Put the cheese cubes in a dish large enough to hold the skewers. Pour over the olive oil. Sprinkle over a little pepper and toss well. Drain the skewers, then thread them with the cheese and drained bay leaves and/or lemon leaves. Put the skewers of cheese back in the oil. Prepare the barbecue.

3 Heat the griddle on the grill rack over hot coals. When hot, lower the heat a little and place the skewers on the griddle, evenly spacing them. Cook for about 5 seconds on each side. The pieces of cheese should have golden-brown lines, and should just be starting to melt. Serve immediately.

COOK'S TIP
Do try to get hold of the recommended cheese, Kefalotiri, which is a mature cheese with a sharp nutty flavour. It originates from the island of Crete.

Energy 213kcal/880kJ; Protein 11.8g; Carbohydrate 0g, of which sugars 0g; Fat 18.4g, of which saturates 10.6g; Cholesterol 48mg; Calcium 316mg; Fibre 0g; Sodium 307mg.

CHILLI AND HERB POLENTA

POLENTA HAS BECOME AS WIDELY ACCEPTED AS MASHED POTATO AND CAN CONFIDENTLY BE CLASSED AS COMFORT FOOD. HERE IT IS FLAVOURED WITH PASILLA CHILLIES, WHICH HAVE A DRIED FRUIT AND SLIGHT LIQUORICE HINT TO THEM. SERVE IT WITH A TANGY SALSA CALLED PEBRE.

SERVES SIX TO TWELVE

INGREDIENTS
- 10ml/2 tsp crushed dried pasilla chilli flakes
- 1.3 litres/2¼ pints/5⅔ cups water
- 250g/9oz/2¼ cups quick-cook polenta
- 50g/2oz/¼ cup butter
- 75g/3oz Parmesan cheese, finely grated
- 30ml/2 tbsp chopped fresh dill
- 30ml/2 tbsp chopped fresh coriander (cilantro)
- 30ml/2 tbsp olive oil
- salt

For the *pebre*
- ½ pink onion, finely chopped
- 4 drained bottled sweet cherry peppers, finely chopped
- 1 fresh medium hot red chilli, seeded and finely chopped
- 1 small red (bell) pepper, quartered and seeded
- 10ml/2 tsp raspberry vinegar
- 30ml/2 tbsp olive oil
- 4 tomatoes, halved, cored, seeded and roughly chopped
- 45ml/3 tbsp chopped fresh coriander (cilantro)

1 Chop the chilli flakes finely. Put them in a pan with the water. Bring to the boil and add salt to taste. Pour the polenta into the water in a continuous stream, whisking all the time. Reduce the heat and continue to whisk for a few minutes. When the polenta is thick and bubbling like a volcano, whisk in the butter, Parmesan and herbs.

2 Pour into a greased 33 x 23cm/ 13 x 9in baking tray and leave to cool. Leave uncovered so that the surface firms up, and chill overnight.

3 About an hour before you plan to serve the meal, make the *pebre*. Place the onion, sweet cherry peppers and chilli in a mortar. Slice the skin from the red pepper quarters. Dice the flesh finely and add it to the mortar with the raspberry vinegar and olive oil.

4 Pound with a pestle for 1 minute, then tip into a serving dish. Stir in the tomatoes and coriander. Cover and chill.

5 Remove the polenta from the refrigerator and leave for about 30 minutes. Cut into 12 even triangles and brush the top with oil.

6 Prepare the barbecue. Heat a griddle on a grill rack over hot coals. Lower the heat to medium and grill the polenta triangles in batches, oiled-side down, for about 2 minutes, then turn through 180 degrees and cook for 1 minute more, to get a striking chequered effect. (Alternatively, you can sear them directly on the oiled grill rack.) Serve the polenta at once, with the chilled *pebre*.

Energy 181kcal/751kJ; Protein 5g; Carbohydrate 17.3g, of which sugars 2g; Fat 10g, of which saturates 4g; Cholesterol 15mg; Calcium 88mg; Fibre 1.2g; Sodium 98mg.

HAM PIZZETTAS WITH MANGO

THESE INDIVIDUAL LITTLE PIZZAS ARE TOPPED WITH AN UNUSUAL BUT VERY SUCCESSFUL COMBINATION OF SMOKED HAM, BRIE AND JUICY CHUNKS OF FRESH MANGO.

2 Turn the dough out on to a floured surface and knead it for about 5 minutes, or until smooth.

3 Return the dough to the bowl and cover it with a damp cloth or oiled clear film (plastic wrap). Leave the dough to rise in a warm place for about 30 minutes, or until is doubled in size and springy to the touch.

4 Prepare the barbecue. Divide the dough into six and roll each piece into a ball. Flatten out with your hand and use your knuckles to press each piece of dough to a round of about 15cm/6in diameter, with a raised lip around the edge.

5 Halve, stone (pit) and peel the mango and cut it into small dice. Arrange with the ham on top of the pizzettas. Top with cheese and tomatoes and sprinkle with salt and ground black pepper.

SERVES SIX

INGREDIENTS
225g/8oz/2 cups strong white
  bread flour
10g/¼ oz sachet easy-blend
  (rapid-rise) dried yeast
150ml/¼ pint/⅔ cup warm water
60ml/4 tbsp olive oil
For the topping
1 ripe mango
150g/5oz smoked ham, sliced
  wafer-thin
150g/5oz Brie, diced
12 yellow cherry tomatoes, halved
salt and ground black pepper

1 In a large bowl, stir together the flour and yeast, with a pinch of salt. Make a well in the centre and stir in the water and 45ml/3 tbsp of the olive oil. Stir until thoroughly mixed.

6 Drizzle the remaining oil over the pizzettas. Place them on the oiled grill rack of a medium-hot barbecue and cook for 8 minutes, or until golden brown and crisp underneath.

Energy 326kcal/1369kJ; Protein 13.6g; Carbohydrate 34g, of which sugars 5.3g; Fat 15.5g, of which saturates 6g; Cholesterol 38mg; Calcium 124mg; Fibre 2.2g; Sodium 444mg.

POTATO WEDGES <u>WITH</u> BASIL <u>AND</u> LEMON DIP

BARBECUED POTATO WEDGES TASTE GREAT SERVED WITH THIS FRESH MAYONNAISE. THE POTATOES ARE PAR-BOILED IN ADVANCE AND NEED ONLY A FEW MINUTES GRILLING ON THE BARBECUE.

SERVES FOUR

INGREDIENTS
  4 large potatoes, peeled
  90ml/6 tbsp olive oil
  sea salt and ground black pepper
For the dip
  2 large egg yolks
  15ml/1 tbsp lemon juice
  150ml/¼ pint/⅔ cup olive oil
  150ml/¼ pint/⅔ cup sunflower oil
  handful of green basil leaves
  handful of dark opal (purple)
    basil leaves
  4 garlic cloves, crushed
  green and dark opal basil leaves and
    sea salt, to garnish

4 Tear both types of basil leaves into small pieces and stir into the mayonnaise with the crushed garlic and seasoning. Transfer to a serving dish, cover and chill until ready to serve, garnished with basil leaves and sea salt.

5 Slice the potatoes into wedges about 7.5cm/3in long and 2.5cm/1in thick. Place the wedges in boiling water and cook for 4–5 minutes (the potato should be just tender but still firm). Drain the potatoes and refresh under cold running water. Dry thoroughly then toss quickly in the olive oil to coat, and season with salt and pepper.

6 Prepare the barbecue. Position a lightly oiled grill rack over the hot coals. Place the potatoes on the grill rack over a medium-high heat and cook them for 3–4 minutes on each side, turning carefully with tongs, so that they are heated through, golden and tender. Serve with the dip.

1 Place the egg yolks and lemon juice in a food processor or blender and process them briefly together.

2 In a jug (pitcher), stir the two oils together. With the machine running, pour in the oil very slowly, a drop at a time.

3 Once half the oil has been added, the remainder can be incorporated more quickly. Continue processing the mixture as you add the oil to form a thick and creamy mayonnaise.

VARIATION
If you prefer, of course, you can serve these wedges with a rich barbecue sauce – such as the homemade recipe in the Accompaniments chapter.

COOK'S TIP
Dark opal basil has crinkled, deep-purple leaves with a hint of blackcurrants.

Energy 680kcal/2803kJ; Protein 3.4g; Carbohydrate 11.1g, of which sugars 0.9g; Fat 69.4g, of which saturates 9.8g; Cholesterol 101mg; Calcium 18mg; Fibre 1.1g; Sodium 11mg.

LITTLE COURGETTE WRAPS

THIS IS A TASTY FIRST COURSE OR VEGETABLE SIDE DISH USING MINI MOZZARELLA BALLS WRAPPED IN SUCCULENT STRIPS OF COURGETTES. ACCOMPANY WITH STRONGLY FLAVOURED SALAD LEAVES.

SERVES SIX

INGREDIENTS
   2 large yellow courgettes (zucchini),
      about 675g/1½lb total weight
   45ml/3 tbsp olive oil
   250g/9oz baby leaf spinach
   250g/9oz mini mozzarella balls
   salad burnet, rocket (arugula) and
      mizuna leaves, to garnish (optional)
For the dressing
   2 whole, unpeeled garlic cloves
   30ml/2 tbsp white wine vinegar
   30ml/2 tbsp olive oil
   15ml/1 tbsp extra virgin olive oil
   45ml/3 tbsp walnut oil
   salt and ground black pepper

COOK'S TIP
Sweeter than the popular green variety, yellow courgettes are quite easy to find.

1 To make the dressing, place the garlic in a small pan with water to cover. Bring to the boil, lower the heat and simmer for 5 minutes. Drain. When cool enough to handle, pop the garlic cloves out of their skins and crush to a smooth paste with a little salt. Scrape into a bowl and add the vinegar. Whisk in the oils and season to taste.

2 Slice each courgette lengthways into six or more broad strips, about 3mm/⅛in wide. Lay them on a tray a little apart from each other. Set aside 5ml/1 tsp of the oil and brush the rest over the strips, making sure each one is evenly coated in the oil.

3 Place a wok over a high heat. When it starts to smoke, add the reserved oil and stir-fry the spinach for 30 seconds.

4 When the spinach is just beginning to wilt over the heat, tip it into a sieve and drain well, then pat the leaves dry with kitchen paper. Tear or slice the mozzarella balls in half and place on kitchen paper to drain.

5 Prepare the barbecue. Position a lightly oiled grill rack over medium-hot coals. Lay the courgettes on the rack. Grill on one side only for 2–3 minutes, or until striped golden. As each strip cooks, return it to the tray, grilled-side up.

6 Place small heaps of spinach towards one end of each courgette strip. Lay two pieces of mozzarella on each pile of spinach. Season well.

7 Using a metal spatula, carefully transfer the topped strips, a few at a time, back to the barbecue rack and grill for about 2 minutes, or until the underside of each is striped with golden-brown grill marks.

8 When the cheese starts to melt, fold the plain section of each courgette over the filling to make a wrap. Lift off carefully and drain on kitchen paper. Serve with the garnish of salad leaves, if you like, and drizzle the dressing over.

COOK'S TIP
You need large courgettes measuring about 19cm/7½in, to create good-sized wraps when cut into strips.

Energy 237kcal/977kJ; Protein 11g; Carbohydrate 2.7g, of which sugars 2.5g; Fat 20.2g, of which saturates 7.4g; Cholesterol 24mg; Calcium 250mg; Fibre 1.9g; Sodium 224mg.

GRILLED BABY ARTICHOKES

THIS IS AN ENJOYABLE WAY TO EAT ARTICHOKES. JUST HOLD THE SKEWER WITH THE ARTICHOKE IN ONE HAND, TEAR OFF A LEAF WITH THE OTHER AND DIP THAT INTO THE HOT MELTED BUTTER.

SERVES SIX

INGREDIENTS
  12 baby artichokes with stalks,
    about 1.3kg/3lb total weight
  1 lemon, halved
  200g/7oz/scant 1 cup butter
  2 garlic cloves, crushed with a pinch
    of salt
  15ml/1 tbsp chopped fresh flat
    leaf parsley
  salt and ground black pepper

1 Soak 12 wooden skewers in cold water for 30 minutes. Drain, then skewer a baby artichoke on to each one. Bring a large pan of salted water to the boil. Squeeze the juice of one lemon half, and add it, with the lemon shell, to the pan.

2 Place the artichokes head first into the pan and boil for 5–8 minutes, or until just tender. Drain well. Set aside for up to 1 hour or use at once.

3 Prepare the barbecue. Put the butter, garlic and parsley into a small pan and squeeze in the juice of the remaining half-lemon.

4 Position a lightly oiled grill rack over the coals to heat over medium heat. If the artichokes have been allowed to cool, wrap the heads in foil and place them on the grill for 3 minutes, then unwrap and return to the heat for 1 minute, turning frequently. If they are still hot, grill without the foil for 4 minutes, turning often.

5 When the artichokes are almost ready, melt the butter sauce in the pan on the barbecue. Either transfer the sauce to six small serving bowls or pour a little on to each plate. Serve it with the artichokes on their skewers.

COOK'S TIP
Have plenty of napkins on hand to catch any stray drops of butter sauce!

Energy 263kcal/1084kJ; Protein 1.4g; Carbohydrate 2.5g, of which sugars 1.2g; Fat 27.7g, of which saturates 17.4g; Cholesterol 71mg; Calcium 49mg; Fibre 1.4g; Sodium 262mg.

HOT AVOCADO HALVES

IF YOU MAKE THE BASIL OIL IN ADVANCE, OR BUY A READY PREPARED BASIL OIL, THIS IS AN ULTRA-SIMPLE DISH THAT CAN BE READY IN A FLASH. IT MAKES AN EYE-CATCHING FIRST COURSE AND IS AN EXCELLENT APPETITE TEASER TO SERVE WHILE THE REST OF THE FOOD IS BARBECUING.

SERVES SIX

INGREDIENTS
   3 ready-to-eat avocados, preferably
     Hass for flavour
   105ml/7 tbsp balsamic vinegar
For the basil oil
   40g/1½oz/1½ cups fresh basil
     leaves, stalks removed
   200ml/7fl oz/scant 1 cup olive oil

COOK'S TIPS
• When choosing Hass avocados, watch out for any with marked indentations in their bumpy skin – this indicates that the flesh underneath may be bruised.
• Remember, the griddle is ready to use when a few drops of water sprinkled on to the surface evaporate instantly.

1 To make the basil oil, place the leaves in a bowl and pour boiling water over. Leave for 30 seconds. Drain, refresh under cold water and drain again. Squeeze dry and pat with kitchen paper to remove as much moisture as possible.

2 Place in a food processor with the oil and process to a purée. Put into a bowl, cover and chill overnight.

3 Next day, line a sieve with muslin (cheesecloth), set it over a deep bowl and pour in the basil purée. Leave undisturbed for 1 hour, or until all the oil has filtered into the bowl. Discard the solids and pour into a bottle, then chill until ready to cook.

4 Prepare the barbecue. Cut each avocado in half and prize out the stone (pit). Brush with a little of the basil oil.

5 Heat the balsamic vinegar gently in a pan, on the stove or on the barbecue. When it starts to boil, simmer for 1 minute, or until it is just beginning to turn slightly syrupy.

6 Heat the griddle on the grill rack over hot coals. Lower the heat a little and place the avocado halves cut-side down on the griddle. Cook for 30–60 seconds until branded with grill marks. (Move the avocados around carefully with tongs to create a chequered effect.) Serve hot with the vinegar and extra oil drizzled over.

Energy 222kcal/916kJ; Protein 1g; Carbohydrate 1g, of which sugars 0.3g; Fat 23.8g, of which saturates 4.1g; Cholesterol 0mg; Calcium 6mg; Fibre 1.7g; Sodium 3mg.

MUSHROOMS WITH GARLIC AND CHILLI SAUCE

WHEN YOU ARE PLANNING A BARBECUE FOR FRIENDS AND FAMILY, IT CAN BE TRICKY FINDING SOMETHING REALLY SPECIAL FOR THE VEGETARIANS IN THE PARTY. THESE TASTY MUSHROOM KEBABS ARE IDEAL BECAUSE THEY LOOK, SMELL AND TASTE WONDERFUL.

SERVES FOUR

INGREDIENTS

12 large field (portabello), chestnut or oyster mushrooms or a mixture, cut in half
4 garlic cloves, coarsely chopped
6 coriander (cilantro) roots, coarsely chopped
15ml/1 tbsp granulated sugar
30ml/2 tbsp light soy sauce
ground black pepper

For the dipping sauce

15ml/1 tbsp granulated sugar
90ml/6 tbsp rice vinegar
5ml/1 tsp salt
1 garlic clove, crushed
1 small fresh red chilli, seeded and finely chopped

1 If using wooden skewers, soak eight of them in cold water for at least 30 minutes to prevent them burning. Prepare the barbecue.

2 Make the dipping sauce by heating the sugar, rice vinegar and salt in a small pan, stirring occasionally until the sugar and salt have dissolved. Add the garlic and chilli, pour into a serving dish and keep warm.

3 Thread three mushroom halves on to each skewer. Lay the filled skewers side by side in a shallow dish.

4 In a mortar or spice grinder pound or blend the garlic and coriander roots. Scrape into a bowl and mix with the sugar, soy sauce and a little pepper.

5 Brush the soy sauce mixture over the mushrooms and leave to marinate for 15 minutes. Cook the mushrooms over medium heat for 5–6 minutes on each side. Serve with the dipping sauce.

Energy 63kcal/267kJ; Protein 4.2g; Carbohydrate 9.6g, of which sugars 9.1g; Fat 1.2g, of which saturates 0.2g; Cholesterol 0mg; Calcium 43mg; Fibre 2.8g; Sodium 1040mg.

BUTTERFLY PRAWNS

THE SUCCESS OF THIS DISH STEMS FROM THE QUALITY OF THE PRAWNS, SO IT IS WORTH GETTING REALLY GOOD ONES, SUCH AS KING PRAWNS, WITH GREAT FLAVOUR AND TEXTURE. A FRUITY, SLIGHTLY SPICY DIP IS SUCH AN EASY BUT FABULOUS ACCOMPANIMENT.

4 Stir the chilli into the raspberry purée. When the dip is cool, cover and place in a cool place until needed.

5 Butterfly each prawn by making an incision down the curved back, just as you would when deveining. Use a piece of kitchen paper to wipe away the dark spinal vein.

6 Mix the oil with a little sea salt in a bowl. Add the prawns and toss to coat, then thread them on to the drained skewers, spearing them head first.

7 Position a lightly oiled grill rack over the coals to heat. Grill the prawns over high heat for about 5 minutes, depending on size, turning them over once. Serve hot, with the chilli and raspberry dip.

SERVES SIX

INGREDIENTS
30 raw king prawns (jumbo shrimp), peeled, with heads removed but tails left on
15ml/1 tbsp sunflower oil
coarse sea salt
For the chilli and raspberry dip
30ml/2 tbsp raspberry vinegar
15ml/1 tbsp sugar
115g/4oz/2⁄3 cup raspberries
1 large fresh red chilli, seeded and finely chopped

1 Prepare the barbecue. Soak 30 wooden skewers in cold water for 30 minutes.

2 Make the dip by mixing the vinegar and sugar in a small pan. Heat gently until the sugar has dissolved, stirring, then add the raspberries.

3 When the raspberry juices start to flow, tip the mixture into a sieve set over a bowl. Push the raspberries through the sieve using the back of a ladle. Discard the seeds.

COOK'S TIP
These prawn dippers also taste delicious with a vibrant chilli and mango dip. Use one large, ripe mango in place of the raspberries and slice the flesh thinly.

Energy 44kcal/185kJ; Protein 5.6g; Carbohydrate 0.9g, of which sugars 0.9g; Fat 2.1g, of which saturates 0.3g; Cholesterol 59mg; Calcium 29mg; Fibre 0.5g; Sodium 58mg.

FETA-STUFFED SQUID

HERE IS A FABULOUS RECIPE FROM GREECE THAT COMBINES TWO OF THE MOST POPULAR INGREDIENTS FROM THAT COUNTRY: SQUID AND FETA CHEESE. SCENTED WITH MARJORAM AND GARLIC, THE SQUID CONTAINS A CREAMY MARINATED FETA CHEESE FILLING. IT IS SIMPLE TO PREPARE AND QUICK TO COOK.

SERVES FOUR

INGREDIENTS
    4 medium squid, about 900g/2lb
      total weight, prepared
    4–8 finger-length slices of
      feta cheese
    lemon wedges, to serve
For the marinade
    90ml/6 tbsp olive oil
    2 garlic cloves, crushed
    3–4 fresh marjoram sprigs, leaves
      removed and chopped
    salt and ground black pepper

COOK'S TIP
Ask your fishmonger to prepare the squid for you so that the bodies are intact. He will sever the tentacles and the two side fins, which you can cook separately.

1 Rinse the squid thoroughly, inside and out, and drain well. Lay the squid bodies and tentacles in a shallow dish that will hold them in a single layer. Tuck the pieces of cheese between the squid.

2 To make the marinade, pour the oil into a jug (pitcher) or bowl and whisk in the garlic and marjoram. Season to taste with salt and pepper. Pour the marinade over the squid and the cheese, then cover and leave in a cool place to marinate for 2–3 hours, turning once. Soak four wooden skewers in water for 30 minutes.

3 Insert 1 or 2 pieces of cheese and a few pieces of marjoram from the marinade into each squid and thread the tentacles on skewers by piercing at the centre to hold them in place.

4 Prepare a barbecue. Position a lightly oiled grill rack over the hot coals. Grill the stuffed squid over medium heat for about 6 minutes, then turn them over carefully. Grill them for 1–2 minutes more, then add the skewered tentacles. Grill them for 2 minutes on each side, until they start to scorch. Serve the stuffed squid with the tentacles. Add a few lemon wedges, for squeezing over the seafood.

Energy 357kcal/1496kJ; Protein 42.5g; Carbohydrate 3.5g, of which sugars 0.8g; Fat 19.4g, of which saturates 8.5g; Cholesterol 541mg; Calcium 209mg; Fibre 0g; Sodium 968mg.

ICED OYSTERS WITH MERGUEZ SAUSAGES

ALTHOUGH IT SEEMS AN UNUSUAL BARBECUE RECIPE, THESE TWO COMPLEMENT EACH OTHER PERFECTLY. MUNCH ON A LITTLE CHILLI-SPICED SAUSAGE, THEN QUELL THE BURNING SENSATION WITH THE CLEAN, COOL TEXTURE OF AN ICE-COLD OYSTER.

SERVES SIX

INGREDIENTS
675g/1½lb merguez sausages
crushed ice for serving
24 oysters
2 lemons, cut into wedges

1 Prepare the barbecue. Position a lightly oiled grill rack over the coals to heat. Place the sausages on the grill rack over medium-high heat. Grill them for 8 minutes, or until cooked through and golden, turning often.

2 Meanwhile, spread out the crushed ice on a platter and keep it chilled while you prepare the oysters. Scrub the oyster shells with a stiff brush to remove any sand. Make sure all the oysters are tightly closed, and discard any that aren't.

3 Place them on the grill rack, a few at a time, with the deep-side down, so that as they open the juices will be retained in the lower shell. They will begin to ease open after 3–5 minutes and must be removed from the heat immediately, so that they don't start to cook.

4 Lay the oysters on the ice. When they have all eased open, get to work with a sharp knife, opening them fully if need be. Remove the oysters from the flat side of the shell and place them with the juices on the deep half shells. Discard any oysters that fail to open. Serve with the hot, cooked sausages, and lemon wedges for squeezing.

Energy 439kcal/1820kJ; Protein 16.3g; Carbohydrate 11.8g, of which sugars 1.6g; Fat 36.6g, of which saturates 13.8g; Cholesterol 76mg; Calcium 102mg; Fibre 0.6g; Sodium 1059mg.

SIZZLING CHILLI SCALLOPS

SCALLOPS HAVE A BEAUTIFUL RICH FLAVOUR AND TASTE WONDERFUL BARBECUED WITH A SUBTLE CHILLI AND HONEY GLAZE. IF YOU ARE ABLE TO BUY QUEEN SCALLOPS IN THE HALF-SHELL THEY WILL BE READY TO GO ON THE BARBECUE ~ NOTHING COULD BE SIMPLER FOR A QUICK AND EXCEPTIONALLY TASTY DISH.

SERVES FOUR TO SIX

INGREDIENTS

   1 fresh fat mild green chilli, seeded
     and finely chopped
   ½–1 fresh Scotch bonnet or
     habañero chilli, seeded and
     finely chopped
   1 small shallot, finely chopped
   15ml/1 tbsp clear honey
   60ml/4 tbsp olive oil
   24 queen scallops on the half shell
   2 lemons, cut into thin wedges
   salt and ground black pepper

1 Prepare the barbecue. While it is heating, mix the chillies, shallot, honey and oil in a bowl.

2 Set out the scallops on a tray. Sprinkle each one with a pinch of salt, then top with a little of the chilli mixture. Position a grill rack over the coals to heat. Place the scallops, on their half shells, on the grill rack over medium-high heat.

3 Cook the scallops for 1½–2 minutes only. If your barbecue has enough space, cook as many as possible at once, moving them from the edge to the centre of the grill rack as necessary. Take care not to overcook them, or they will toughen. Place them on a serving platter, with the lemon wedges for squeezing. Serve immediately.

Energy 133kcal/554kJ; Protein 11.7g; Carbohydrate 3.6g, of which sugars 1.9g; Fat 8g, of which saturates 1.3g; Cholesterol 24mg; Calcium 15mg; Fibre 0g; Sodium 90mg.

CHARGRILLED TUNA SLICES

USE SASHIMI-QUALITY TUNA FROM A JAPANESE FOOD STORE OR FIRST-RATE FISHMONGER, WHO WILL TRIM IT TO A NEAT RECTANGULAR SHAPE. SERVE WITH JAPANESE SHISO LEAVES, OR SWEET BASIL.

SERVES FOUR

INGREDIENTS
15g/½oz dried arame seaweed,
  soaked in water
60ml/4 tbsp tamari
30ml/2 tbsp mirin
120ml/4fl oz/½ cup water
5ml/1 tsp white sesame seeds
15ml/1 tbsp black sesame seeds
10ml/2 tsp dried pink peppercorns
2.5ml/½ tsp sunflower oil
250g/9oz sashimi tuna
16 fresh shiso leaves
7.5ml/1½ tsp wasabi paste
50g/2oz mooli (daikon),
  finely grated

1 Drain the arame, then soak it in a bowl with the tamari, mirin and water for 1 hour. Pour the liquid from the arame into a small pan and put the arame in a serving bowl.

2 Bring the liquid to a simmer. Cook for 3–5 minutes, or until syrupy, cool for 2 minutes and pour over the arame. Scatter with the white sesame seeds and cover until needed.

3 Prepare the barbecue. Lightly grind the black sesame seeds and pink peppercorns in a spice mill. Brush the oil over the tuna, then roll the tuna into the spice mixture to coat it evenly.

4 Heat a griddle on a grill rack over hot coals. Sear the tuna for 30 seconds on each of the four sides. Using a very sharp knife, slice it into 5mm/¼in wide pieces and arrange on plates with the shiso leaves, a blob of wasabi and a mound each of arame and grated mooli.

Energy 96kcal/404kJ; Protein 15.3g; Carbohydrate 1.3g, of which sugars 1.2g; Fat 3.3g, of which saturates 0.8g; Cholesterol 18mg; Calcium 18mg; Fibre 0.2g; Sodium 743mg.

HOT TROUT WITH RED VEGETABLES

ROAST THE VEGETABLES IN ADVANCE FOR THIS FLAVOURSOME AND BRIGHTLY COLOURED MEDITERRANEAN-STYLE SANDWICH AND THEN HAVE EVERYTHING READY TO ASSEMBLE WHEN THE TROUT IS COOKED.

SERVES FOUR

INGREDIENTS
    2 red (bell) peppers
    8 cherry tomatoes
    60ml/4 tbsp extra virgin olive oil
    30ml/2 tbsp lemon juice
    4 thin trout fillets, each about
      115g/4oz, skinned
    2 small ciabatta rolls
    15ml/1 tbsp red pesto
    30ml/2 tbsp mayonnaise
    115g/4oz rocket (arugula)
    salt and ground black pepper

1 Preheat the oven to 180°C/350°F/ Gas 4. Place the peppers and tomatoes in a roasting pan and drizzle half the olive oil over. Bake for 25–30 minutes or until the pepper skins are blackened. Set aside to cool.

2 In a small bowl or jug (pitcher), whisk the remaining oil with the lemon juice and a little salt and freshly ground black pepper. Place the trout in a shallow, non-metallic dish and pour over the oil and lemon juice. Turn the fish to make sure they are well coated.

3 Peel the skin off the cooked peppers and discard the core and seeds. Cut the pepper flesh into strips. Slice each ciabatta bread in half vertically, then cut each half in half horizontally.

4 Prepare the barbecue. Heat a griddle on the grill rack over hot coals. Lift the trout fillets carefully out of the marinade and grill them for 1–2 minutes, without adding any oil, until just cooked.

5 Mix the pesto and mayonnaise together and spread over the bread. Divide the rocket among four halves of the bread and top with the trout, pepper strips and roasted tomatoes. Place the remaining bread on top and serve.

COOK'S TIPS
• You can use any bread you like but make sure you slice it thickly.
• This recipe would be delicious using smoked fish fillets as a filling for the sandwich. Try smoking trout or salmon fillets over the barbecue using aromatic wood chips – you can follow the technique for hot smoked salmon that appears in the Fish and Shellfish chapter.
• Small loaves of olive-oil bread, such as ciabatta and focaccia, are ideal for these sandwiches. Try the sun-dried tomato and black olive versions, too.
• If you can't find any red pesto, use 30ml/2 tbsp chopped fresh basil mixed with 15ml/1 tbsp sun-dried tomato paste.

Energy 538kcal/2253kJ; Protein 32.6g; Carbohydrate 46.7g, of which sugars 9.8g; Fat 25.7g, of which saturates 3.8g; Cholesterol 9mg; Calcium 206mg; Fibre 4.2g; Sodium 588mg.

CHICKEN SATAY STICKS

PANDANUS LEAVES ARE COMMON TO THAI AND SOUTH-EAST ASIAN COOKING, AND ARE SOMETIMES ALSO KNOWN AS SCREWPINE OR BANDAN LEAVES. THEY ARE ENORMOUSLY VERSATILE, AND ARE USED HERE FOR THE DELICATE FLAVOUR THEY BRING TO THE CHICKEN, AS WELL AS THEIR VISUAL APPEAL.

SERVES SIX

INGREDIENTS
  about 1kg/2¼lb skinless chicken
    breast fillets
  30ml/2 tbsp olive oil
  5ml/1 tsp ground coriander
  2.5ml/½ tsp ground cumin
  2.5cm/1in piece of fresh root ginger,
    finely grated
  2 garlic cloves, crushed
  5ml/1 tsp caster (superfine) sugar
  2.5ml/½ tsp salt
  18 long pandanus leaves, each
    halved to give 21cm/8½in lengths
For the hot cashew nut sambal
  2 garlic cloves, roughly chopped
  4 small fresh hot green chillies (not
    tiny birdseye chillies), seeded and
    sliced
  50g/2oz/⅓ cup cashew nuts
  10ml/2 tsp sugar, preferably
    palm sugar
  75ml/5 tbsp light soy sauce
  juice of ½ lime
  30ml/2 tbsp coconut cream

1 To make the sambal, place the garlic and chillies in a mortar and grind them quite finely with a pestle. Add the nuts and continue to grind until the mixture is almost smooth, with just a bit of texture. Pound in the remaining ingredients, cover and put in a cool place until needed.

2 Soak 36 long bamboo or wooden skewers in water for 30 minutes. Slice the chicken horizontally into thin pieces and then into strips about 2.5cm/1in wide. Toss in the oil. Mix the coriander, cumin, ginger, garlic, sugar and salt together. Rub this mixture into the strips of chicken. Leave to marinate while you prepare the barbecue.

3 Thread a strip of pandanus leaf and a piece of chicken lengthways on to each skewer. Once the flames have died down, rake the coals to one side. Position a lightly oiled grill rack over the coals to heat.

4 Place the satays meat-side down over the coals and cover with a lid or some tented heavy-duty foil and cook for 5–7 minutes. Once the meat has seared, move the satays around so that they are not cooking directly over the coals. This will avoid the leaves becoming scorched. Serve hot with the sambal.

COOK'S TIP
The easiest way to make the sambal is to use a deep Thai mortar. The resulting mixture will have a satisfying crunch rather than being a smooth purée.

Energy 280kcal/1178kJ; Protein 42.3g; Carbohydrate 5.9g, of which sugars 4.6g; Fat 9.8g, of which saturates 1.9g; Cholesterol 117mg; Calcium 19mg; Fibre 0.5g; Sodium 1026mg.

MINI CHICKEN FILLETS

THE AJI AMARILLO IS A YELLOWY ORANGE PERUVIAN CHILLI, VERY FRUITY AND QUITE HOT, WHICH IS WHY IT IS A GOOD IDEA TO PREPARE THE MARMALADE THE DAY BEFORE SO THAT THE FLAVOURS CAN MELLOW AND BLEND. PERFECT SERVED WITH GARLICKY CHICKEN FILLETS.

SERVES FOUR

INGREDIENTS
  500g/1¼lb mini chicken breast
    fillets or skinless chicken breast
    fillets, each cut into 4 long strips
  2 garlic cloves, crushed to a paste
    with 2.5ml/½ tsp salt
  30ml/2 tbsp olive oil
  ground black pepper
For the aji amarillo marmalade
  50g/2oz dried aji
    amarillo chillies
  120ml/4fl oz/½ cup water
  20ml/4 tsp olive oil
  2 onions, finely chopped
  3 garlic cloves, crushed
  5ml/1 tsp ground cumin
  10ml/2 tsp Mexican oregano
  130g/4½oz/scant ¾ cup sugar
  200ml/7fl oz/scant 1 cup cider or
    white wine vinegar
  2 small orange (bell) peppers,
    quartered and seeded

1 To make the aji amarillo marmalade, heat a heavy frying pan, add the dried chillies and roast them by stirring them continuously over the heat for about 1½ minutes without letting them scorch.

2 Put them in a bowl with just enough almost-boiling water to cover. Use a saucer to keep them submerged and leave to rehydrate for about 2 hours, or longer if you prefer.

3 Slit the chillies, remove the seeds and chop the flesh into small dice. Place in a blender, add the water and process to a purée.

4 Heat the oil in a heavy pan, add the onions and garlic and cook over a gentle heat for 5 minutes. Add the cumin, Mexican oregano and the chilli purée. Add the sugar and stir until turning syrupy, then add the vinegar and stir well. Bring the mixture to the boil, then lower the heat and simmer for 30 minutes.

5 Meanwhile, heat a griddle on the stove. Roast the peppers, placed with skin-side down so that the skins char. Put the peppers underneath an upturned bowl. When they are cool enough to handle, rub off the skin and finely dice the flesh. Add to the chilli mixture and continue to simmer for about 25 minutes, or until the marmalade thickens. Transfer to a bowl. When cool, cover and chill until 30 minutes before serving.

COOK'S TIP
The aji amarillo marmalade will keep, chilled, for a week. It is also good eaten with hot smoked salmon.

6 Spread out the chicken pieces in a shallow dish and add the garlic, oil and pepper. Turn the fillets in the mixture, cover and set aside in a cool place for 30–45 minutes, turning occasionally.

7 Prepare the barbecue. Position a lightly oiled grill rack over the coals to heat. Grill the chicken pieces over medium-high heat for 2½–3 minutes on each side, or until cooked through and branded with grill marks. Using tongs, carefully move the food about while cooking to avoid over-charring. Transfer to a platter, cover and leave in a warm place for 5 minutes before serving with the marmalade.

Energy 401kcal/1689kJ; Protein 32.2g; Carbohydrate 47.5g, of which sugars 44.9g; Fat 10.4g, of which saturates 1.7g; Cholesterol 88mg; Calcium 56mg; Fibre 2.8g; Sodium 84mg.

GRILLED CHICKEN BALLS

THESE TASTY JAPANESE CHICKEN BALLS, KNOWN AS TSUKUNE, ARE POPULAR WITH CHILDREN AS WELL AS ADULTS. YOU CAN MAKE THE BALLS IN ADVANCE UP TO THE END OF STEP 2, AND THEY FREEZE VERY WELL.

SERVES FOUR

INGREDIENTS
300g/11oz skinless chicken,
   minced (ground)
2 eggs
2.5ml/½ tsp salt
10ml/2 tsp plain (all-purpose) flour
10ml/2 tsp cornflour (cornstarch)
90ml/6 tbsp dried breadcrumbs
2.5cm/1in piece of fresh root
   ginger, grated
For the *yakitori* sauce
60ml/4 tbsp sake
75ml/5 tbsp shoyu
15ml/1 tbsp mirin
15ml/1 tbsp caster (superfine) sugar
2.5ml/½ tsp cornflour (cornstarch)
   blended with 5ml/1 tsp water
shichimi togarashi or sansho
   (optional), to serve

1 Soak eight bamboo skewers for 30 minutes in water. Put all the ingredients for the chicken balls, except the ginger, in a food processor and blend well.

2 Wet your hands and scoop about a tablespoonful of the mixture into your palm. Shape it into a small ball about half the size of a golf ball. Make a further 30–32 balls in the same way.

3 Squeeze the juice from the grated ginger into a small mixing bowl. Discard the pulp.

4 Add the ginger juice to a small pan of boiling water. Add the chicken balls, and boil for about 7 minutes, or until the colour of the meat changes and the balls float to the surface. Scoop out using a slotted spoon and drain on a plate covered with kitchen paper.

5 In a small pan, mix all the ingredients for the *yakitori* sauce, except for the cornflour liquid. Bring to the boil, then reduce the heat and simmer for about 10 minutes, or until the sauce has slightly reduced. Add the cornflour liquid and stir until the sauce is thick. Transfer to a small bowl.

6 Prepare the barbecue. Position a lightly oiled grill rack over the hot coals. Thread three to four balls on each skewer and turn over the heat for a few minutes until the balls start to brown. Brush with sauce and return to the heat. Repeat the process twice. Serve, sprinkled with shichimi togarashi or sansho, if you like.

COOK'S TIP
Sansho is a Japanese spice, made by grinding the black seeds of pricky ash berries, that is often sprinkled on soups and stews. It is an important ingredient in the seven-spice blend shichimi togarash, which may also contain ground chilli, sesame seeds, seaweed and citrus peel. Shichimi togarash can be made at home but also bought ready-made.

Energy 263kcal/1111kJ; Protein 24.1g; Carbohydrate 25.9g, of which sugars 4.8g; Fat 4.1g, of which saturates 1g; Cholesterol 148mg; Calcium 54mg; Fibre 0.6g; Sodium 520mg.

PORK <u>ON</u> LEMON GRASS STICKS

THIS SIMPLE RECIPE MAKES A SUBSTANTIAL APPETIZER, AND THE LEMON GRASS STICKS NOT ONLY ADD A SUBTLE FLAVOUR BUT ALSO LOOK MOST ATTRACTIVE.

SERVES FOUR

INGREDIENTS

   300g/11oz minced (ground) pork
   4 garlic cloves, crushed
   4 fresh coriander (cilantro) roots,
    finely chopped
   2.5ml/½ tsp granulated sugar
   15ml/1 tbsp soy sauce
   8 x 10cm/4in lengths of lemon
    grass stalk
   salt and ground black pepper
   sweet chilli sauce,
    to serve

VARIATION
Slimmer versions of these pork sticks are perfect for parties. The mixture will be enough for 12 lemon grass sticks if you use it sparingly.

1 Place the minced pork, crushed garlic, chopped coriander root, sugar and soy sauce in a large bowl. Season with salt and pepper to taste, and mix well.

2 Divide into eight portions and mould each one into a ball. It may help to dampen your hands before shaping the mixture to prevent it from sticking.

3 Stick a length of lemon grass halfway into each ball, then press the meat mixture around it.

4 Prepare the barbecue. Position a lightly oiled grill rack over the hot coals. Cook the pork sticks for 3–4 minutes on each side, until golden and cooked through. Serve with the chilli sauce for dipping.

Energy 97kcal/409kJ; Protein 16.6g; Carbohydrate 0.7g, of which sugars 0.6g; Fat 3.2g, of which saturates 1.1g; Cholesterol 47mg; Calcium 31mg; Fibre 0.6g; Sodium 324mg.

Mini Burgers with Mozzarella

These Italian-style patties are made with beef and topped with creamy melted mozzarella and savoury anchovies. They make a substantial and unusual appetizer.

SERVES SIX

INGREDIENTS
- ½ slice white bread, crusts removed
- 45ml/3 tbsp milk
- 675g/1½lb minced (ground) beef
- 1 egg, beaten
- 50g/2oz/⅔ cup dry breadcrumbs
- olive oil, for brushing
- 2 beefsteak or other large tomatoes, sliced
- 15ml/1 tbsp chopped fresh oregano
- 1 mozzarella, cut into 6 slices
- 6 drained, canned anchovy fillets, cut in half lengthways
- salt and ground black pepper

1 Put the bread and milk into a small pan and heat gently, until the bread absorbs all the milk. Mash and leave to cool.

2 Put the minced beef into a bowl and add the cooled bread mixture. Stir in the beaten egg and season with plenty of salt and freshly ground black pepper. Mix well.

3 Shape the mixture into six patties, using your hands. Sprinkle the dry breadcrumbs on to a plate and dredge the patties, coating them thoroughly all over.

4 Prepare the barbecue. Position a lightly oiled grill rack over the hot coals. Brush the patties with olive oil and cook them on a hot barbecue for 2–3 minutes on one side, or until brown. Turn them over.

5 Without removing the patties from the barbecue, lay a slice of tomato on top of each patty, sprinkle with chopped oregano and season with salt and pepper. Place a mozzarella slice on top and arrange two strips of anchovy in a cross over the cheese.

6 Cook for a further 4–5 minutes, or until the patties are cooked through and the mozzarella has melted.

Energy 360kcal/1499kJ; Protein 28.6g; Carbohydrate 9.6g, of which sugars 2.2g; Fat 23.2g, of which saturates 10.9g; Cholesterol 82mg; Calcium 121mg; Fibre 0.7g; Sodium 374mg.

GRILLED FOIE GRAS

THE RICH AND LUXURIOUS TEXTURE OF THE FOIE GRAS IS TEAMED HERE WITH A SHARP, TANGY JAPANESE SAUCE, PONZU JOYU. THE CARAMELIZED FLAVOUR OF THE ASIAN PEAR BALANCES THE DISH PERFECTLY.

SERVES FOUR

INGREDIENTS
2 Asian (nashi) pears, each cut into eight wedges
15ml/1 tbsp clear honey mixed with 45ml/3 tbsp water
225g/8oz duck or goose foie gras, chilled and cut into eight 1cm/½in slices
For the ponzu joyu
  45ml/3 tbsp mirin
  120ml/4fl oz/½ cup tamari
  75ml/5 tbsp dried bonito flakes
  45ml/3 tbsp rice vinegar
  juice of 1 large lemon
  4 strips dried kombu seaweed

1 To make the ponzu joyu, place the mirin in a small pan, bring to the boil and cook for about 30 seconds.

2 Pour into a small bowl and add all the remaining ingredients. Cool, then cover and chill for about 24 hours. Strain the mixture into a screw-topped jar and chill until needed.

COOK'S TIP
You will find the ingredients for the ponzu joyu sauce in a Japanese supermarket. Bonito flakes are the dried shavings or flakes of Pacific bonito (a kind of small tuna). They are used to add flavour and always strained once their flavour has been absorbed. They are often used to season Japanese-style salads and vegetable dishes.

3 Toss the pear wedges in the honey mixture. Heat a griddle on the grill rack over hot coals. Griddle the pear wedges for about 30 seconds on each cut side.

4 Wipe the pan with kitchen paper and heat again. When it is searing hot, grill the foie gras for 30 seconds on each side. Serve immediately with the ponzu joyu and pear wedges.

Energy 238kcal/988kJ; Protein 7.5g; Carbohydrate 11.1g, of which sugars 10.9g; Fat 18.5g, of which saturates 5.4g; Cholesterol 96mg; Calcium 18mg; Fibre 1.7g; Sodium 692mg.

FISH AND SHELLFISH

Fresh seafood tastes great when it is barbecued, and there are so many ways that fish and shellfish can be prepared. Wrap them in leaves or steam inside foil parcels, cut them into chunks and skewer, stuff them or simply brush with oil or a fresh marinade and cook straight on the barbecue. Some of the fastest foods to cook over coals are shellfish, so they are perfect for that impromptu meal. Small whole fish are also an ideal choice for a quick bite to eat, but if you have a little more time, try some of the rewarding recipes that include sauces or relishes, or those dishes that require marinating a little way in advance; these simple touches and techniques will transform barbecued seafood — and the cooking aromas, with their promise of flavour, will tempt the tastebuds of any party guest. If you are planning to eat on the beach, there is even a Seafood Bake where you can cook locally caught shellfish without using a conventional barbecue.

CLAMS AND MUSSELS IN BANANA LEAVES

THESE PRETTY RAFFIA-TIED PARCELS CAN EITHER BE COOKED AS SOON AS THEY ARE READY OR CHILLED FOR UP TO 30 MINUTES, OFFERING A MOMENT'S RESPITE BEFORE THE COOKING BEGINS. BANANA LEAVES MAKE NEAT LITTLE PARCELS BUT YOU COULD ALSO USE DOUBLE FOIL.

3 Top a sheet of foil with a piece of banana leaf, placing it smooth-side up. Place another piece of leaf on top, at right angles, so that the leaves form a cross. Don't worry if the leaves are slightly wet – it's more important to work quickly with the leaves at this stage, while they remain soft and pliable.

4 Pile one-sixth of the seafood mixture into the centre, then bring up the leaves and tie them into a money-bag shape, using the raffia. Do the same with the foil, scrunching slightly to seal the top. Make the remaining parcels in the same way, then chill the parcels until needed.

5 Prepare the barbecue. Position a lightly oiled grill rack over the coals to heat. Cook the parcels over medium-high heat for about 15 minutes. Carefully remove the outer layer of foil from each and put the parcels back on the grill rack for 1 minute.

6 Transfer to individual plates. The parcels retain heat for a while, so can be left to stand for up to 5 minutes. Untie the raffia and eat from the leaves. Serve with bread sticks, if you wish.

COOK'S TIP
Have a quick peek into all of the bags to make sure the shells have opened before serving. Discard any shellfish that haven't opened.

SERVES SIX

INGREDIENTS
  15ml/1 tbsp olive oil
  1 large onion, finely chopped
  2 garlic cloves, crushed
  1.5ml/¼ tsp saffron threads
  60ml/4 tbsp Noilly Prat or other
    dry vermouth
  30ml/2 tbsp water
  30ml/2 tbsp chopped fresh flat
    leaf parsley
  500g/1¼lb clams, scrubbed
  900g/2lb mussels, cleaned
  6 banana leaves
  salt and ground black pepper
  raffia, for tying
  bread sticks, for serving

1 Heat the oil in a pan and add the chopped onion and garlic with the saffron threads. Cook over a gentle heat for 4 minutes. Add the vermouth and water, increase the heat and simmer for 2 minutes. Stir in the parsley, with salt and pepper to taste. Transfer to a bowl and leave to cool completely.

2 Tap the clam and mussel shells and discard any that stay open. Stir them into the bowl containing the onion mixture. Trim the hard edge from each banana leaf. Cut the leaves in half lengthways. Soak them in hot water for 10 minutes, then drain. Wipe any white residue from the leaves. Rinse, then pour over boiling water to soften.

Energy 116kcal/488kJ; Protein 14g; Carbohydrate 6.2g, of which sugars 4g; Fat 3.1g, of which saturates 0.5g; Cholesterol 40mg; Calcium 131mg; Fibre 0.9g; Sodium 498mg.

GIANT PRAWNS WRAPPED IN LIME LEAVES

THESE HUGE PRAWNS CAN GROW UP TO 33CM/13IN IN LENGTH, AND ARE PERFECT FOR GRILLING ON A BARBECUE. THIS DISH IS FAST AND EASY, YET IMPRESSIVE; IDEAL FOR A RELAXED POOLSIDE LUNCH WITH SALAD OR FOR SERVING AS AN APPETIZER WHILE THE MAIN COURSE IS COOKING.

SERVES SIX

INGREDIENTS
  6 giant Mediterranean prawns
    (extra large jumbo shrimp),
    total weight about 900g/2lb
  juice of 2 limes
  60ml/4 tbsp olive oil
  12 large kaffir lime leaves
  12 pandanus leaves
  2 limes cut into wedges, to serve

VARIATION
Serve these with a really easy dip made by mixing together 150ml/¼ pint/⅔ cup mayonnaise and 20ml/4 tsp Thai sweet chilli sauce.

1 Soak six wooden cocktail sticks (toothpicks) in water for 30 minutes. Make a shallow cut down the curved back of each prawn.

2 Put the giant prawns into a shallow dish, large enough to avoid cramming them on top of each other. In a separate bowl, mix the lime juice and oil together and pour over the prawns. Set aside for 15 minutes to allow the flavour to soak in.

3 Take each marinated prawn, lay two kaffir lime leaves on top, wrap two pandanus leaves around it and skewer with a cocktail stick.

4 Prepare the barbecue. Position a lightly oiled grill rack over the coals to heat. When the coals are medium-hot, grill the wrapped prawns for 3 minutes on each side. Serve with lime wedges. Unwrap the prawns, peel off the shell and remove the black vein with your fingers before eating.

COOK'S TIP
Many barbecue meals are hands-on affairs, so a few finger bowls are often useful. You can scent the water with citrus slices, herbs and flower essences, such as rose. Float fresh petals on top for a decorative touch, if you like.

Energy 122kcal/512kJ; Protein 12.9g; Carbohydrate 0.1g, of which sugars 0.1g; Fat 7.8g, of which saturates 1.2g; Cholesterol 158mg; Calcium 65mg; Fibre 0g; Sodium 900mg.

SEAFOOD ON SUGAR CANE

TOLEE MOLEE IS A BURMESE TERM FOR THE BITS AND PIECES THAT GO WITH A MAIN COURSE, SUCH AS BOWLS OF HERBS, CRISPY FRIED ONIONS AND BALACHAUNG, A CHILLI AND PRAWN PASTE. IF YOU PREFER, SPIKE THE PRAWNS ON SKEWERS RATHER THAN SUGAR CANE.

MAKES TWELVE

INGREDIENTS
  400g/14oz king prawns (jumbo
    shrimp), peeled
  225g/8oz skinned cod or halibut
    fillet, roughly cut into pieces
  pinch of ground turmeric
  1.5ml/¼ tsp ground white pepper
  1.5ml/¼ tsp salt
  60ml/4 tbsp chopped fresh coriander
    (cilantro)
  1 fresh long red chilli, seeded and
    finely chopped
  a piece of sugar cane cut into
    12 spikes (see Cook's Tip)
    or 12 wooden skewers
  30ml/2 tbsp sunflower oil
For the tolee molee
  25g/1oz/1 cup coriander
    (cilantro) leaves
  45ml/3 tbsp olive oil
  300g/11oz sweet onions, halved and
    finely sliced
  90ml/6 tbsp balachaung
  15ml/1 tbsp sugar
  juice of ½ lime
  30ml/2 tbsp water

1 Soak the sugar cane spikes or skewers in water for 30 minutes. Make a shallow cut down the centre of the curved back of the prawns. Pull out the black veins with a cocktail stick (toothpick). Slice the prawns roughly and place in a food processor with the fish, turmeric, pepper and salt.

2 Pulse until the mixture forms a paste. Add the coriander and chilli, and pulse lightly to combine with the other ingredients. Spoon into a bowl and chill for 30 minutes.

3 To make the tolee molee, place the coriander leaves in a small serving bowl filled with cold water. Chill. Heat the olive oil in a large frying pan and fry the sliced onions over a medium heat for 10 minutes, stirring occasionally and increasing the heat for the last few minutes so that the onions become golden and crisp.

4 Pile the cooked onions into a serving bowl. Place the balachaung in another serving bowl, and mix in the sugar, lime juice and measured water. Stir the mixture thoroughly and set aside.

5 Using damp hands, mould the seafood mixture around the drained sugarcane spikes or wooden skewers, so that it forms an oval sausage shape.

6 Prepare the barbecue. Position a lightly oiled grill rack over the hot coals. Brush the seafood with the sunflower oil and grill over medium-high heat for about 3 minutes on each side until just cooked through. Serve with the tolee molee.

COOK'S TIP
To make sugar cane spikes, chop through the length using a cook's knife and split into 1cm/½in shards. The sugar cane can be bought from ethnic grocers.

Energy 98kcal/410kJ; Protein 9.9g; Carbohydrate 3.5g, of which sugars 2.9g; Fat 5.1g, of which saturates 0.7g; Cholesterol 74mg; Calcium 52mg; Fibre 0.8g; Sodium 78mg.

MARINATED OCTOPUS ON STICKS

OCTOPUS THAT IS FROZEN AND THEN THAWED BECOMES TENDER IN THE PROCESS, AND SO IT COOKS QUICKLY. CHECK WITH THE FISHMONGER BEFORE BUYING, BECAUSE FRESH OCTOPUS WILL NEED CONSIDERABLY MORE SIMMERING TIME. SERVE WITH RED PIPIAN FOR A SPICY PUNCH.

SERVES EIGHT

INGREDIENTS
  1kg/2¼lb whole octopus
  1 onion, quartered
  2 bay leaves
  30ml/2 tbsp olive oil
  grated rind and juice of 1 lemon
  15ml/1 tbsp chopped fresh coriander
    (cilantro)
For the red pipian
  1 ancho chilli (dried poblano)
  4 whole garlic cloves, peeled
  1 small pink onion, chopped
  500g/1¼lb plum tomatoes, cored
    and seeded
  30ml/2 tbsp olive oil
  5ml/1 tsp sugar
  30ml/2 tbsp pine nuts
  30ml/2 tbsp pumpkin seeds
  pinch of ground cinnamon
  15ml/1 tbsp chipotles in adobo
    or other sweet and smoky chilli
    sauce
  45ml/3 tbsp vegetable stock
  leaves from 4 large fresh thyme
    sprigs, finely chopped
  salt
  fresh coriander (cilantro) sprigs,
    to garnish

1 Make the red pipian. Preheat the oven to 200°C/400°F/Gas 6. Put the ancho chilli in a bowl and cover with hot water. Leave to soak for about 20 minutes. Meanwhile place the garlic, onion and tomatoes in a roasting pan and drizzle with the oil, then sprinkle the sugar and a little salt over the top. Roast for 15 minutes. Add the pine nuts, pumpkin seeds and cinnamon to the top of the mixture and roast for a further 5 minutes. Meanwhile, drain the ancho chilli, remove the seeds and chop the flesh.

2 Transfer the roasted mixture and the ancho chilli to a food processor with the chipotles or chilli sauce, vegetable stock and thyme. Pulse to a purée, then scrape into a serving bowl and leave to cool.

COOK'S TIP
Cook the skewered octopus on a griddle, if you prefer. The timing will be the same.

3 Trim the tentacles from the head of the octopus. Leave the skin on, but trim any large flaps with kitchen scissors. Discard the head. Place the tentacles in a large pan, cover with cold water and add the onion and bay leaves. Bring slowly to the boil, lower the heat and simmer for about 20 minutes if pre-frozen, and up to 2 hours if fresh.

4 Drain the tentacles and rinse under cold water, rubbing off any loose dark membrane. Thread the tentacles on to eight metal skewers and put in a plastic bag with the olive oil, lemon rind and juice, and chopped coriander. Tie shut and shake to mix. Leave to marinate in a cool place for at least 1 hour or up to 12 hours.

5 Prepare the barbecue. Position a lightly oiled grill rack over the hot coals. Grill the octopus skewers over medium-high heat for 2–4 minutes each side, or until nicely golden. Serve with the red pipian, garnished with the coriander sprigs.

Energy 149kcal/627kJ; Protein 23.2g; Carbohydrate 3.8g, of which sugars 3.4g; Fat 4.7g, of which saturates 0.8g; Cholesterol 60mg; Calcium 62mg; Fibre 1.2g; Sodium 8mg.

SEAFOOD AND SPRING ONION SKEWERS

MONKFISH IS A FINE FISH FOR BARBECUING, AS ITS FIRM FLESH HOLDS ITS SHAPE WELL AND IS EASY TO SPEAR ON TO SKEWERS. IT HAS A LOVELY SWEET FLAVOUR, VERY SIMILAR TO SHELLFISH, AND HERE IT IS PARTNERED WITH SCALLOPS OR KING PRAWNS, MAKING AN ATTRACTIVE AND DELICIOUS COMBINATION.

MAKES NINE

INGREDIENTS
    675g/1½lb monkfish, filleted,
      skinned and membrane removed
    1 bunch thick spring onions
      (scallions), cut into 5cm/2in pieces
    75ml/5 tbsp olive oil
    1 garlic clove, finely chopped
    15ml/1 tbsp lemon juice
    5ml/1 tsp dried oregano
    30ml/2 tbsp chopped fresh flat
      leaf parsley
    12–18 small scallops or raw king
      prawns (jumbo shrimp)
    75g/3oz/1½ cups fine fresh
      breadcrumbs
    salt and ground black pepper
For the tartare sauce
    2 egg yolks
    300ml/½ pint/1¼ cups olive oil,
      or vegetable oil and olive oil mixed
    15–30ml/1–2 tbsp lemon juice
    5ml/1 tsp French mustard, preferably
      tarragon mustard
    15ml/1 tbsp chopped gherkin or
      pickled cucumber
    15ml/1 tbsp chopped capers
    30ml/2 tbsp chopped fresh flat
      leaf parsley
    30ml/2 tbsp chopped fresh chives
    5ml/1 tsp chopped fresh tarragon

1 Soak nine wooden skewers in water for 30 minutes to prevent them from scorching on the barbecue.

2 To make the tartare sauce, whisk the egg yolks and a pinch of salt. Whisk in the oil, a drop at a time at first. When about half the oil is incorporated, add it in a thin stream, whisking constantly. Stop when the mayonnaise is thick.

3 Whisk in 15ml/1 tbsp lemon juice, then a little more oil. Stir in the mustard, gherkin or cucumber, capers, parsley, chives and tarragon. Add more lemon juice and seasoning to taste.

4 Cut the monkfish into 18 pieces. In a bowl, mix the oil, garlic, lemon juice, oregano and half the parsley with seasoning. Add the seafood and spring onions. Leave to marinate for 15 minutes.

5 Mix the breadcrumbs and remaining parsley together. Toss the seafood and spring onions in the mixture to coat.

6 Prepare the barbecue. Position a lightly oiled grill rack over the hot coals. Drain the wooden skewers and thread the monkfish, scallops or prawns and spring onions on to them. Drizzle with a little marinade then cook over medium heat for 7–8 minutes in total, turning once and drizzling with the marinade, until the fish is just cooked. Serve immediately with the tartare sauce.

Energy 352kcal/1462kJ; Protein 16.6g; Carbohydrate 6.9g, of which sugars 0.6g; Fat 28.9g, of which saturates 4.3g; Cholesterol 88mg; Calcium 41mg; Fibre 0.4g; Sodium 111mg.

WHOLE STUFFED SQUID

BEAUTIFULLY FRESH SQUID TASTES WONDERFUL WHEN IT IS BARBECUED, AND THE SQUID BODY IS PERFECT FOR A RICH WALNUT STUFFING. THE TENTACLES ARE PARTICULARLY TASTY, SO BE SURE TO SKEWER THEM AND COOK THEM AS WELL.

SERVES SIX

INGREDIENTS
12 whole small squid, total weight about 675g/1½lb
45ml/3 tbsp extra virgin olive oil, plus extra for coating
2 onions, finely chopped
3 garlic cloves, crushed
25g/1oz/2 tbsp walnuts, finely chopped
7.5ml/1½ tsp ground sumac or a squeeze of lemon juice
1.5ml/¼ tsp chilli flakes, finely chopped
75–90g/3–3½oz rocket (arugula), any tough stalks removed
115g/4oz/1 cup cooked rice
salt and ground black pepper
lemon and lime wedges, to serve

1 To prepare the squid, hold the body firmly in one hand and grasp the tentacles at their base with the other. Pull the head away from the body, bringing the entrails with it. Cut the tentacles (and part of the head above the eyes) away from the entrails. Snip out the hard beak in the middle of the clump of tentacles and discard this, along with the entrails attached to the remainder of the head.

2 Peel the purplish membrane away from the body, then pull out the hard transparent quill and discard. Wash the clumps of tentacles and body well, inside and out, under cold running water.

3 Put the tentacles on a plate, cover and chill. Pull the side flaps or wings away from the body, chop them finely and set aside. Reserve the squid body with the tentacles.

COOK'S TIPS
• You can ask your fishmonger to prepare the squid for you, if you prefer.
• If you stuff the squid in advance and chill them, remember to let them return to room temperature before cooking.

4 Heat a frying pan. Add the oil, onions and garlic and fry for 5 minutes, or until the onions are soft and golden. Add the chopped squid wings and fry for about 1 minute, then stir in the walnuts, sumac and chilli flakes. Add the rocket and continue to stir-fry until it has wilted. Stir in the rice, season well and tip into a bowl to cool. Soak six wooden skewers in water for 30 minutes.

5 Prepare the barbecue. Stuff each squid with the cold mixture and thread two on to each skewer, with two clumps of tentacles. Toss in oil and salt. Position a lightly oiled grill rack over the coals to heat. Grill the squid over medium-high heat for about 1½ minutes on each side.

6 Once they are pale golden, move them to a cooler part of the grill to cook for 1½ minutes more on each side to ensure the filling is hot. Baste with any remaining oil and salt mixture as they are turned. Serve them with the lemon and lime wedges.

Energy 212kcal/887kJ; Protein 19.3g; Carbohydrate 10.3g, of which sugars 2.2g; Fat 10.7g, of which saturates 1.6g; Cholesterol 253mg; Calcium 56mg; Fibre 1g; Sodium 146mg.

TIGER PRAWN SKEWERS

LARGE PRAWNS ARE FULL OF FLAVOUR AND IDEAL FOR BARBECUING — AND THEY ARE SO QUICK TO COOK. IN THIS RECIPE THEY ARE MARINATED IN AN UNUSUAL WALNUT PESTO, WHICH IS SIMPLE TO PREPARE AND CAN BE MADE THE DAY BEFORE. MARINATE OVERNIGHT FOR THE BEST RESULTS.

SERVES FOUR

INGREDIENTS
  12–16 large, raw, shell-on tiger
    prawns (jumbo shrimp)
  50g/2oz/½ cup walnut pieces
  60ml/4 tbsp chopped fresh flat
    leaf parsley
  60ml/4 tbsp chopped fresh basil
  2 garlic cloves, chopped
  45ml/3 tbsp grated fresh
    Parmesan cheese
  30ml/2 tbsp extra virgin olive oil
  30ml/2 tbsp walnut oil
  salt and ground black pepper

1 Peel the prawns, removing the head but leaving the tail. Devein the prawns using a cocktail stick (toothpick) and then put the prawns in a large mixing bowl.

VARIATION
For garlic prawns, clean the prawns and thread on skewers. Brush with oil and grill as before. Melt 50g/2oz/¼ cup butter in a small pan on the barbecue. Add 2 crushed garlic cloves, 30ml/2 tbsp chopped fresh parsley, the grated rind of ¼ lemon and 15ml/1 tbsp lemon juice. Serve with the prawns.

2 To make the pesto, place the walnuts, parsley, basil, garlic, cheese and oils in a food processor and process until finely chopped. Season.

3 Add half the pesto to the prawns in the bowl, toss them well, then cover and chill for a minimum of 1 hour, or leave them overnight.

4 Soak four wooden skewers in water for 30 minutes. Prepare the barbecue. Position a lightly oiled grill rack over the hot coals. Thread the prawns on to the skewers and cook them over high heat for 3–4 minutes, turning once. Serve with the remaining pesto and a green salad, if you like.

Energy 256kcal/1062kJ; Protein 13.9g; Carbohydrate 0.9g, of which sugars 0.8g; Fat 21.9g, of which saturates 4.2g; Cholesterol 90mg; Calcium 209mg; Fibre 1.3g; Sodium 578mg.

MARINATED MONKFISH AND MUSSEL KEBABS

THIS RECIPE COMBINES SEAFOOD WITH TURKEY, GIVING THE KEBABS EXTRA RICHNESS. THE SIMPLE MARINADE TAKES NO TIME AT ALL TO PREPARE. THE MARINADE WILL MAKE THE MONKFISH BOTH DELICIOUSLY FLAVOURED AND QUICKER TO BARBECUE, SO OBSERVE THE COOKING TIME CLOSELY.

SERVES FOUR

INGREDIENTS
    450g/1lb monkfish, skinned
        and boned
    5ml/1 tsp olive oil
    30ml/2 tbsp lemon juice
    5ml/1 tsp paprika
    1 garlic clove, crushed
    4 turkey rashers
    8 cooked mussels
    8 large raw prawns (shrimp)
    15ml/1 tbsp chopped fresh dill
    salt and ground black pepper
    lemon wedges, to garnish
    salad and rice, to serve

1 Mix together the oil, lemon juice, paprika, and garlic in a bowl and season with pepper.

2 Cut the monkfish into 2.5cm/1in cubes and place in a shallow glass dish.

3 Pour the marinade over the fish and toss to coat evenly. Cover and leave in a cool place for 30 minutes.

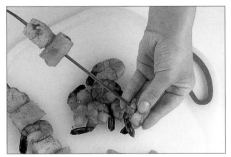

4 Cut the turkey rashers in half and wrap each strip around a mussel. Thread on to skewers alternating with the fish cubes and raw prawns.

COOK'S TIP
If you thread your kebabs on to two parallel skewers you will find they are easier to turn over.

5 Prepare the barbecue. Position a lightly oiled grill rack over the hot coals. Cook the kebabs over high heat for 7–8 minutes, turning once and basting with the marinade. Sprinkle with chopped dill and salt. Garnish with the lemon wedges and serve with salad and rice.

Energy 126kcal/534kJ; Protein 26.5g; Carbohydrate 0.3g, of which sugars 0g; Fat 2.1g, of which saturates 0.5g; Cholesterol 67mg; Calcium 26mg; Fibre 0g; Sodium 103mg.

GRILLED LOBSTER

THIS IS A SMART YET UNPRETENTIOUS DISH AND WELL WORTH THE LITTLE BIT OF EXTRA EFFORT.
LOBSTER IS A FANTASTIC INGREDIENT TO COOK WITH BUT, IF YOU ARE A BIT SQUEAMISH, DISPATCHING
IT IS A VERY HARD THING TO DO, IN WHICH CASE IT IS A JOB PROBABLY BEST LEFT TO THE
FISHMONGER. INSTRUCTIONS FOR KILLING IT HUMANELY ARE GIVEN BELOW.

SERVES TWO TO FOUR

INGREDIENTS
  15 fresh basil leaves, roughly
    chopped
  60ml/4 tbsp olive oil
  1 garlic clove, crushed
  2 freshly killed lobsters, cut in
    half lengthways and cleaned
    (see Cook's Tip)
  salt and ground black pepper
  2 limes, halved, to serve
For the basil oil and mayonnaise
  40g/1½oz/1½ cups basil leaves
    stripped from their stalks
  175ml/6fl oz/¾ cup sunflower oil,
    plus extra if needed
  45ml/3 tbsp olive oil
  1 small garlic clove, crushed
  2.5ml/½ tsp dry English (hot)
    mustard
  10ml/2 tsp lemon juice
  2 egg yolks
  ground white pepper

1 To make the basil oil, place the basil leaves in a bowl and pour boiling water over them. Leave for about 30 seconds until the leaves turn a brighter green. Drain, refresh under cold running water, drain again, then squeeze dry in kitchen paper. Place the leaves in a food processor. Add both oils and process to a purée. Scrape into a bowl, cover and chill overnight.

2 Line a sieve with muslin and set it over a deep bowl. Pour in the basil and oil purée and leave undisturbed for about 1 hour, or until all the oil has filtered through into the bowl. Discard the solids left behind. Cover and chill.

3 To make the mayonnaise, you will need 200ml/7fl oz/ scant 1 cup of the basil oil. If you do not have enough, make it up with more sunflower oil. Place the crushed garlic in a bowl. Add the mustard with 2.5ml/ ½ tsp of the lemon juice and a little salt and white pepper.

4 Whisk in the egg yolks, then start adding the basil oil, a drop at a time, whisking continuously until the mixture starts to thicken. At this stage it is usually safe to start adding the oil a little faster. When you have 45ml/3 tbsp oil left, whisk in the remaining lemon juice and then add the rest of the oil. Finally, whisk in 7.5ml/1½ tsp cold water. Cover the mayonnaise and chill.

5 Prepare the barbecue. Chop the basil and mix it with the oil and garlic in a bowl. Season lightly. Once the flames have died down, rake the coals to get more on one side than the other. Position a lightly oiled grill rack over the coals to heat.

6 Brush some of the oil mixture over the cut side of each lobster half. Place cut-side down on the grill rack on the side away from the bulk of the coals. Grill for 5 minutes. Turn the lobsters over, baste with more oil mixture and cook for 10–15 minutes more, basting and moving them about the rack.

7 Grill the lime halves at the same time, placing them cut-side down for 3 minutes to caramelize. Serve the lobster with the mayonnaise and the grilled lime halves.

COOK'S TIP
If you have to kill a lobster yourself, you can do so humanely. Either put the live lobster in a freezerproof dish or tray and cover with crushed ice to render it unconscious, or by put it into the freezer for 2 hours. When the lobster is very cold and no longer moving, place it on a chopping board and drive the tip of a large, sharp and heavy knife or a very strong skewer through the centre of the cross on its head. According to experts, death is instantaneous.

   To clean, split in half by laying the lobster on its back and stretching out the body. Use a sharp, heavy knife to cut the lobster neatly in half along the entire length. Discard the whitish sac and the feathery gills from the head and the grey-black intestinal sac that runs down the tail. The greenish tomalley (liver) and the coral (roe) are delicious, so retain these.

Energy 518kcal/2144kJ; Protein 21.8g; Carbohydrate 0.4g, of which sugars 0.3g; Fat 47.9g, of which saturates 6.5g; Cholesterol 201mg; Calcium 92mg; Fibre 0.6g; Sodium 309mg.

SEAFOOD BAKE

A BEACH BAKE IS GREAT FUN AND A SEMI-PRECISE SCIENCE, WHICH REQUIRES COMMITMENT BY AT LEAST TWO HIGHLY MOTIVATED PARTIES WITH A PENCHANT FOR DIGGING HOLES. BASE YOUR CATCH ON THE INGREDIENTS BELOW, MULTIPLIED AS REQUIRED.

SERVES ONE

INGREDIENTS
  2 freshwater crayfish
  4 langoustines
  2 large clams, about 6cm/2½in
    across
  6 small clams
  3 whelks
  12 cockles
  lemons, bread and good quality
    olive oil
Other things you will need
  sand or earth
  shovels and buckets
  dry pebbles
  plenty of dry firewood, newspaper
    and twigs
  matches or a lighter
  long-handled rake
  seaweed, well washed and soaked
    in water
  a large piece of canvas, soaked
    in water
  12 heavy stones
  heatproof gloves
  cocktail sticks (toothpicks)

1 Dig a pit at least 90cm/3ft square x 30cm/1ft deep; larger if you are catering for a crowd. Line the base with pebbles, taking them part of the way up the sides. Build a pyramid-shaped mound of kindling in the middle of the square, with some scrunched-up newspaper at the base.

2 Start the fire. When the wood is burning well, add larger pieces to the fire so that it eventually covers the entire surface area of the pit. Keep the fire well stoked up for about 45–60 minutes, then let it burn down to a stage where small glowing embers remain. Using a long-handled rake, pull as many of the dying embers as possible from the pit without dislodging the pebbles.

3 At this point it is important to retain the oven-like temperature of the pebbles so, working quickly, spread half the seaweed evenly over the pebbles. Arrange the seafood over the seaweed, with the smallest items towards the edges for easy access, as these will cook first. Cover with the rest of the seaweed, then cover the lot with the wet canvas. This should extend beyond the perimeter of the pit and should be weighted down with 12 heavy stones, placed well away from the pit.

4 Leave the seafood to bake undisturbed for 1–2 hours. The hotter the pebbles get, the faster the food will cook, so after 1 hour, have a sneaky peek to see if the cockles and small clams are cooked. These can be taken out at this stage and eaten, and the rest of the seafood enjoyed when it is ready.

COOK'S TIP
Before leaving the site, take care to douse any discarded embers with water to ensure they are not left hot.

Energy 175kcal/742kJ; Protein 38.9g; Carbohydrate 0.9g, of which sugars 0g; Fat 1.8g, of which saturates 0.4g; Cholesterol 268mg; Calcium 164mg; Fibre 0g; Sodium 1139mg.

SCALLOPS <u>WITH</u> LIME BUTTER

CHARGRILLING FENNEL RELEASES ITS ANISEED FLAVOUR, WHICH TASTES GREAT WITH SWEET AND RICH SCALLOPS. THESE WONDERFUL SHELLFISH ARE IDEAL FOR THE BARBECUE BECAUSE THEY HAVE FIRM FLESH THAT COOKS QUICKLY — SIMPLY TOSS IN LIME JUICE BEFORE COOKING.

SERVES FOUR

INGREDIENTS
   1 head fennel
   2 limes
   12 large scallops, cleaned
   1 egg yolk
   90ml/6 tbsp melted butter
   olive oil for brushing
   salt and ground black pepper

COOK'S TIP
When choosing fennel, look for bulbs that are white and firm.

1 Trim any feathery leaves from the fennel and reserve them. Slice the rest lengthways into thin wedges.

2 Cut one lime into wedges. Finely grate the rind and squeeze the juice of the other lime and toss half the juice and rind on to the scallops. Season well with salt and ground black pepper.

3 Place the egg yolk and remaining lime rind and juice in a small bowl and whisk until pale and smooth.

4 Gradually whisk in the melted butter and continue whisking until thick and smooth. Finely chop the reserved fennel leaves and stir them in, with seasoning.

5 Prepare the barbecue. Position a lightly oiled grill rack over the hot coals. Brush the fennel wedges with olive oil and cook them over high heat for 3–4 minutes, turning once.

6 Add the scallops and cook for a further 3–4 minutes, turning once. Serve with the lime and fennel butter and the lime wedges.

COOK'S TIP
Thread small scallops on to flat skewers to make turning them easier.

Energy 232kcal/961kJ; Protein 10g; Carbohydrate 2.2g, of which sugars 0.9g; Fat 20.5g, of which saturates 12.3g; Cholesterol 116mg; Calcium 31mg; Fibre 1.1g; Sodium 211mg.

GRILLED SALTED SARDINES

WHOLE GRILLED SARDINES ARE CLASSIC MEDITERRANEAN BEACH FOOD, EVOKING MEMORIES OF LAZY LUNCHES UNDER RUSTIC AWNINGS, JUST A STEP AWAY FROM THE SEA. HERE THEY ARE SERVED WITH SALMORIGLIO, AN ITALIAN HERB SALSA POUNDED WITH SEA SALT.

SERVES FOUR TO EIGHT

INGREDIENTS
  8 sardines, total weight about
    800g/1¾lb, scaled and gutted
  50g/2oz/¼ cup salt
  oil, for brushing
  focaccia, to serve
For the salmoriglio
  5ml/1 tsp sea salt flakes
  60ml/4 tbsp chopped fresh tarragon
    leaves
  40g/1½oz/generous 1 cup chopped
    flat leaf parsley
  1 small red onion, very finely
    chopped
  105ml/7 tbsp extra virgin olive oil
  60ml/4 tbsp lemon juice

1 Rub the sardines inside and out with salt. Cover and put in a cool place for 30–45 minutes. Make the salmoriglio by putting the salt in a mortar and pounding all the ingredients one at a time with a pestle.

2 Meanwhile, prepare the barbecue. Rinse the salt off the sardines. Pat them dry with kitchen paper, then leave to air-dry for 15 minutes. Position a lightly oiled grill rack over the hot coals.

3 Brush the sardines with a little oil and put them in a small, hinged, wire barbecue fish basket. Grill them over medium-high heat for about 3 minutes on one side and about 2½ minutes on the other. When ready, lift out of the basket and serve hot with the salmoriglio and focaccia.

COOK'S TIP
Hinged wire fish baskets come in various shapes and sizes, often oval to accommodate a whole fish, square to hold fillets and steaks, or more elaborate in design to hold a number of smaller fish (see left). The idea is that you turn the basket over the barbecue rather than the fish, which is ideal for delicate dishes. If you do not have one, you can of course grill the fish directly on the rack. Do make sure to oil it well first, and only turn the fish when the undersides are crisp.

Energy 210kcal/873kJ; Protein 15.7g; Carbohydrate 0.8g, of which sugars 0.6g; Fat 16g, of which saturates 3.2g; Cholesterol 0mg; Calcium 90mg; Fibre 0.4g; Sodium 87mg.

ROLLED SARDINES WITH PLUM PASTE

MAKE THIS SIMPLE AND DELIGHTFUL JAPANESE RECIPE WHEN SARDINES ARE IN SEASON. PERFECTLY FRESH SARDINES ARE ROLLED UP AROUND LAYERS OF SHISO LEAVES AND UMEBOSHI, A JAPANESE APRICOT (OFTEN CALLED 'JAPANESE PLUM') THAT IS PICKLED IN SALT.

SERVES FOUR

INGREDIENTS
   8 sardines, cleaned and filleted
   5ml/1 tsp salt
   4 umeboshi, about 30g/1¼oz total
      weight (choose the soft type)
   5ml/1 tsp sake
   5ml/1 tsp toasted sesame seeds
   16 shiso leaves, cut in
      half lengthways
   1 lime, thinly sliced, the centre
      hollowed out to make rings,
      to garnish

COOK'S TIP
Sardines deteriorate very quickly and must be bought and eaten on the same day. Be careful when buying: the eyes and gills should not be too pink. If the fish "melts" like cheese when grilled, don't bother to eat it.

1 Carefully cut the sardine fillets in half lengthways and place them side by side in a large, shallow container. Sprinkle with salt on both sides.

2 Remove the stones (pits) from the umeboshi and put the fruit in a small mixing bowl with the sake and toasted sesame seeds. With the back of a fork, mash the umeboshi, mixing well to form a smooth paste.

3 Wipe the sardine fillets with kitchen paper. With a butter knife, spread some umeboshi paste thinly on to one of the sardine fillets, then press some shiso leaves on top. Roll up the sardine starting from the tail and pierce with a wooden cocktail stick (toothpick). Repeat to make 16 rolled sardines.

4 Prepare the barbecue. Position a lightly oiled grill rack over the hot coals. Grill the rolled sardines over medium-high heat for 4–6 minutes on each side, or until golden brown, turning once.

5 Lay a few lime rings on four individual plates and arrange the rolled sardines alongside. Serve hot.

Energy 248kcal/1037kJ; Protein 31.1g; Carbohydrate 0.7g, of which sugars 0.7g; Fat 13.3g, of which saturates 3.7g; Cholesterol 0mg; Calcium 161mg; Fibre 0.2g; Sodium 171mg.

MACKEREL <u>WITH</u> NUTTY BACON STUFFING

THIS MACKEREL RECIPE WAS INSPIRED BY A POPULAR TURKISH DISH CALLED USKUMRU DOLMASI. THE FISH ARE STUFFED, TIED WITH RAFFIA AND THEN GRILLED. THEY TASTE JUST AS GOOD COLD, SO MAKE EXTRA FOR LUNCH NEXT DAY AND SERVE WITH HORSERADISH MAYONNAISE.

SERVES SIX

INGREDIENTS
45ml/3 tbsp olive oil
2 onions, finely chopped
2 garlic cloves, crushed
6 rindless smoked bacon rashers
  (strips), diced
50g/2oz/½ cup pine nuts
45ml/3 tbsp chopped fresh
  sweet marjoram
6 mackerel, about 300g/11oz each,
  cleaned but with heads left on
salt and ground black pepper
raffia, soaked in water
lemon wedges, to serve

1 Heat the oil in a large frying pan and sweat the chopped onions and garlic over a medium heat for 5 minutes.

2 Increase the heat and add the bacon and pine nuts. Fry for a further 5–7 minutes, stirring occasionally, until golden. Tip into a bowl to cool. Gently fold in the sweet marjoram, season lightly, cover and chill until needed.

3 To prepare each fish, snip the backbone at the head end. Extend the cavity opening at the tail end so that you can reach the backbone more easily. Turn the fish over and, with the heel of your hand, press firmly along the entire length of the backbone to loosen it. Snip the bone at the tail end and it will lift out surprisingly easily. Season the insides lightly.

COOK'S TIPS
• If you are cooking these mackerel on a charcoal kettle barbecue, and the heat becomes too intense very suddenly, you can reduce it a little by half-closing the air vents.
• If your barbecue has a lid, it is especially useful for this recipe. This will help you achieve an even golden skin without needing to move the fish about.

4 Stuff the cavity in each mackerel with some of the chilled onion mixture, then tie the mackerel along its entire length with raffia to hold in the stuffing. Chill the fish for at least 15 minutes. They can be chilled for up to 2 hours, but if so, allow them to come to room temperature for about 15 minutes before grilling.

5 Prepare the barbecue. Position a lightly oiled grill rack over the hot coals. Transfer the mackerel to the grill rack and cook for about 8 minutes on each side over medium-high heat, or until cooked and golden.

6 Transfer the cooked fish to warmed serving plates, and snip the raffia in several places, but otherwise leave it wrapped around the fish to add visual appeal. Serve the mackerel with lemon wedges and black pepper.

COOK'S TIP
Raffia is a strong, pliable and water-resistant fibre obtained from the raffia palm, native to Madagascar. After being dried in the sun, it is often used in crafts such as weaving or flower arranging.

Energy 858kcal/3561kJ; Protein 64.5g; Carbohydrate 5.8g, of which sugars 4.3g; Fat 64.1g, of which saturates 12.9g; Cholesterol 175mg; Calcium 69mg; Fibre 1.5g; Sodium 641mg.

Hot Smoked Salmon

Hickory chips added to the coals while the food cooks give it an authentic smoky flavour, which is perfect for this quickly smoked salmon dish that is served with a fruity mojo.

4 Place the fillets skin side down on the grill rack over medium-high heat. Cover the barbecue with a lid or tented heavy-duty foil and cook the fish for 3–5 minutes.

5 Drain the hickory chips into a colander and sprinkle about a third of them as evenly as possible over the coals. Carefully drop them through the slats in the grill rack, taking care not to scatter the ash as you do so.

6 Replace the barbecue cover and continue cooking for a further 8 minutes, adding a small handful of hickory chips twice more during this time. Serve the salmon hot or cold, with the mojo.

SERVES SIX

INGREDIENTS
  6 salmon fillets, each about
    175g/6oz, with skin
  15ml/1 tbsp sunflower oil
  salt and ground black pepper
  2 handfuls hickory wood chips,
    soaked in cold water for as much
    time as you have available,
    preferably 30 minutes
For the mojo
  1 ripe mango, diced
  4 drained canned pineapple
    slices, diced
  1 small red onion, finely chopped
  1 fresh long mild red chilli, seeded
    and finely chopped
  15ml/1 tbsp good quality sweet
    chilli sauce
  grated rind and juice of 1 lime
  leaves from 1 small lemon basil
    plant or 45ml/3 tbsp fresh
    coriander (cilantro) leaves,
    shredded or chopped

1 First, make the mojo by putting the mango, pineapple, onion, and chilli together in a bowl.

2 Add the chilli sauce, lime rind and juice, and the herb leaves. Stir to mix well. Cover tightly and leave in a cool place until needed.

3 Prepare the barbecue. Position a lightly oiled grill rack over the hot coals. Rinse the salmon fillets and pat dry, then brush each with a little oil.

COOK'S TIPS
• When sweet pineapples are in season, you may prefer to use fresh ones in the mojo. You will need about half a medium pineapple. Slice off the skin, remove the core and cut the flesh into chunks.
• To dice a mango, slice alongside the stone (pit) on both sides. Cut the flesh in a criss-cross pattern, then turn it inside out and slice off the cubes.

Energy 365kcal/1522kJ; Protein 36g; Carbohydrate 7.8g, of which sugars 7.5g; Fat 21.3g, of which saturates 3.6g; Cholesterol 88mg; Calcium 61mg; Fibre 1.3g; Sodium 83mg.

MEXICAN BARBECUE SALMON

THESE SALMON FILLETS COOK QUICKLY ON THE BARBECUE, AND BECAUSE THEY'VE BEEN MARINATED IN THE TOMATO SAUCE, THEY REMAIN BEAUTIFULLY MOIST AND SUCCULENT.

SERVES FOUR

INGREDIENTS

   25g/1oz/2 tbsp butter
   1 small red onion, finely chopped
   1 garlic clove, crushed
   6 plum tomatoes, diced
   45ml/3 tbsp tomato ketchup
   30ml/2 tbsp Dijon mustard
   30ml/2 tbsp soft dark brown sugar
   15ml/1 tbsp clear honey
   5ml/1 tsp ground cayenne pepper
   15ml/1 tbsp ancho chilli powder
   15ml/1 tbsp paprika
   15ml/1 tbsp Worcestershire sauce
   4 salmon fillets, about 175g/6oz each
   fresh flat leaf parsley sprigs,
     to garnish

3 Add the tomato ketchup, Dijon mustard, brown sugar, honey, cayenne pepper, chilli powder, paprika and Worcestershire sauce. Stir well, then simmer for a further 20 minutes. Pour the mixture into a food processor and process until smooth. Leave to cool.

4 Put the salmon in a shallow dish, brush with the sauce and chill for 2 hours. Prepare the barbecue. Position a lightly oiled grill rack over the hot coals. Cook the salmon over medium-high heat for 2–3 minutes on each side, brushing with the sauce. Garnish and serve.

1 Melt the butter in a large, heavy pan and cook the onion and garlic gently for about 5 minutes until softened and translucent. Do not let the onion brown.

2 Add the plum tomatoes. Bring to the boil, then reduce the heat and simmer for 15 minutes. Stir the tomatoes occasionally with a wooden spoon so that they do not catch on the base of the pan.

Energy 437kcal/1827kJ; Protein 36.9g; Carbohydrate 17.5g, of which sugars 17g; Fat 24.9g, of which saturates 6.7g; Cholesterol 101mg; Calcium 65mg; Fibre 1.8g; Sodium 360mg.

TANGY GRILLED SALMON WITH PINEAPPLE

FRESH PINEAPPLE REALLY BRINGS OUT THE FLAVOUR OF SALMON. HERE, IT IS COMBINED WITH LIME JUICE TO MAKE A LIGHT AND REFRESHING DISH, WHICH TASTES GREAT WITH WILD RICE AND A SIMPLE GREEN SALAD TOSSED WITH A GRAPEFRUIT VINAIGRETTE DRESSING.

SERVES FOUR

INGREDIENTS
    4 salmon fillets, each about
      200g/7oz
    1 small pineapple
    30ml/2 tbsp sesame seeds
    fresh chives, to garnish
    wild rice and a green salad,
      to serve
For the marinade
    grated rind and juice of 2 limes
    15ml/1 tbsp olive oil
    1cm/½in piece of fresh root ginger,
      peeled and grated
    1 garlic clove, crushed
    30ml/2 tbsp clear honey
    15ml/1 tbsp soy sauce
    ground black pepper

1 To make the marinade, put the lime rind in a jug (pitcher) and stir in the lime juice, olive oil, ginger, garlic, honey and soy sauce. Taste and add a little ground black pepper. The inclusion of soy sauce in the marinade means that salt will probably not be needed.

2 Place the salmon fillets in a single layer in a shallow, non-metallic dish. Pour the marinade over the salmon. Cover and chill for at least 1 hour, turning the salmon halfway through.

3 Carefully cut the skin off the pineapple, removing as many of the small black "eyes" as possible. Cut the pineapple into four thick rings. Use an apple corer to remove the tough central core from each slice and cut away any remaining eyes with a small knife.

COOK'S TIPS
• To cook wild rice, put it in a pan of cold salted water. Bring to the boil, then simmer for 30–40 minutes, or as directed on the packet, until tender. This would make a perfect salad lightly dressed with oil and vinegar and flavoured with chopped fresh herbs.
• Serve the grilled salmon with a mixed leaf salad. For the dressing, mix 45ml/3 tbsp grapefruit juice with 10ml/2 tsp balsamic vinegar and a pinch each of salt, ground black pepper and sugar, then whisk in 120ml/4fl oz/ ½ cup mild olive oil.

4 Preheat the grill (broiler) to high. Sprinkle the sesame seeds over a piece of foil and place under the grill for a minute or two until they turn golden brown. Set aside.

5 Prepare the barbecue. Position a lightly oiled grill rack over the hot coals. Using a slotted spoon, remove the salmon fillets from the marinade and place them on the grill rack with the pineapple rings.

6 Grill the fish and pineapple for 10 minutes over medium-high heat, brushing occasionally with the marinade and turning everything over once, until the fish is cooked through and the pineapple rings are golden brown. Brush over the final layer of marinade no less than 2 minutes before the end of cooking to ensure it cooks thoroughly.

7 Transfer the fish to serving plates, placing each fillet on a bed of wild rice. Top with the pineapple slices. Sprinkle the sesame seeds over the top and garnish with the chives. Serve with a green salad.

Energy 487kcal/2036kJ; Protein 42.4g; Carbohydrate 17.1g, of which sugars 17.1g; Fat 28.2g, of which saturates 4.6g; Cholesterol 100mg; Calcium 120mg; Fibre 2.4g; Sodium 95mg.

SALMON KEBABS WITH COCONUT

KEBABS MAKE EXCITING BARBECUE FOOD, BECAUSE YOU CAN COOK A VARIETY OF FLAVOURS TOGETHER WITHOUT LOSING THEIR INDIVIDUAL IDENTITIES. INSPIRED BY FLAVOURS FROM THE WEST INDIES, THIS RECIPE COMBINES COCONUT AND LIME TO COMPLEMENT THE SUBTLE TASTE OF THE SEAFOOD.

3 Cut each lime into six slices. Thread the coconut, salmon, scallops and pieces of lime alternately on to the skewers.

4 Add the lime juice, soy sauce, honey and sugar to the coconut liquor to make the marinade. Season with pepper.

5 Place the prepared kebabs in a single layer in a shallow non-metallic dish. Pour the marinade over. Cover and chill for at least 3 hours.

6 Preheat the barbecue. Position a lightly oiled grill rack over the hot coals. Transfer the kebabs to the barbecue and cook for 4 minutes on each side, basting with the marinade.

SERVES SIX

INGREDIENTS
450g/1lb salmon fillet, skinned
1 small fresh coconut
2 limes
12 scallops
45ml/3 tbsp freshly squeezed
  lime juice
30ml/2 tbsp soy sauce
30ml/2 tbsp clear honey
15ml/1 tbsp soft light brown sugar
ground black pepper

COOK'S TIP
The easiest way to open a coconut is to hold it in the palm of your left hand, with the "eyes" just above your thumb. The fault line lies between the eyes. Hold the coconut over a bowl to catch the liquid, then carefully hit the line with the blunt side of a cleaver or hammer so that it splits into two halves.

1 Soak six wooden skewers in water for 30 minutes. Using a sharp knife, cut the salmon into bite size chunks and place these in a shallow bowl.

2 Halve the coconut as instructed (see cook's tip) and pour the liquor into a jug (pitcher). Using a small, sharp knife, remove the coconut flesh from the inside of the shell and cut it into chunks, making them about the same size as the salmon.

Energy 265kcal/1102kJ; Protein 20.8g; Carbohydrate 3.2g, of which sugars 2.5g; Fat 18.9g, of which saturates 10.4g; Cholesterol 47mg; Calcium 26mg; Fibre 2.3g; Sodium 193mg.

HERBY WRAPPED SALMON

THIS PARSI DISH, WITH ITS ORIGINS IN PERSIAN COOKING, USES A TOPPING FOR SALMON THAT IS BURSTING WITH THE FLAVOURS OF COCONUT, GARLIC, CHILLI, FRESH HERBS AND FENUGREEK. IT IS WRAPPED IN MOIST BANANA LEAVES TO SEAL IN THE FLAVOUR AND COOK THE FISH PERFECTLY.

SERVES SIX

INGREDIENTS

- 50g/2oz fresh coconut, skinned and finely grated, or 65g/2½oz/scant 1 cup desiccated (dry unsweetened shredded) coconut, soaked in 30ml/2 tbsp water
- 1 large lemon, skin, pith and seeds removed, roughly chopped
- 4 large garlic cloves, crushed
- 3 large fresh mild green chillies, seeded and chopped
- 50g/2oz/2 cups fresh coriander (cilantro), roughly chopped
- 25g/1oz/1 cup fresh mint leaves, roughly chopped
- 5ml/1 tsp ground cumin
- 5ml/1 tsp sugar
- 2.5ml/½ tsp fenugreek seeds, finely ground
- 5ml/1 tsp salt
- 2 large, whole banana leaves
- 6 salmon fillets, about 1.2kg/2½lb total weight, skinned

1 Place all the ingredients except the banana leaves and salmon in a food processor. Pulse to a fine paste. Scrape the mixture into a bowl, cover and chill for 30 minutes.

2 Prepare the barbecue. To make the parcels, cut each banana leaf widthways into three and cut off the hard outside edge from each piece. Put the pieces of leaf and the edge strips in a bowl of hot water. Leave for about 10 minutes. Drain, gently wipe off any white residue, rinse the leaves and strips, and pour over boiling water to soften. Drain, then place the leaves, smooth-side up, on a clean board.

3 Smear the top and bottom of each fillet with the coconut paste, then place one on each leaf. Bring the trimmed edge of the leaf over the salmon, then fold in the sides. Bring up the remaining edge to cover the salmon and make a neat parcel. Tie securely with a leaf strip.

4 Lay each parcel on a sheet of heavy-duty foil, bring up the edges and scrunch the tops together to seal. Position a lightly oiled grill rack over the hot coals. Place the salmon parcels on the grill rack and cook over medium-high heat for about 10 minutes, turning them over once.

5 Place the foil-wrapped parcels on individual plates and leave to stand for 2–3 minutes – the salmon will continue to cook for a while in the residual heat of the parcel. Remove the foil, then carefully unwrap so that the fish is resting on the opened leaves, then eat straight out of the banana leaf parcel.

COOK'S TIP
Serve little rice parcels with the fish. Fill six more banana leaf packages with cooked basmati rice coloured with ground turmeric, secure each one with a skewer and reheat on the barbecue.

Energy 430kcal/1789kJ; Protein 41.4g; Carbohydrate 1.1g, of which sugars 0.9g; Fat 28.9g, of which saturates 9.6g; Cholesterol 100mg; Calcium 70mg; Fibre 1.9g; Sodium 96mg.

GRILLED SWORDFISH SKEWERS

FOR A HINT OF THE GREEK ISLANDS, TRY THESE TANTALIZING SWORDFISH KEBABS. BARBECUED WITH PEPPERS AND ONIONS, THEY ALSO HAVE A HINT OF OREGANO. TRY THROWING SOME OREGANO SPRIGS OVER THE COALS AS YOU COOK, FOR ADDED FLAVOUR.

SERVES FOUR

INGREDIENTS

2 red onions, quartered
2 red or green (bell) peppers,
  quartered and seeded
20–24 thick cubes of swordfish,
  prepared weight
  675–800g/1½–1¾lb
75ml/5 tbsp extra virgin olive oil
1 garlic clove, crushed
large pinch of dried oregano
salt and ground black pepper

1 Carefully separate the onion quarters in pieces, each composed of two or three layers. Slice each pepper quarter in half widthways.

2 Make the kebabs by threading five or six pieces of swordfish on to each of four long metal skewers, alternating with pieces of the pepper and onion. Lay the kebabs across a grill pan or roasting tray and set aside while you make the basting sauce.

3 Whisk the olive oil, crushed garlic and oregano in a bowl. Add salt and pepper, and whisk again. Brush the kebabs generously on all sides with the basting sauce.

4 Prepare the barbecue. Position a lightly oiled grill rack over the hot coals. Transfer the skewers to the barbecue. Cook for 8–10 minutes over medium heat, turning the skewers several times, until the fish is cooked and the peppers and onions have begun to scorch around the edges. Every time you turn the skewers, brush them with the basting sauce.

5 Serve the kebabs immediately, with a cucumber, onion and olive salad.

COOK'S TIP
The fishmonger will prepare the cubes of swordfish for you, but if you prefer to do this yourself you will need to buy about 800g/1¾lb swordfish. The cubes should be fairly big – about 5cm/2in square.

Energy 322kcal/1345kJ; Protein 32.5g; Carbohydrate 13.5g, of which sugars 11g; Fat 15.7g, of which saturates 2.8g; Cholesterol 69mg; Calcium 39mg; Fibre 2.8g; Sodium 226mg.

SWORDFISH <u>WITH</u> ROASTED TOMATOES

SUN-RIPENED TOMATOES ARE NATURALLY FULL OF FLAVOUR AND SWEETNESS, AND IN THIS MOROCCAN RECIPE THEY ARE ROASTED WITH SUGAR AND SPICES SO THAT THEY SIMPLY MELT IN THE MOUTH. AS AN ACCOMPANIMENT TO CHARGRILLED FISH OR POULTRY, THEY ARE SENSATIONAL.

SERVES FOUR

INGREDIENTS

1kg/2¼lb large vine or plum
  tomatoes, peeled, halved and seeded
5–10ml/1–2 tsp ground cinnamon
pinch of saffron threads
15ml/1 tbsp orange flower water
60ml/4 tbsp olive oil
45–60ml/3–4 tbsp sugar
4 swordfish steaks, about
  225g/8oz each
rind of ½ preserved lemon,
  finely chopped
small bunch of fresh coriander
  (cilantro), finely chopped
handful of blanched almonds
knob (pat) of butter
salt and ground black pepper

1 Preheat the oven to 110°C/225°F/ Gas ¼. Place the tomatoes on a baking sheet. Sprinkle with the cinnamon, saffron and orange flower water. Trickle half the oil over, being sure to moisten every tomato half, and sprinkle with sugar. Place the tray in the bottom of the oven and cook the tomatoes for about 3 hours, then turn the oven off and leave them to cool.

2 Prepare the barbecue. Heat a griddle on a grill rack over hot coals. Brush the remaining olive oil over the swordfish steaks and season with salt and pepper. Cook the steaks for 3–4 minutes on each side. Sprinkle the chopped preserved lemon rind and coriander over the steaks towards the end of the cooking time.

3 In a separate pan, fry the almonds in the butter until golden and sprinkle them over the tomatoes. Then serve the steaks immediately with the tomatoes.

VARIATIONS

If swordfish steaks are not available, tuna or shark steaks can be cooked in the same way with excellent results. Or, if you prefer, try the recipe with a lean sirloin or thinly cut fillet steak (beef tenderloin). The lemon and coriander flavours lift the meat beautifully.

Energy 463kcal/1941kJ; Protein 47.2g; Carbohydrate 19.9g, of which sugars 19.8g; Fat 22.2g, of which saturates 4.1g; Cholesterol 103mg; Calcium 59mg; Fibre 3.1g; Sodium 352mg.

FISH BROCHETTES <u>WITH</u> PEPERONATA

IN THIS DISH, THE PEPPERS FOR THE PEPERONATA ARE ROASTED AND SKINNED, GIVING IT A LOVELY SMOKY FLAVOUR AND SMOOTH TEXTURE, WHILE THE VERJUICE, AN UNFERMENTED GRAPE JUICE, ADDS AN UNDERLYING TARTNESS. IT IS EXCELLENT SERVED WITH FISH KEBABS.

SERVES FOUR

INGREDIENTS
    8 fresh sprigs of bay leaves
    675g/1½lb mahi-mahi, swordfish or
        marlin fillet, skinned
    1 lime, halved
    1 lemon, halved
    60ml/4 tbsp olive oil
    1 small garlic clove, crushed
    salt and ground black pepper
For the peperonata
    2 large red (bell) peppers, quartered
        and seeded
    2 large yellow (bell) peppers,
        quartered and seeded
    90ml/6 tbsp extra virgin olive oil
    2 sweet onions, thinly sliced
    1 garlic clove, thinly sliced
    5ml/1 tsp sugar
    4 tomatoes, peeled, seeded and
        roughly chopped
    2 bay leaves
    1 large fresh thyme sprig
    15ml/1 tbsp red verjuice or red wine

1 To make the peperonata, spread out the peppers on a board and brush the skin side with oil. Heat the remaining oil in a pan and add the onions and garlic. Fry over a medium-high heat for 6–8 minutes, or until lightly golden.

2 Prepare the barbecue. Heat a griddle on a grill rack over hot coals. Add the peppers, skin-side down. Lower the heat a little and grill them for 5 minutes until the skins are charred. Remove from the heat and put them under an upturned bowl. When cool enough to handle, rub off the skins and slice each piece into six or seven strips.

3 Add the pepper strips to the onion mixture, stir in the sugar and cook over a medium heat for about 2 minutes. Add the tomatoes and herbs and bring to the boil. Transfer the pan to the barbecue. Stir in the verjuice or wine, and simmer, uncovered, for about 30 minutes. Remove from the heat and cover to keep warm.

4 Meanwhile, soak eight wooden skewers with the bay leaf sprigs in a bowl of cold water for 30 minutes. Cut the fish into 12 large cubes and place in a bowl. Squeeze the juice from half a lime and half a lemon into a small bowl. Whisk in 45ml/3 tbsp of the oil. Cream the garlic and plenty of seasoning to a paste, add to the oil mixture and pour over the fish. Marinate for 30 minutes.

5 Cut the remaining lime and lemon halves into four wedges each. Using two skewers placed side by side instead of the usual one, thread alternately with three pieces of fish, one lime and one lemon wedge and two sprigs of bay leaves. Make three more brochettes in the same way.

6 Replace the griddle over a high heat and test that it is hot. Brush the brochettes with the remaining oil and grill for 3–4 minutes on each side, or until the fish is cooked through and nicely branded. Cover the kebabs and keep them warm for up to 5 minutes before serving with the peperonata in a little bowl on the side.

COOK'S TIPS
• The brochettes can also be cooked on an oiled grill rack over a medium to high heat. Cook for 8–10 minutes, turning the skewers several times, until the fish is cooked and the rind of the citrus fruits has begun to scorch.
• You may prefer to quickly re-heat the peperonata while keeping the kebabs warm.

Energy 426kcal/1777kJ; Protein 34g; Carbohydrate 22.2g, of which sugars 19.4g; Fat 22.6g, of which saturates 3.9g; Cholesterol 69mg; Calcium 53mg; Fibre 5.2g; Sodium 239mg.

GRIDDLED HALIBUT

ANY THICK WHITE FISH FILLETS CAN BE COOKED IN THIS VERSATILE DISH; TURBOT AND BRILL ARE ESPECIALLY DELICIOUS, BUT THE FLAVOURSOME SAUCE OF TOMATOES, CAPERS, ANCHOVIES AND HERBS ALSO GIVES HUMBLER FISH SUCH AS COD, HADDOCK OR HAKE A REAL LIFT.

SERVES FOUR

INGREDIENTS

2.5ml/½ tsp fennel seeds
2.5ml/½ tsp celery seeds
5ml/1 tsp mixed peppercorns
105ml/7 tbsp olive oil
5ml/1 tsp chopped fresh
  thyme leaves
5ml/1 tsp chopped fresh rosemary
  leaves
5ml/1 tsp chopped fresh oregano or
  marjoram leaves
675–800g/1½–1¾lb middle cut of
  halibut, about 3cm/1¼in thick, cut
  into 4 pieces
coarse sea salt
For the sauce
105ml/7 tbsp extra virgin olive oil
juice of 1 lemon
1 garlic clove, finely chopped
2 tomatoes, peeled, seeded
  and diced
5ml/1 tsp small capers
2 drained canned anchovy
  fillets, chopped
5ml/1 tsp chopped fresh chives
15ml/1 tbsp chopped fresh
  basil leaves
15ml/1 tbsp chopped fresh chervil

1 Prepare the barbecue. Heat a griddle on the grill rack over the hot coals. Mix the fennel and celery seeds with the peppercorns in a mortar. Crush with a pestle, and then stir in coarse sea salt to taste. Spoon the mixture into a shallow dish large enough to hold the fish in one layer and stir in the herbs and the olive oil.

2 Add the halibut pieces to the olive oil mixture, turning them to coat them thoroughly, then arrange them with the dark skin uppermost in the griddle. Cook for about 6–8 minutes, or until the fish is cooked all the way through and the skin has browned.

3 Combine all the sauce ingredients except the fresh herbs in a pan and heat gently on the grill rack until warm but not hot. Stir in the chives, basil and chervil.

4 Place the halibut on four warmed plates. Spoon the sauce around and over the fish and serve immediately.

Energy 363kcal/1513kJ; Protein 37.4g; Carbohydrate 1.9g, of which sugars 1.8g; Fat 22.9g, of which saturates 3.3g; Cholesterol 60mg; Calcium 82mg; Fibre 1.1g; Sodium 169mg.

BARBECUED RED SNAPPER

THE RED SNAPPER IS A LINE-CAUGHT REEF FISH FROM THE INDIAN OCEAN AND THE CARIBBEAN. ALTHOUGH BEAUTIFUL TO LOOK AT, IT HAS VICIOUS SPINES AND A FAIRLY IMPENETRABLE ARMOUR OF SCALES, SO PERHAPS IT WOULD BE BEST IF YOU ASK THE FISHMONGER TO SCALE IT. LEAVE THE FINS ON, HOWEVER, SO THAT IT RETAINS ITS LOVELY FISH-LIKE QUALITY.

SERVES FOUR

INGREDIENTS
  2 red snapper, about 900g/2lb each,
    cleaned and scaled, or tilapia
  15ml/1 tbsp olive oil
  5cm/2in piece of fresh root ginger,
    thinly sliced
  4 banana shallots, total weight about
    150g/5oz, thinly sliced
  3 garlic cloves, thinly sliced
  30ml/2 tbsp sugar
  3 lemon grass stalks, 1 thinly sliced
  grated rind and juice of 1 lime
  5ml/1 tsp salt
  4 small fresh green or red chillies,
    thinly sliced
  2 whole banana leaves
  30ml/2 tbsp chopped fresh coriander
    (cilantro)
For the dipping sauce
  1 large fresh red chilli, seeded and
    finely chopped
  juice of 2 limes
  30ml/2 tbsp fish sauce
  5ml/1 tsp sugar
  60ml/4 tbsp water

1 Soak six wooden skewers in cold water for 30 minutes. Make four slashes in either side of each fish and rub the skin with oil.

2 Make the dipping sauce by mixing together all the ingredients in a bowl. Cover and chill until needed.

3 Place half the ginger and shallots and the garlic in a mortar. Add half the sugar, the thinly sliced lemon grass, a little of the lime juice, the salt and the chillies and pound to break up and bruise. Mix in the remaining sugar and lime juice, with the lime rind. Rub a little of the mixture into the slashes and the bulk of it into the cavity of each fish.

4 Trim the hard edge from each banana leaf and discard it. Soak the banana leaves in hot water for 10 minutes, then drain. Wipe any white residue from the leaves. Rinse, then pour over boiling water to soften. Drain again.

5 Lay a fish on each leaf and scatter the remaining ginger and shallots over them. Split the whole lemon grass stalks lengthways and lay the pieces over each fish. Bring the sides of the leaves up over the fish and secure using three wooden skewers for each envelope. Wrap in clear film (plastic wrap) to keep the wooden skewers moist, and chill for at least 30 minutes, but no more than 6 hours.

COOK'S TIPS
• Serve leaf-wrapped rice parcels with the fish. Heat them up in foil next to the fish for the last 5 minutes. They can be found in larger Asian food stores.
• Banana shallots have longer bulbs than most shallots or onions, and varieties include Long Red Florence and Longor.

6 Prepare the barbecue. Bring the dipping sauce to room temperature. Remove the clear film from each banana leaf envelope and place each on a sheet of foil. Bring the sides of the foil up around each envelope to enclose it loosely. This will protect the base of each banana leaf wrapper.

7 Position a lightly oiled grill rack over the hot coals. Lay the envelopes on the grill rack and cook for 15 minutes over medium-high heat. Turn the envelopes around 180 degrees and cook for about 10 minutes more, opening up the foil for the last 5 minutes.

8 Remove from the barbecue and leave to stand for a further 5 minutes, then check to see if the fish is cooked by inserting a skewer – it should flake easily when the skewer is removed. Place on a large serving dish, open the envelopes and sprinkle the fish with the chopped coriander. Serve the fish in individual serving bowls, with smaller bowls for the dipping sauce.

Energy 305kcal/1293kJ; Protein 57.3g; Carbohydrate 2.9g, of which sugars 2.9g; Fat 7.5g, of which saturates 1.4g; Cholesterol 104mg; Calcium 157mg; Fibre 1.2g; Sodium 541mg.

SEA BASS WRAPPED IN VINE LEAVES

THIS DISH IS EFFORTLESS BUT MUST BE STARTED IN ADVANCE BECAUSE THE RICE NEEDS TO BE COLD BEFORE IT IS USED IN THE LITTLE PARCELS. ONCE THE FISH HAVE BEEN WRAPPED, ALL YOU HAVE TO DO IS KEEP THEM CHILLED, READY TO POP ON TO THE BARBECUE.

3 Season the sea bass fillets. Wash the vine leaves in water, then pat dry with kitchen paper. Lay each leaf in the centre of a double layer of foil. Top with a sea bass fillet. Divide the rice mixture among the fillets, spooning it towards one end. Fold the fillet over the rice, trickle over the remaining oil, lay the second vine leaf on top and bring the foil up around the fish and scrunch it together to seal. Chill the packages for up to 3 hours, or until needed.

4 Take the fish out of the refrigerator and prepare the barbecue. Position a lightly oiled grill rack over the hot coals. Place the parcels on the edge of the grill rack. Cook for 5 minutes over high heat, turning them around by 90 degrees halfway through. Open up the top of the foil a little and cook for 2 minutes more. Gently remove from the foil and transfer the vine parcels to individual plates and serve.

COOK'S TIP

For a quick salsa, chop half a seeded cucumber and half a pink onion. Place in a bowl and add 30ml/2 tbsp seasoned sushi vinegar and mix well. Add a little chilli to put a bit of a kick in it.

MAKES SIXTEEN

INGREDIENTS
  90g/3½oz/½ cup Chinese
    black rice
  400ml/14fl oz/1⅔ cups boiling water
  45ml/3 tbsp extra virgin olive oil
  1 small onion, chopped
  1 fresh mild chilli, seeded and
    finely chopped
  8 sea bass fillets, about 75g/3oz
    each, with skin
  16 large fresh vine leaves
  salt and ground black pepper

1 Place the Chinese black rice in a large pan. Add the measured boiling water and simmer for 15 minutes. Add a little salt to taste and simmer for a further 10 minutes, or until tender. Drain well and tip into a bowl.

2 Meanwhile, heat half the oil in a frying pan. Fry the onion gently for 5 minutes until softened but not browned. Add the chilli. Stir into the rice mixture and season with salt and pepper according to taste. Cool the rice completely and cover and chill until needed.

Energy 157kcal/656kJ; Protein 15.5g; Carbohydrate 9.9g, of which sugars 0.7g; Fat 6.1g, of which saturates 0.9g; Cholesterol 60mg; Calcium 105mg; Fibre 0.2g; Sodium 52mg.

Sea Bass with Fennel

The classic combination of sea bass and fennel works particularly well when the fish is cooked over charcoal. Fennel twigs are traditionally used inside the fish but this version of the recipe uses fennel seeds, which flavour the fish beautifully.

SERVES SIX

INGREDIENTS

   1 sea bass, about 1.3–1.6kg/
     3–3½lb, cleaned and scaled
   60ml/4 tbsp olive oil
   10ml/2 tsp fennel seeds
   2 large fennel bulbs
   60ml/4 tbsp Pernod
   salt and ground black pepper

1 Make four deep slashes in each side of the fish. Brush the fish with olive oil and season well with salt and freshly ground black pepper. Sprinkle the fennel seeds in the cavity and slashes of the fish.

2 Trim and slice the fennel bulbs thinly, reserving any leafy fronds to use as a garnish. Prepare the barbecue. Part the coals in the centre and position a drip tray. Position a lightly oiled grill rack over the hot coals. Put the fish inside a hinged wire grill or straight on to the grill rack over the drip tray. Cook over indirect medium heat using a cover, for 20 minutes, basting occasionally and turning once.

3 Meanwhile, brush the slices of fennel with olive oil and barbecue for about 8–10 minutes, turning the fennel occasionally, until tender. Remove the fish and fennel from the heat.

4 Scatter the fennel slices on a serving plate. Lay the fish on top and garnish with the reserved fennel fronds.

5 When ready for eating, heat the Pernod in a small pan on the side of the barbecue, light it and pour it, flaming, over the fish. Serve at once.

Energy 180kcal/750kJ; Protein 19.9g; Carbohydrate 1.2g, of which sugars 1.1g; Fat 8.1g, of which saturates 1.2g; Cholesterol 80mg; Calcium 146mg; Fibre 1.6g; Sodium 76mg.

SEARED TUNA WITH GINGER

THIS NORTH AFRICAN RECIPE IS UNBEATABLE FAST, NUTRITIOUS FARE FOR THE BARBECUE. TUNA STEAKS ARE RUBBED WITH HARISSA AND THEN GRIDDLED QUICKLY OVER HIGH HEAT AND SERVED WITH A DELICIOUS WARM SALAD SPICED WITH GINGER AND CHILLIES. NO MARINATING TIME IS NEEDED.

SERVES FOUR

INGREDIENTS

30ml/2 tbsp olive oil
5ml/1 tsp harissa
5ml/1 tsp clear honey
4 tuna steaks, about 200g/7oz each
salt and ground black pepper
lemon wedges, to serve
For the salad
30ml/2 tbsp olive oil
a little butter
25g/1oz fresh root ginger, peeled and
   finely sliced
2 garlic cloves, finely sliced
2 green chillies, seeded and
   finely sliced
6 spring onions (scallions), cut into
   bite size pieces
2 large handfuls of watercress or
   rocket (arugula)
juice of ½ lemon

1 Prepare the barbecue. While the coals are heating up, combine the olive oil, harissa, honey and salt in a bowl, and rub the mixture over the tuna steaks using your fingers.

2 Heat a griddle on the grill rack over hot coals. Sear the tuna steaks for about 2 minutes on each side. They should still be pink on the inside when pierced with a skewer.

3 Keep the tuna warm while you quickly prepare the salad: heat the olive oil and butter in a heavy pan on the side of the barbecue. Add the ginger, garlic, chillies and spring onions. Cook until the mixture begins to colour, then add the watercress or rocket. When it begins to wilt, toss in the lemon juice and season well.

4 Tip the warm salad on to a serving dish or individual plates. Slice the tuna steaks and arrange on top of the salad. Serve immediately with lemon wedges for squeezing over.

VARIATION
Prawns (shrimp) and scallops can be cooked in the same way. The shellfish will just need to be cooked briefly – too long and they will become rubbery.

Energy 176kcal/731kJ; Protein 12.3g; Carbohydrate 1.6g, of which sugars 1.6g; Fat 13.4g, of which saturates 2.2g; Cholesterol 14mg; Calcium 18mg; Fibre 0.4g; Sodium 25mg.

MARINATED SEA TROUT

SEA TROUT HAS A SUPERB TEXTURE AND A FLAVOUR LIKE THAT OF WILD SALMON. IT'S BEST SERVED WITH STRONG BUT COMPLEMENTARY FLAVOURS SUCH AS CHILLIES AND LIME THAT CUT THE RICHNESS OF THE FLESH. USE HINGED WIRE BASKETS TO MAKE COOKING AND TURNING EASIER.

SERVES SIX

INGREDIENTS

- 6 sea trout cutlets, about 115g/4oz each, or wild or farmed salmon
- 2 garlic cloves, chopped
- 1 fresh long red chilli, seeded and chopped
- 45ml/3 tbsp chopped Thai basil
- 15ml/1 tbsp palm sugar or granulated sugar
- 3 limes
- 400ml/14fl oz/1⅔ cups coconut milk
- 15ml/1 tbsp Thai fish sauce

1 Place the sea trout cutlets in a shallow dish. Using a pestle, pound the garlic and chilli in a large mortar to break it up roughly. Add 30ml/2 tbsp of the Thai basil with the sugar and continue to pound to a rough paste.

2 Grate the rind from 1 lime and squeeze it. Mix the rind and juice into the chilli paste, with the coconut milk. Pour the mixture over the cutlets, cover and chill the mixture for about 1 hour. Cut the remaining limes into wedges.

COOK'S TIP

This recipe uses the marinade as a sauce to accompany the fish. You can do this with most marinades as long as you boil them up thoroughly first. Put a small pan on to the barbecue to boil up the marinade and then move it to the side while it simmers for about 5 minutes. Never use a marinade to brush over food just before serving or as a sauce unless it has been thoroughly cooked first.

3 Remove the fish from the refrigerator so that it can return to room temperature before you cook it on the barbecue. Prepare the barbecue. Position a lightly oiled grill rack over the hot coals. Remove the cutlets from the marinade and reserve the marinade. Place them in an oiled hinged wire fish basket or directly on the grill rack. Cook the fish over medium-high heat for 4 minutes on each side, trying not to move them. They may stick to the grill rack if not seared first.

4 Strain the remaining marinade into a pan, reserving the contents of the sieve. Bring the marinade to the boil, simmer gently for 5 minutes, then stir in the contents of the sieve and continue to simmer for 1 minute more.

5 Add the Thai fish sauce and the remaining Thai basil. Lift each fish cutlet on to a plate, pour over the sauce and serve with the lime wedges.

Energy 157kcal/662kJ; Protein 23.1g; Carbohydrate 5.9g, of which sugars 5.9g; Fat 4.7g, of which saturates 0.1g; Cholesterol 0mg; Calcium 46mg; Fibre 0.4g; Sodium 141mg.

HAM-WRAPPED TROUT

SERRANO HAM IS USED TO STUFF AND WRAP TROUT FOR THIS UNUSUAL RECIPE FROM SPAIN, ENSURING A SUCCULENT FLAVOUR. ONE OF THE BEAUTIES OF THIS METHOD IS THAT THE SKINS COME OFF IN ONE PIECE, LEAVING THE SUCCULENT, MOIST FLESH TO BE EATEN WITH THE CRISPED, SALT HAM.

SERVES FOUR

INGREDIENTS

    4 brown or rainbow trout, about
       250g/9oz each, cleaned
    16 thin slices Serrano ham, about
       200g/7oz
    50g/2oz/¼ cup melted butter, plus
       extra for greasing
    salt and ground black pepper
    buttered potatoes, to
       serve (optional)

1 Extend the belly cavity of each trout, cutting up one side of the backbone. Slip a knife behind the rib bones to loosen them (sometimes just flexing the fish makes them pop up). Snip these off from both sides with scissors, and season the fish well inside.

2 Fold a piece of ham into each belly. Use smaller or broken bits of ham for this, and reserve the eight best slices.

COOK'S TIP
Serrano ham is a good choice for this recipe, as it is less fatty than prosciutto, which should help to avoid flare ups.

3 Prepare the barbecue. Position a lightly oiled grill rack over the hot coals. Brush each trout with a little butter, seasoning the outside lightly with salt and pepper. Wrap two ham slices round each one, crossways, tucking the ends into the belly.

4 Put the fish into oiled hinged wire fish baskets or directly on to the grill rack. The combined grilling time should be 4 minutes on each side, though it is wise to turn the fish every 2 minutes to ensure that the ham does not become charred.

5 Serve the trout hot, with the butter spooned over the top. Diners should open the trout on their plates, and eat them from the inside, pushing the flesh off the skin.

Energy 369kcal/1546kJ; Protein 48g; Carbohydrate 0.6g, of which sugars 0.6g; Fat 19.4g, of which saturates 8.8g; Cholesterol 216mg; Calcium 66mg; Fibre 0g; Sodium 821mg.

PAPRIKA-CRUSTED MONKFISH

SUCH A CHUNKY FISH AS MONKFISH IS JUST PERFECT FOR SKEWERING, AS IT IS NOT LIKELY TO DISINTEGRATE BEFORE YOUR EYES AND FALL BETWEEN THE GRILL BARS AS YOU COOK. MONKFISH CAN ALSO TAKE SOME STRONG FLAVOURS, SUCH AS THIS SMOKY PAPRIKA CRUST WITH CHORIZO.

SERVES FOUR

INGREDIENTS

    1 monkfish tail, about 1kg/2¼lb,
      trimmed and filleted
    10ml/2 tsp smoked red paprika
    2 red (bell) peppers, halved
      and seeded
    15ml/1 tbsp extra virgin olive oil
    16 thin slices of chorizo
    salt and ground black pepper
For the cucumber and mint sauce
    150ml/¼ pint/⅔ cup Greek
      (US strained plain) yogurt
    ½ cucumber, halved lengthways
      and seeded
    30ml/2 tbsp chopped fresh
      mint leaves

1 Place both monkfish fillets in a flat dish. Rub them all over with 5ml/1 tsp salt, then cover and leave in a cool place for 20 minutes. To make the sauce, pour the yogurt into a food processor. Cut the cucumber into it, season with a little salt and pulse to a pale green purée. Transfer to a serving bowl and stir in the mint.

2 Prepare the barbecue. Rinse the salt off the pieces of monkfish and lightly pat them dry with kitchen paper. Mix the smoked red paprika with a pinch of salt and gently rub the mixture evenly over the fish. Slice each pepper into 12 long strips and cut each monkfish fillet into ten equal pieces. Thread six pieces of pepper and five pieces of fish on to each of four long skewers and brush one side with a little extra virgin olive oil.

3 Position a lightly oiled grill rack over the hot coals. Grill the skewered food, oiled-side down over medium-high heat, for about 3½ minutes. Lightly brush the top side with oil, turn over and cook for 3–4 minutes more. Remove the skewers from the heat and keep warm.

4 Grill the chorizo slices for a second or two until just warm. Thread one piece of chorizo on to the end of each skewer and serve the rest alongside on individual plates. Serve with the prepared cucumber and mint sauce.

COOK'S TIP
If it is easier, fry the chorizo on a hot griddle set on the grill rack for 30 seconds on each side.

Energy 375kcal/1572kJ; Protein 51.7g; Carbohydrate 7.1g, of which sugars 6.8g; Fat 15.9g, of which saturates 5.6g; Cholesterol 57mg; Calcium 115mg; Fibre 2.1g; Sodium 445mg.

POULTRY

Chicken is one of the most popular barbecue meats, and the reason is perhaps that it can be transformed in so many ways by using different marinades, stuffings or quick glazes. Small portions are always popular because they cook quickly, and the pages that follow contain a host of different ways to prepare breast fillets, drumsticks and bite size pieces threaded on to skewers, and achieve exceptionally flavourful results. However, if you're planning to feed a gathering of family and friends, and have a little time to spare, you can also roast a whole chicken — even without the aid of a rotisserie. You do need a lid, but a home-made one will do nicely. This chapter includes a turkey recipe as well as ways to barbecue the ever-popular duck, which achieves fantastically crispy skin while retaining moist flesh. Small birds are also great for grilling either whole or spatchcocked: try the recipes for poussins and delicate quail on the following pages.

STUFFED CORN-FED CHICKEN

THIS IS ONE OF THOSE DISHES THAT IS IDEAL TO COOK FOR FRIENDS. IT DOES NOT REQUIRE ANY EFFORT BUT LOOKS AND TASTES AS IF YOU HAVE GONE TO HUGE AMOUNTS OF TROUBLE. SERVE GRILLED MEDITERRANEAN VEGETABLES, OR USE SIMPLY DRESSED SALAD LEAVES WITH THE CHICKEN.

SERVES FOUR TO SIX

INGREDIENTS
  4–6 chicken breast fillets, preferably
    from a corn-fed bird
  115g/4oz firm goat's cheese
  60ml/4 tbsp chopped fresh oregano
  20ml/4 tsp maple syrup
  juice of 1 lemon
  oil, for brushing
  salt and ground black pepper

1 Slash a pocket horizontally in each chicken fillet. Mix the goat's cheese, chopped oregano and 10ml/2 tsp of the maple syrup in a small bowl. Stuff the pockets in the chicken with the mixture. Don't overfill.

2 Put the remaining maple syrup into a shallow dish large enough to hold the chicken fillets in a single layer. Stir in the lemon juice and add the chicken fillets. Rub them all over with the maple syrup mixture, then cover and leave in a cool place for 20 minutes, turning them occasionally. Season with salt and pepper and marinate for 10 minutes more.

3 Prepare the barbecue. Once the flames have died down, rake the hot coals to one side and insert a drip tray flat beside them. Position a lightly oiled grill rack over the hot coals. Lay the chicken breast portions, skin-side up, on the grill rack over the drip tray. Cover with a lid or tented heavy-duty foil.

4 Grill the chicken over high heat for about 15 minutes in total, turning and moving the pieces around the grill rack so that they cook evenly without getting too charred. Baste with any remaining marinade 5 minutes before the end of cooking.

5 Transfer the chicken to a dish to rest and keep warm for about 5 minutes before serving.

COOK'S TIP
You can cook these successfully on a hot griddle. They will take about 20 minutes. Sear on a high heat then lower the heat. Turn frequently.

Energy 180kcal/756kJ; Protein 28.3g; Carbohydrate 3g, of which sugars 3g; Fat 6.1g, of which saturates 3.7g; Cholesterol 88mg; Calcium 44mg; Fibre 0.3g; Sodium 186mg.

TANDOORI DRUMSTICKS

No self-respecting book on barbecuing could leave out a tandoori dish — in this case, served with a chilli onion salad. When making kachumbar, use the pink onions available in West Indian markets if you can, but white sweet Italian ones would do.

SERVES SIX

INGREDIENTS
- 12 small chicken drumsticks, skinned
- 3 garlic cloves, crushed to a paste with a pinch of salt
- 150ml/¼ pint/⅔ cup Greek (US strained plain) yogurt
- 10ml/2 tsp ground coriander
- 5ml/1 tsp ground cumin
- 5ml/1 tsp ground turmeric
- 1.5ml/¼ tsp cayenne pepper
- 2.5ml/½ tsp garam masala
- 15ml/1 tbsp curry paste
- juice of ½ lemon
- salt
- warmed naan breads, to serve

For the kachumbar
- 2 pink onions, halved and thinly sliced
- 10ml/2 tsp salt
- 4cm/1½in piece of fresh root ginger, finely shredded
- 2 fresh long green chillies, seeded and finely chopped
- 20ml/4 tsp sugar, preferably palm sugar
- juice of ½ lemon
- 60ml/4 tbsp chopped fresh coriander (cilantro)

1 Cut each drumstick around the flesh that attaches itself to the tip of the bone. Place the drumsticks in a bowl. Put the garlic, yogurt, spices, curry paste and lemon juice in a food processor and whizz until smooth. Pour the mixture over the drumsticks to coat, then cover and chill overnight.

2 Two hours before serving, make the kachumbar. Put the onion slices in a bowl, sprinkle them with the salt, cover and leave to stand for 1 hour. Tip into a sieve, rinse well under cold running water, then drain and pat dry. Roughly chop the slices and put them in a serving bowl. Add the remaining ingredients and mix well.

3 About an hour before cooking, drain the drumsticks in a sieve set over a bowl. Remove the wobbly knuckle bone at the end of each drumstick with a sharp knife and scrape the flesh down a little to make the bone look clean. Return the drumsticks to the bowl of marinade.

4 Prepare the barbecue. About 30 minutes before you are ready to cook, salt the drumsticks. Once the flames have died down, part the coals in the centre and insert a drip tray. Position a lightly oiled grill rack over the hot coals. Carefully lift the drumsticks out of the marinade. Wrap the tips with strips of foil to prevent them from burning, then place on the grill rack so that they are not directly over the coals.

5 Cover with a lid or tented heavy-duty foil and cook for 5 minutes, turning frequently. Brush the drumsticks with a little of the marinade and cook for 5–7 minutes more, or until cooked. Serve hot with the kachumbar and naan breads.

Energy 155kcal/654kJ; Protein 23g; Carbohydrate 6.4g, of which sugars 6.1g; Fat 4.5g, of which saturates 1.3g; Cholesterol 108mg; Calcium 81mg; Fibre 0.6g; Sodium 160mg.

CHARGRILLED CAJUN DRUMMERS

THIS IS A CLASSIC AMERICAN DEEP-SOUTH METHOD OF COOKING IN A SPICED COATING, WHICH CAN BE USED FOR POULTRY, MEAT OR FISH AS WELL AS DELICIOUS CORN ON THE COB. THE COATING SHOULD BEGIN TO CHAR AND BLACKEN SLIGHTLY AT THE EDGES DURING GRILLING.

2 Pull the husks and silks off the corn cobs, then rinse them under cold running water and pat them dry with kitchen paper. Cut the cobs into thick slices, using a heavy kitchen knife.

3 Mix together all the spices. Brush the chicken and corn with the melted butter and sprinkle the spices over. Toss well to coat evenly. Prepare the barbecue.

SERVES FOUR

INGREDIENTS
8 chicken joints (drumsticks, thighs or wings)
2 whole corn on the cob
10ml/2 tsp garlic salt
10ml/2 tsp ground black pepper
7.5ml/1½ tsp ground cumin
7.5ml/1½ tsp paprika
5ml/1 tsp cayenne pepper
45ml/3 tbsp melted butter
chopped fresh parsley, to garnish

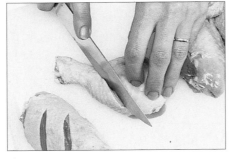

1 Trim any excess fat from the chicken, but leave the skin in place. Slash the thickest parts with a knife to allow the flavours to penetrate the meat as much as possible.

4 Prepare a lightly oiled grill rack over the hot coils. Cook the chicken pieces over medium-high heat for about 25 minutes, turning occasionally. Add the corn after 15 minutes, and grill, turning often, until golden brown. Serve garnished with chopped parsley.

Energy 266kcal/1108kJ; Protein 22g; Carbohydrate 5.9g, of which sugars 0.8g; Fat 17.3g, of which saturates 8g; Cholesterol 132mg; Calcium 20mg; Fibre 0.8g; Sodium 174mg.

BARBECUED CHICKEN TIKKA

MARINATED IN LOW-FAT YOGURT AND SPICES, THE CHICKEN HAS ALL THE FLAVOUR YOU WOULD EXPECT FROM A BARBECUED DISH AND YET IT IS A HEALTHY LOW-FAT MEAL. LEAVE IT OVERNIGHT TO MARINATE, IF YOU CAN, FOR THE BEST FLAVOUR. RED FOOD COLOURING ADDS A DASH OF TRADITIONAL COLOUR.

SERVES FOUR

INGREDIENTS
    4 skinless chicken breast fillets
    lemon wedges and mixed salad
        leaves, such as frisée and oakleaf
        lettuce or radicchio, to serve
For the marinade
    150ml/1/4 pint/2/3 cup low-fat natural
        (plain) yogurt
    5ml/1 tsp paprika
    10ml/2 tsp grated fresh root ginger
    1 garlic clove, crushed
    10ml/2 tsp garam masala
    2.5ml/1/2 tsp salt
    few drops of red food
        colouring (optional)
    juice of 1 lemon

3 Remove the chicken pieces from the marinade and cook over high heat for 30–40 minutes, or until tender, turning occasionally and basting with a little of the marinade.

4 Arrange the chicken pieces on a bed of salad leaves with two lemon wedges and serve either hot or cold.

1 Mix all the marinade ingredients in a large dish. Add the chicken pieces to coat for at least 4 hours or overnight in the refrigerator to allow the flavours to penetrate the flesh.

2 Prepare the barbecue. Position a lightly oiled grill rack over the hot coals.

COOK'S TIP
This is an example of a dish that is usually very high in fat, but with a few basic changes this level can be dramatically reduced. This can also be achieved with other similar dishes, by substituting low-fat yogurt for full-fat versions and creams, and by removing the skin from the chicken, as well as by reducing the amount of oil.

Energy 169kcal/716kJ; Protein 36.8g; Carbohydrate 1.3g, of which sugars 1.3g; Fat 1.9g, of which saturates 0.5g; Cholesterol 105mg; Calcium 38mg; Fibre 0.2g; Sodium 199mg.

BARBECUED CHICKEN SALAD

THIS DISH IS REMARKABLY SIMPLE BUT TASTES ABSOLUTELY WONDERFUL. SIMPLY BARBECUED CHICKEN IS TOSSED IN A CRISP SALAD OF BABY SPINACH AND CHERRY TOMATOES WITH A HERBY AND NUTTY DRESSING. THIS WOULD MAKE A SUPER FILLING TO POP INTO WARMED AND SPLIT PITTA BREADS.

SERVES FOUR

INGREDIENTS

   30ml/2 tbsp olive oil, plus extra
     for brushing
   30ml/2 tbsp hazelnut oil
   15ml/1 tbsp white wine vinegar
   1 garlic clove, crushed
   15ml/1 tbsp chopped fresh
     mixed herbs
   225g/8oz baby spinach leaves
   250g/9oz cherry tomatoes, halved
   1 bunch spring onions
     (scallions), chopped
   2 skinless chicken breast fillets
   salt and ground black pepper

COOK'S TIP
Remember to cut up your cooked chicken on a different plate to that which held the raw chicken, as it is essential to avoid cross-contamination when cooking meat or poultry.

1 First make the dressing. Place 30ml/ 2 tbsp of the olive oil, the hazelnut oil, vinegar, garlic and herbs in a small bowl or jug (pitcher) and whisk together until thoroughly mixed. Set the dressing aside.

2 Trim any long stalks from the spinach leaves and discard, then place the leaves in a large serving bowl with the tomatoes and spring onions, and toss together to mix.

3 Prepare the barbecue. Position a lightly oiled grill rack over the hot coals. Brush the chicken breasts all over with oil and then grill them over medium heat for 15–20 minutes, turning regularly, until cooked through and golden brown. Brush them with oil if necessary during cooking to keep them moist. Cut the chicken into thin slices.

4 Scatter the chicken pieces over the salad, give the dressing a quick whisk to blend, then drizzle it over the salad and gently toss all the ingredients together to mix. Season to taste and serve immediately.

VARIATION
You can try out different dressings for this salad. For example, try a piquant combination of 20ml/4 tsp olive oil, 15ml/1 tbsp balsamic vinegar, 10ml/ 2 tsp honey and 30ml/2 tbsp mustard.

Energy 436kcal/1830kJ; Protein 37.3g; Carbohydrate 34.6g, of which sugars 12.8g; Fat 17.5g, of which saturates 4.6g; Cholesterol 105mg; Calcium 96mg; Fibre 3.9g; Sodium 194mg.

CHICKEN FAJITAS

FAJITAS BURSTING WITH TENDER CHICKEN AND A WONDERFUL BLEND OF VEGETABLES AND SALSA ARE ALWAYS A GREAT HIT, AND THEY MAKE PERFECT BARBECUE FOOD BECAUSE YOU CAN EAT THEM WITH YOUR FINGERS WITHOUT GETTING MESSY. KIDS JUST LOVE THEM.

SERVES SIX

INGREDIENTS
  finely grated rind of 1 lime and the
    juice of 2 limes
  105ml/7 tbsp olive oil, plus extra
    for brushing
  1 garlic clove, finely chopped
  2.5ml/½ tsp dried oregano
  good pinch of dried red chilli flakes
  5ml/1 tsp coriander seeds, crushed
  6 chicken breast fillets
  3 Spanish onions, thickly sliced
  2 large red, yellow or orange (bell)
    peppers, seeded and cut into strips
  30ml/2 tbsp chopped fresh
    coriander (cilantro)
  salt and ground black pepper
For the tomato salsa
  450g/1lb tomatoes, peeled, seeded
    and chopped
  2 garlic cloves, finely chopped
  1 small red onion, finely chopped
  1–2 green chillies, seeded
    and chopped
  finely grated rind of ½ lime
  30ml/2 tbsp chopped fresh
    coriander (cilantro)
  pinch of caster (superfine) sugar
  2.5–5ml/½–1 tsp ground roasted
    cumin seeds
To serve
  12–18 soft flour tortillas
  guacamole
  120ml/4fl oz/½ cup sour cream
  crisp lettuce leaves
  coriander (cilantro) sprigs
  lime wedges

1 In an ovenproof dish, combine the lime rind and juice, 75ml/5 tbsp of the oil, the garlic, oregano, chilli flakes and coriander seeds. Season with salt and pepper. Slash the skin on the chicken breast fillets several times and put them into the garlic mixture. Turn them in the mixture, then cover and set aside to marinate for several hours.

2 To make the tomato salsa, combine the tomatoes, garlic, onion, chillies, lime rind and chopped coriander. Season to taste with salt, pepper, caster sugar and cumin seeds. Set aside for 30 minutes, then taste and adjust the seasoning, adding more cumin and sugar, if necessary. Put in a bowl.

3 Prepare the barbecue. Position a lightly oiled grill rack over the hot coals. Thread the onion slices on to a metal skewer. Brush them with the remaining oil and season. Grill until softened and slightly charred in places.

4 Grill the chicken breast fillets over medium heat for 15–20 minutes, turning regularly, until cooked through and golden brown. Baste with the marinade during cooking, but add the final basting no less than 5 minutes before the end of the cooking time to ensure the marinade is fully cooked.

5 Heat a griddle on the grill rack over hot coals. Brush the pepper strips with oil and cook in the griddle for 8–10 minutes, or until softened and browned in places. Add the grilled onions and mix together for 2 minutes. Stir in the chopped coriander. Put in a bowl.

6 Reheat the tortillas by putting them on to the grill rack very briefly, about 30 seconds on each side. Stack the warm tortillas on a serving plate and cover them with a clean dish towel. Using a sharp knife, cut the grilled chicken into strips and transfer to a serving dish.

7 Serve the dishes of chicken, onions and peppers, and salsa with the tortillas, guacamole, sour cream, lettuce and coriander for people to help themselves. Serve with lime wedges.

Per Fajita: Energy 174kcal/732kJ; Protein 14.9g; Carbohydrate 13.9g, of which sugars 5.1g; Fat 7g, of which saturates 1.8g; Cholesterol 42mg; Calcium 38mg; Fibre 1.6g; Sodium 78mg.

CARIBBEAN CHICKEN KEBABS

RUM, LIME JUICE AND CINNAMON MAKE A ROBUST MARINADE FOR CHICKEN, WHICH IS THEN BARBECUED WITH MANGOES TO MAKE AN UNUSUAL AND FRESH-TASTING DISH. YOU CAN SERVE THE KEBABS WITH RICE, OR SLIDE THEM OFF THE SKEWERS STRAIGHT INTO PITTA BREAD FOR AN INFORMAL BARBECUE MEAL.

2 Soak four wooden skewers in water for 30 minutes. Cut the mangoes into cubes by cutting slices, scoring into cubes and slicing away from the skin.

3 Prepare the barbecue. Position a lightly oiled grill rack over the hot coals. Drain the chicken, saving the juices, and thread on to the wooden skewers, alternating with the mango cubes.

4 Grill the skewers over high heat for 8–10 minutes, turning occasionally and basting with the juices, until the chicken is tender and golden brown. Serve at once with rice and a salad.

SERVES FOUR

INGREDIENTS
   500g/1¼lb skinless chicken
      breast fillets
   finely grated rind of 1 lime
   30ml/2 tbsp fresh lime juice
   15ml/1 tbsp rum or sherry
   15ml/1 tbsp light muscovado
      (brown) sugar
   5ml/1 tsp ground cinnamon
   2 mangoes, peeled and cubed
   rice and salad, to serve

1 Cut the chicken into bite size chunks, and place in a bowl with the lime rind and juice, rum or sherry, sugar and cinnamon. Toss well, cover and leave to stand for 1 hour in a cool place.

Energy 195kcal/826kJ; Protein 30.6g; Carbohydrate 14.6g, of which sugars 14.3g; Fat 1.5g, of which saturates 0.5g; Cholesterol 88mg; Calcium 18mg; Fibre 2g; Sodium 77mg.

GRIDDLED CHICKEN WITH SALSA

THINLY POUNDED CHICKEN BREAST FILLETS COOK IN THE MINIMUM OF TIME WHEN USING THE GRIDDLE. MARINATE THEM FIRST TO MAKE THEM EXTRA DELICIOUS AND MOIST, AND THEN SERVE WITH A SALSA OF FRESH SUMMER INGREDIENTS WITH ROASTED CHILLI TO MAKE A SIMPLE DISH THAT IS FULL OF FLAVOUR.

SERVES FOUR

INGREDIENTS

- 4 boneless, skinless chicken breast fillets, about 175g/6oz each
- 30ml/2 tbsp fresh lemon juice
- 30ml/2 tbsp olive oil
- 10ml/2 tsp ground cumin
- 10ml/2 tsp dried oregano
- 15ml/1 tbsp coarse black pepper

For the salsa

- 1 green chilli
- 450g/1lb plum tomatoes, seeded and chopped
- 3 spring onions (scallions), chopped
- 15ml/1 tbsp chopped fresh parsley
- 30ml/2 tbsp chopped fresh coriander (cilantro)
- 30ml/2 tbsp fresh lemon juice
- 45ml/3 tbsp olive oil

1 With a meat mallet, pound the chicken fillets between two sheets of clear film (plastic wrap) until thin.

2 In a shallow dish, combine the lemon juice, oil, cumin, oregano and pepper. Add the chicken and turn to coat. Cover and leave to marinate for 2 hours, or in the refrigerator overnight.

3 To make the salsa, char the chilli skin either over a gas flame or under the grill (broiler). Leave to cool for 5 minutes. Carefully rub off the charred skin, taking care to wash your hands afterwards. For a less hot flavour, discard the seeds.

4 Chop the chilli very finely and place in a bowl. Add the tomatoes, the spring onions, parsley and coriander, lemon juice and olive oil, and mix well.

5 Prepare the barbecue. Heat a griddle on the grill rack over hot coals. Remove the chicken from the marinade. Griddle the chicken on one side until browned, for about 3 minutes. Turn over and cook for a further 4 minutes. Serve with the chilli salsa.

Energy 312kcal/1309kJ; Protein 43.4g; Carbohydrate 4.5g, of which sugars 4.4g; Fat 13.5g, of which saturates 2.2g; Cholesterol 123mg; Calcium 46mg; Fibre 2g; Sodium 121mg.

CHARGRILLED CHICKEN WITH PEPPERS

CHICKEN REALLY LENDS ITSELF TO IMAGINATIVE MARINADES USING ALL KINDS OF AROMATIC INGREDIENTS. HERE FRENCH MUSTARD, GARLIC AND CHILLIES MAKE A PIQUANT COMBINATION THAT TASTES REALLY GREAT ON THE CHICKEN AS WELL AS THE ACCOMPANYING PEPPERS AND TOMATOES.

2 Beat together all the marinade ingredients in a large bowl. Add the chicken pieces and turn them over to coat them thoroughly in the marinade. Cover the bowl with clear film (plastic wrap) and place in the refrigerator for 4–8 hours, turning the chicken pieces over in the marinade a couple of times.

3 Prepare the barbecue. Position a lightly oiled grill rack over the hot coals. Transfer the chicken pieces to the grill. Add the pepper pieces and the tomatoes to the marinade and set it aside for 15 minutes. Grill the chicken pieces for 20–25 minutes over medium heat. Watch them closely and move them away from the area where the heat is most fierce if they start to burn.

SERVES FOUR TO SIX

INGREDIENTS
  1½ chickens, total weight about
  2.25kg/5lb, jointed, or
  12 chicken pieces
  2–3 red or green (bell) peppers,
  quartered and seeded
  4–5 tomatoes, halved horizontally
  lemon wedges, to serve
For the marinade
  90ml/6 tbsp extra virgin olive oil
  juice of 1 large lemon
  5ml/1 tsp French mustard
  4 garlic cloves, crushed
  2 fresh red or green chillies, seeded
  and chopped
  5ml/1 tsp dried oregano
  salt and ground black pepper

1 If you are jointing the chicken yourself, divide the legs into two. Make a couple of slits in the deepest part of the flesh of each piece of chicken, using a small sharp knife. This will help the marinade to be absorbed more efficiently and allow the chicken to cook thoroughly.

COOK'S TIP
You can, of course, cook these chicken pieces indoors under the grill (broiler). Have the heat fairly high, but don't place the chicken too close to the source. They will probably need less time than when cooked over the coals – allow about 15 minutes each side.

4 Turn the chicken pieces over and cook them for 20–25 minutes more. Meanwhile, thread the peppers on two long metal skewers. Add them to the barbecue grill, with the tomatoes, for the last 15 minutes of cooking. Remember to keep an eye on them and turn them over at least once. Serve with the lemon wedges.

Energy 337kcal/1419kJ; Protein 57.6g; Carbohydrate 7.2g, of which sugars 6.9g; Fat 8.7g, of which saturates 1.6g; Cholesterol 163mg; Calcium 48mg; Fibre 2.5g; Sodium 154mg.

SMOKED CHICKEN <u>WITH</u> BUTTERNUT PESTO

WHOLE CHICKEN SMOKED OVER HICKORY WOOD CHIPS ACQUIRES A PERFECTLY TANNED SKIN AND SUCCULENT PINKISH FLESH. THE BUTTERNUT SQUASH ROASTS ALONGSIDE IT, WRAPPED IN FOIL, AND IS LATER TRANSFORMED INTO A DELICIOUS PESTO. THE CHICKEN ALSO TASTES GREAT COLD.

SERVES FOUR TO SIX

INGREDIENTS
- 1.3kg/3lb roasting chicken
- 1 lemon, quartered
- 8–10 fresh bay leaves
- 3 branches fresh rosemary
- 15ml/1 tbsp olive oil
- salt and ground black pepper
- 4 handfuls hickory wood chips
  soaked in cold water for at least
  30 minutes

For the pesto
- 1 butternut squash, about
  675g/1½lb, halved and seeded
- 2 garlic cloves, sliced
- 2 fresh thyme sprigs
- 45ml/3 tbsp olive oil
- 25g/1oz/⅓ cup freshly grated
  Parmesan cheese

1 Prepare the barbecue. Cut away any excess fat from the opening to the chicken cavity, season the inside and stuff with lemon quarters, bay leaves and sprigs from one rosemary branch. Tie the legs together with kitchen string (twine) and rub the bird all over with the oil. Season the skin lightly.

2 Prepare the butternut squash for the pesto. Cut it into eight pieces and lay them on a piece of double foil. Season well and scatter with the garlic and thyme leaves. Drizzle over 15ml/1 tbsp of the olive oil and a sprinkling of water. Bring the sides of the foil up to completely enclose the squash and secure the parcel.

3 Once the flames have died down, rake the hot coals to one side and insert a drip tray beside them. Fill the drip tray with water. Position a lightly oiled grill rack over the hot coals. Place the chicken on the grill rack above the drip tray, with the squash next to it, over the coals. Cover with a lid or tented heavy-duty foil. Cook the squash for 35 minutes, or until tender.

4 Drain the hickory chips and carefully add a handful to the coals, then replace the lid. Cook the chicken for 1–1¼ hours more, adding a handful of hickory chips every 15 minutes. Add the remaining rosemary to the coals with the last batch of hickory chips. When the chicken is done, transfer it to a plate, cover with tented foil and leave to stand for 10 minutes.

5 Unwrap the butternut squash. Leaving the thyme stalk behind, scoop the flesh and the garlic into a food processor. Pulse until the mixture forms a thick purée. Add the Parmesan, then the remaining oil, pulsing to ensure it is well combined. Spoon into a bowl and serve with the hot chicken. If the chicken is to be eaten cold, cover it once cool.

COOK'S TIP
With small barbecues, the coals may need to be replenished during cooking. Lift off the rack and chicken before the heat is too low and re-fuel. The coals will take about 10 minutes to heat sufficiently to continue. Allow for this when timing.

Energy 257kcal/1078kJ; Protein 34.4g; Carbohydrate 2.5g, of which sugars 1.9g; Fat 12.2g, of which saturates 2.7g; Cholesterol 98mg; Calcium 89mg; Fibre 1.1g; Sodium 126mg.

TURKEY SOSATIES WITH APRICOT SAUCE

CHUNKS OF TURKEY FILLET ARE MARINATED IN A FABULOUS SWEET-AND-SOUR SPICED SAUCE IN THIS RECIPE FROM SOUTH AFRICA. MOP IT UP WITH SOME CRUSTY BREAD.

SERVES FOUR

INGREDIENTS
    5ml/1 tsp vegetable oil
    1 onion, finely chopped
    1 garlic clove, crushed
    2 bay leaves
    juice of 1 lemon
    30ml/2 tbsp curry powder
    60ml/4 tbsp apricot jam
    60ml/4 tbsp apple juice
    675g/1½lb turkey fillet
    30ml/2 tbsp low-fat crème fraîche
    salt

COOK'S TIP
If serving the sosaties indoors, serve with couscous and grilled vegetables.

1 Heat the oil in a pan. Add the onion, garlic and bay leaves and cook over a low heat for 10 minutes, or until the onions are soft. Add the lemon juice, curry powder, apricot jam and apple juice, with salt to taste. Cook gently for 5 minutes. Transfer to a bowl and cool.

2 Cut the turkey into 2cm/³⁄₄in cubes and add to the bowl. Mix well, cover and leave to marinate for at least 2 hours or chill overnight.

3 Prepare the barbecue. Position a lightly oiled grill rack over the hot coals. Thread the turkey on to four metal skewers, allowing the marinade to run back into the bowl. Cook the sosaties for 6–8 minutes over medium heat, turning several times, until done.

4 Meanwhile, transfer the marinade to a pan and simmer on the grill rack for 2 minutes. Stir in the crème fraîche, allow to heat through gently, and serve the sauce with the sosaties.

SPICY INDONESIAN CHICKEN SATAY

CHILLIES, GARLIC AND SOY SAUCE GIVE THESE INDONESIAN CHICKEN SATAYS PIQUANCY, AND THE REMAINING MARINADE IS COOKED TO MAKE A TASTY ACCOMPANYING DIP.

SERVES FOUR

INGREDIENTS
    ½ onion, sliced
    oil, for deep-frying
    4 chicken breast fillets, about
        175g/6oz each, skinned and cut
        into 2.5cm/1in cubes
For the sambal kecap
    1 fresh red chilli, seeded and finely
        chopped
    2 garlic cloves, crushed
    60ml/4 tbsp dark soy sauce
    20ml/4 tsp lemon juice or 15–25ml/
        1–1½ tbsp tamarind juice
    30ml/2 tbsp hot water

1 Deep-fry the onion until golden. Set aside.

2 To make the sambal kecap, mix all the ingredients in a bowl. Leave to stand for 30 minutes.

3 Place the chicken breast cubes in a bowl with the sambal kecap. Mix thoroughly. Cover and leave in a cool place to marinate for 1 hour.

4 Meanwhile, soak eight wooden skewers in water for 30 minutes.

5 Tip the chicken and marinade into a sieve placed over a pan and leave to drain for a few minutes. Set the sieve with the chicken aside.

6 Add 30ml/2 tbsp hot water to the marinade and bring to the boil. Lower the heat and simmer for 2 minutes, then pour into a bowl and leave to cool. When cool, add the deep-fried onion.

7 Prepare the barbecue. Position a lightly oiled grill rack over the hot coals. Thread the skewers with the chicken and cook over medium heat for about 10 minutes, turning regularly, until golden brown and cooked through. Serve with the sambal kecap as a dip.

Above: Energy 325kcal/1381kJ; Protein 59.4g; Carbohydrate 12.2g, of which sugars 12.1g; Fat 4.8g, of which saturates 1.9g; Cholesterol 125mg; Calcium 18mg; Fibre 0g; Sodium 162mg.
Below: Energy 197kcal/835kJ; Protein 42.5g; Carbohydrate 2.5g, of which sugars 2g; Fat 2g, of which saturates 0.5g; Cholesterol 123mg; Calcium 15mg; Fibre 0.4g; Sodium 640mg.

SKEWERED POUSSINS WITH LIME AND CHILLI

THE POUSSINS IN THIS RECIPE ARE FLATTENED OUT — SPATCHCOCKED — SO THAT THEY WILL COOK EVENLY AND QUICKLY. THE BREAST IS STUFFED WITH CHILLI AND SUN-DRIED TOMATO BUTTER, WHICH KEEPS THE MEAT MOIST AND MAKES IT TASTE WONDERFUL.

SERVES FOUR

INGREDIENTS

   4 poussins, about 450g/1lb each
   40g/1¹/₂oz/3 tbsp butter
   30ml/2 tbsp sun-dried tomato paste
   finely grated rind of 1 lime
   10ml/2 tsp chilli sauce
   juice of ¹/₂ lime
   flat leaf parsley sprigs, to garnish
   lime wedges, to serve

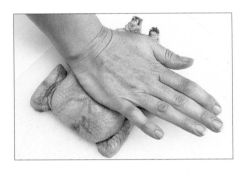

1 Place each poussin on a board, breast side up, and press down firmly with the palm of your hand, to break the breastbone.

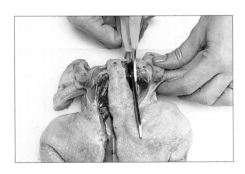

2 Turn the poussin over and, with poultry shears or strong kitchen scissors, cut down either side of the backbone and remove it.

3 Turn the poussin breast side up and flatten it neatly. Lift the breast skin carefully and gently ease your fingertips underneath, to loosen it from the flesh.

4 Mix together the butter, sun-dried tomato paste, lime rind and chilli sauce. Spread about three-quarters of the mixture under the skin of the poussins, smoothing it evenly.

COOK'S TIP
If you wish to serve half a poussin per portion, use poultry shears or a large sharp knife to cut through the breastbone and then the backbone.

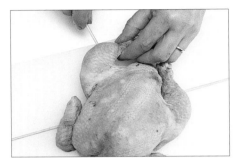

5 To hold the poussins flat during cooking, thread two skewers through each bird, crossing at the centre. Each skewer should pass through a wing and then out through a drumstick on the other side.

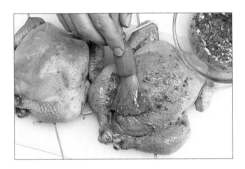

6 Prepare the barbecue. Position a lightly oiled grill rack over the hot coals. Mix the remaining tomato and butter mixture with the lime juice and brush it over the skin of the skewered poussins. Cook them over a medium-high heat, turning occasionally, for 25–30 minutes, or until the juices run clear when the thickest part of the leg is pierced. Garnish with flat leaf parsley and serve with lime wedges.

Energy 607kcal/2526kJ; Protein 50.4g; Carbohydrate 1.1g, of which sugars 1.1g; Fat 44.7g, of which saturates 15.1g; Cholesterol 282mg; Calcium 23mg; Fibre 0.2g; Sodium 259mg.

QUAIL WITH A FIVE-SPICE MARINADE

BLENDING AND GRINDING YOUR OWN FIVE-SPICE POWDER WILL GIVE THE FRESHEST-TASTING RESULTS FOR THIS VIETNAMESE-STYLE DISH OF SPATCHCOCKED QUAIL. IF YOU ARE SHORT OF TIME, BUY A GOOD-QUALITY READY-MIXED BLEND FROM THE SUPERMARKET.

SERVES FOUR TO SIX

INGREDIENTS
    6 quails, cleaned
To garnish
    mandarin orange or satsuma
    2 spring onions (scallions),
      roughly chopped
    banana leaves, to serve
For the marinade
    2 pieces star anise
    10ml/2 tsp ground cinnamon
    10ml/2 tsp fennel seeds
    10ml/2 tsp Sichuan pepper
    a pinch ground cloves
    1 small onion, finely chopped
    1 garlic clove, crushed
    60ml/4 tbsp clear honey
    30ml/2 tbsp dark soy sauce

COOK'S TIP
If you prefer, or if quails are not available, you could use other small poultry such as poussins. Poussins will take around 25–30 minutes to cook using the method given in this recipe.

1 Soak 12 wooden skewers in water for 30 minutes. Remove the backbones from the quails by cutting down either side with a pair of strong kitchen scissors.

2 Flatten the birds with the palm of your hand and secure each bird using two bamboo skewers.

3 To make the marinade, place the spices in a mortar or spice mill and grind into a fine powder. Add the onion, garlic, clear honey and soy sauce, and combine until thoroughly mixed.

4 Arrange the quails on a flat dish and pour over the marinade. Cover with clear film (plastic wrap) and leave in the refrigerator for 8 hours or overnight for the flavours to mingle.

5 Preheat the barbecue. Position a lightly oiled grill rack over the hot coals. Cook the quails over medium-high heat for 5 minutes then cover with a lid or tented heavy-duty foil and cook for 10 minutes more until golden brown. Baste occasionally with the marinade during cooking.

6 To make the garnish, remove the outer zest from the mandarin orange or satsuma, using a vegetable peeler. Shred the zest finely and combine with the chopped spring onions. Arrange the quails on a bed of banana leaves and garnish with the orange zest and spring onions.

Energy 159kcal/664kJ; Protein 13.2g; Carbohydrate 5.6g, of which sugars 5.6g; Fat 9.5g, of which saturates 2.6g; Cholesterol 68mg; Calcium 7mg; Fibre 0.1g; Sodium 404mg.

SPATCHCOCKED QUAIL <u>WITH</u> COUSCOUS

THESE DELICATE BABY BIRDS CAN BE COOKED VERY EFFICIENTLY ON A KETTLE BARBECUE WITH A LID. IF YOUR BARBECUE DOESN'T HAVE ITS OWN LID, IMPROVISE WITH A LARGE UPTURNED WOK WITH A WOODEN HANDLE OR USE TENTED FOIL. SERVE WITH A HERBY CHERRY TOMATO SALAD.

SERVES EIGHT

INGREDIENTS
8 quail
400ml/14fl oz/1⅔ cups water
2 lemons
60ml/4 tbsp extra virgin olive oil
45ml/3 tbsp chopped fresh
  tarragon leaves
125g/4¼oz/¾ cup couscous
15g/½oz dried (bell) peppers,
  finely chopped
8 black olives, pitted and chopped
salt and ground black pepper
16 wooden or metal skewers

1 Cut the backbones away from each quail and place them in a pan. Add the measured water and bring to the boil, then simmer gently to reduce the liquid by half. While the stock is cooking, wipe the insides of each bird with kitchen paper. If you find a heart inside, add it to the stock pot. Place each quail in turn, breast uppermost, on a board, and flatten it by pressing firmly on the breastbone. Carefully loosen the quail skin over the breasts with your fingers, creating a pocket for stuffing later.

COOK'S TIP
A lid is important for these fragile quail as it is best not to turn them. When enclosed, the heat circulates around the food, cooking it on all sides.

2 Grate the rind from the lemons. Set half the rind aside and put the rest in a flat dish. Squeeze both lemons and add the juice to the dish with 30ml/2 tbsp of the oil and 15ml/1 tbsp of the tarragon. Add the quail, turn to coat them well, cover and leave to marinate while you prepare the couscous stuffing.

3 Place the couscous in a medium bowl and add the dried peppers and salt and pepper. The stock should have reduced considerably by now. Strain 200ml/7fl oz/scant 1 cup over the couscous, cover with a dry cloth and leave to stand for 10 minutes.

4 Mix the reserved lemon rind into the couscous with the olives and the remaining tarragon and oil. Spread the mixture on a plate to cool, then cover and chill. When cold, ease a little stuffing into the breast pocket of each quail. If using wooden skewers, soak them in cold water for 30 minutes.

5 Prepare the barbecue. Pin the legs and wings of each quail to the body by driving a long skewer right through from either side to form a cross. If you want, wrap the leg tips with foil to prevent them from getting too charred.

6 Once the flames have died down, position a lightly oiled grill rack over the hot coals. Place the spatchcocked quail on the grill rack and cook over medium-high heat for about 5 minutes, moving the birds around occasionally. Cover with a lid or tented heavy-duty foil and cook for 10 minutes. Check if they are cooked; if they are plump and nicely browned they will almost certainly be done. If not, allow them to cook for a further 5 minutes. Let them stand for a few minutes to cool a little before serving, as they are best eaten with the fingers.

Energy 314kcal/1308kJ; Protein 23.2g; Carbohydrate 8.3g, of which sugars 0.2g; Fat 21.2g, of which saturates 5.1g; Cholesterol 116mg; Calcium 15mg; Fibre 0.2g; Sodium 221mg.

DUCK SAUSAGES WITH SPICY PLUM SAUCE

THE RICH FLAVOUR OF DUCK SAUSAGES GOES EXTREMELY WELL WITH SWEET POTATO MASH AND A PLUM SAUCE. THE RECIPE WOULD ALSO WORK WELL WITH PORK OR GAME SAUSAGES — OR A LUXURIOUS HICKORY-SMOKED SAUSAGE FOR A REAL BOOST TO FLAVOUR.

SERVES FOUR

INGREDIENTS
    8–12 duck sausages
For the sweet potato mash
    1.5kg/3¼lb sweet potatoes, cut
        into chunks
    25g/1oz/2 tbsp butter or 30ml/2 tbsp
        olive oil
    60ml/4 tbsp milk
    sea salt and ground black pepper
For the plum sauce
    30ml/2 tbsp olive oil
    1 small onion, chopped
    1 small red chilli, seeded
        and chopped
    450g/1lb plums, stoned (pitted)
        and chopped
    30ml/2 tbsp red wine vinegar
    45ml/3 tbsp clear honey

1 Put the sweet potatoes in a pan and add water to cover. Bring to the boil, then reduce the heat and simmer for 20 minutes, or until tender.

2 To make the plum sauce, heat the oil in a small pan and fry the onion and chilli gently for 5 minutes. Stir in the plums, vinegar and honey, then simmer gently for 10 minutes.

3 Drain and mash the potatoes and leave them in the pan.

VARIATION
If you'd rather not go to the bother of cooking the sweet potato mash, try a quick and easy polenta mash, perhaps combined with steamed spinach.

4 Prepare the barbecue. Arrange the duck sausages on the grill rack and cook over medium heat for 25–30 minutes, turning the sausages two or three times during cooking to ensure that they brown and cook evenly.

5 Place the pan with the mash on the grill rack and reheat. Stir frequently for about 5 minutes to dry out the mashed potato. Beat in the butter or oil and milk, and season to taste.

6 Serve the freshly cooked sausages accompanied by the sweet potato mash and plum sauce.

Energy 894kcal/3755kJ; Protein 17.8g; Carbohydrate 110.8g, of which sugars 42.9g; Fat 45.5g, of which saturates 17.9g; Cholesterol 67mg; Calcium 170mg; Fibre 11.6g; Sodium 1052mg.

RARE GINGERED DUCK

THIS IS JAPANESE AND CHINESE FUSION FOOD: THE TARE IS JAPANESE BUT THE PANCAKES ARE CHINESE.
YOU CAN COOK THE DUCK USING A GRIDDLE OR DIRECTLY ON THE GRILL RACK OF THE BARBECUE. BOTH
METHODS USE HIGH HEAT TO SEAR THE FLESH AND REMOVE THE FAT FOR SUCCULENT AND TASTY MEAT.

SERVES FOUR

INGREDIENTS

    4 large duck breast fillets, total
      weight about 675g/1½lb
    5cm/2in piece of fresh root ginger,
      finely grated
    ½ large cucumber
    12 Chinese pancakes
    6 spring onions (scallions),
      finely shredded
For the tare
    105ml/7 tbsp tamari
    105ml/7 tbsp mirin
    25g/1oz/2 tbsp sugar
    salt and ground black pepper

1 Make four slashes in the skin of each duck breast fillet, then lay them skin-side up on a plate. Squeeze the grated ginger over the duck to extract every drop of juice; discard the pulp. Generously rub the juice all over the duck, especially into the slashes. Using a vegetable peeler, peel the cucumber in strips, then cut it in half, scoop out the seeds and chop the flesh. Set aside in a bowl.

2 To make the tare, mix the tamari, mirin and sugar in a heavy pan and heat gently together until the sugar has dissolved. Increase the heat and simmer for 4–5 minutes, or until the syrup has reduced by about one-third.

3 Prepare the barbecue. Heat a griddle on the grill rack over hot coals. Sear the duck breasts in batches, placing them skin-side down.

4 When the fat has been rendered, and the skin is nicely browned, remove the duck from the pan. Drain off the fat and wipe the pan clean with kitchen paper. Reheat it, return the duck, flesh-side down and cook over a medium heat for about 3 minutes.

5 Brush on a little of the tare, turn the duck over, then, using a clean brush, brush the other side with tare and turn again. This should take about 1 minute, by which time the duck should be cooked rare. You can test for this by pressing the meat lightly: there should be some give in the flesh.

6 Remove from the pan and let the duck rest for a few minutes before slicing each breast across at an angle.

7 Warm the pancakes in a steamer for about 3 minutes. Serve with the duck, tare, spring onions and cucumber.

COOK'S TIP
To cook straight on the grill rack, part the hot coals in the centre and put a drip tray in the space. Position a lightly oiled grill rack over the hot coals. Sear the duck breasts directly over the coals, then move them over the drip tray. Cover with a lid or tented heavy-duty foil and cook as above, from step 4.

Energy 558kcal/2332kJ; Protein 36.4g; Carbohydrate 29.6g, of which sugars 7.6g; Fat 36.4g, of which saturates 6.1g; Cholesterol 186mg; Calcium 73mg; Fibre 1.2g; Sodium 293mg.

APRICOT DUCK <u>WITH</u> BEANSPROUTS

DUCK IS A RICHLY FLAVOURED BIRD AND IT GOES EXTREMELY WELL WHEN COOKED WITH FRUIT. HERE APRICOTS ARE USED TO STUFF DUCK BREASTS, WHICH ARE THEN BARBECUED WITH A HONEY GLAZE, MAKING DELICIOUSLY CRISPY SKIN ENCLOSING BEAUTIFULLY MOIST MEAT.

SERVES FOUR

INGREDIENTS

    4 plump duck breast portions
    1 small red onion, thinly sliced
    115g/4oz/½ cup ready-to-eat
      dried apricots
    15ml/1 tbsp clear honey
    5ml/1 tsp sesame oil
    10ml/2 tsp ground star anise
    salt and ground black pepper
For the salad
    ½ head Chinese leaves,
      finely shredded
    150g/5oz/2 cups beansprouts
    2 spring onions (scallions), shredded
    15ml/1 tbsp light soy sauce
    15ml/1 tbsp groundnut (peanut) oil
    5ml/1 tsp sesame oil
    5ml/1 tsp clear honey

1 Place the duck breast portions, skin side down, on a chopping board or clean work surface and cut a long slit down one side with a sharp kitchen knife, cutting not quite through, to form a large pocket.

2 Tuck the slices of onion and the apricots inside the pocket and press the breast firmly back into shape. Secure with metal skewers.

3 Prepare the barbecue. Position a lightly oiled grill rack over the hot coals. Mix together the clear honey and sesame oil, and brush generously over the duck, particularly the skin. Sprinkle over the star anise and season with plenty of salt and black pepper.

4 Cook the duck over medium-high heat for 12–15 minutes, turning once, until golden brown. The duck should be slightly pink in the centre.

5 Meanwhile, make the salad. Mix together the Chinese leaves, beansprouts and spring onions in a large bowl. Shake together the soy sauce, groundnut oil, sesame oil and honey in a screw-topped jar. Season to taste with salt and pepper.

6 Toss the salad with the dressing and serve with the duck.

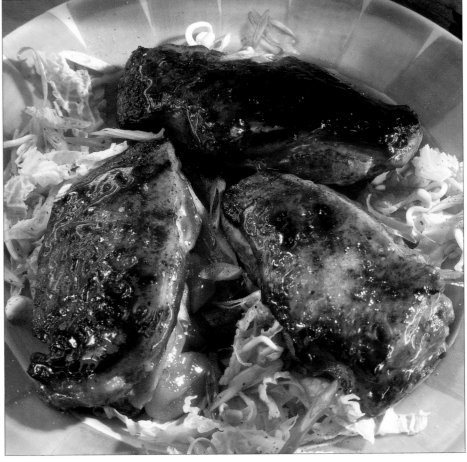

Energy 338kcal/1420kJ; Protein 36.5g; Carbohydrate 19.7g, of which sugars 18.6g; Fat 16g, of which saturates 2.9g; Cholesterol 186mg; Calcium 79mg; Fibre 3.7g; Sodium 197mg.

GLAZED DUCK BREASTS

IN THIS CAJUN RECIPE, SLICED AND BARBECUED SWEET POTATOES GO PARTICULARLY WELL WITH DUCK BREASTS THAT HAVE BEEN BRUSHED WITH A SWEET GLAZE. THE DISH IS QUICK TO PREPARE AND COOK, MAKING IT IDEAL FOR A FUSS-FREE BARBECUE.

SERVES TWO

INGREDIENTS

2 duck breast portions
1 sweet potato, about 400g/14oz
30ml/2 tbsp red pepper jelly
15ml/1 tbsp sherry vinegar
50g/2oz/4 tbsp butter, melted
coarse sea salt and ground
   black pepper

COOK'S TIP
Choose cylindrical sweet potatoes for the neatest slices.

1 Prepare the barbecue. Position a lightly oiled grill rack over the hot coals. Slash the skin of the duck breast portions diagonally at 2.5cm/1in intervals and rub plenty of salt and pepper over the skin and into the cuts.

2 Scrub the sweet potato and cut into 1cm/½in slices, discarding the ends.

3 Cook the duck breast portions over medium heat, skin side down, for 5 minutes. Turn and cook for a further 8–10 minutes, according to preference.

4 Meanwhile, brush the sweet potato slices with melted butter and sprinkle with coarse sea salt. Cook on the hottest part of the barbecue for 8–10 minutes until soft, brushing regularly with more butter and sprinkling liberally with salt and pepper every time you turn them. Keep an eye on them so that they do not char.

5 Warm the red pepper jelly and sherry vinegar together in a bowl set over a pan of hot water, stirring to mix them as the jelly melts. Brush the skin of the duck with the jelly and return to the barbecue, skin side down, for 2–3 minutes to caramelize it. Slice and serve with the sweet potatoes.

Energy 643kcal/2702kJ; Protein 42.1g; Carbohydrate 53.1g, of which sugars 21.9g; Fat 34.2g, of which saturates 15.8g; Cholesterol 273mg; Calcium 79mg; Fibre 4.8g; Sodium 456mg.

MEAT

It is surprising how many types and cuts of meat are appropriate for successful barbecuing. Meat can be minced and formed into koftas or burgers, or cut into chunks for kebabs. Finely minced meat can be made into wonderfully spiced home-made sausages, while whole joints of meat can be cooked on the barbecue - try the Barbecue Roast Beef, which is 'mopped' with a horseradish and beer sauce during cooking to keep it beautifully succulent and moist. As well as steaks, chops of all kinds are great favourites for barbecuing, and are made even more mouthwatering by the addition of fragrant marinades or a herb butter. This chapter includes recipes for lamb, bacon, pork, beef and venison that are a step away from the ordinary. Even old favourites have a new slant, such as beef burgers with a melted Stilton centre or the richly flavoured Indonesian Beef Burgers, which contain coconut. These classic meaty barbecue recipes have never tasted so good.

LAMB KEBABS <u>WITH</u> MINT CHUTNEY

THESE LITTLE ROUND LAMB KEBABS OWE THEIR EXOTIC FLAVOUR TO RAS EL HANOUT, A NORTH AFRICAN SPICE WHOSE HEDONISTIC QUALITIES ARE ACHIEVED BY ADDING HIGHLY PERFUMED DRIED DAMASK ROSE PETALS TO OVER TEN DIFFERENT SPICES. THE RESULT IS SUBLIME.

SERVES FOUR TO SIX

INGREDIENTS
  30ml/2 tbsp extra virgin
    olive oil
  1 onion, finely chopped
  2 garlic cloves, crushed
  35g/1¼oz/5 tbsp pine nuts
  500g/1¼lb/2½ cups minced
    (ground) lamb
  10ml/2 tsp ras el hanout spice mix
  10ml/2 tsp dried pink rose petals
    (optional)
  salt and ground black pepper
For the fresh mint chutney
  40g/1½oz/1½ cups fresh
    mint leaves
  10ml/2 tsp sugar
  juice of 2 lemons
  2 eating apples, peeled and
    finely grated
To serve (optional)
  150ml/¼ pint/⅔ cup Greek
    (US strained plain) yogurt
  7.5ml/1½ tsp rose harissa

1 If using wooden skewers, soak 18 in cold water for 30 minutes. Heat the oil in a frying pan on the stove. Add the onion and garlic, and fry gently for 7 minutes. Stir in the pine nuts. Fry for about 5 minutes more, or until the mixture is slightly golden, then set aside to cool.

2 Make the fresh mint chutney. Chop the mint finely by hand or in a food processor, then add the sugar, lemon juice and grated apple. Stir or pulse to mix.

3 Prepare the barbecue. Place the minced lamb in a large bowl and add the ras el hanout and rose petals, if using. Tip in the cooled onion mixture and add salt and pepper. Using your hands, mix well, then form into 18 balls. Drain the skewers and mould a ball on to each one. Once the flames have died down, rake a few hot coals to one side. Position a lightly oiled grill rack over the hot coals.

4 Place the kebabs on the grill over the part with the most coals to cook over medium heat. If it is easier, cover the barbecue with a lid or tented heavy-duty foil so that the heat will circulate and they will cook evenly all over. Otherwise, you will need to stay with them, turning them frequently for about 10 minutes. This prevents the kebabs from forming a hard crust before the meat is cooked right through to the centre.

5 Serve with the yogurt, mixed with the rose harissa, if you like. The kebabs can also be wrapped in Middle Eastern flat bread such as lavash with a green salad and cucumber slices piled in with them.

COOK'S TIPS
• You can also cook these kebabs on a hot griddle. They will take about 10 minutes. Sear on a high heat then lower the heat and turn frequently.
• The dried pink rose petals can be bought at Middle Eastern food stores.

Energy 257kcal/1070kJ; Protein 17.2g; Carbohydrate 5.1g, of which sugars 4.5g; Fat 18.8g, of which saturates 6g; Cholesterol 64mg; Calcium 33mg; Fibre 0.6g; Sodium 59mg.

SHISH KEBABS

SUMAC IS A SPICE, GROUND FROM A DRIED PURPLE BERRY WITH A SOUR, FRUITY FLAVOUR. IN THIS RECIPE IT BLISSFULLY COMPLEMENTS THE RICHNESS OF THE LAMB AND YOGURT. THESE KEBABS ARE EXCELLENT SERVED WITH LITTLE BOWLS OF INDIVIDUAL HERBS DRESSED AT THE LAST MINUTE.

MAKES EIGHT

INGREDIENTS
  675g/1½lb lamb neck (US shoulder
    or breast) fillet, trimmed and cut
    into 2.5cm/1in pieces
  5ml/1 tsp each fennel, cumin and
    coriander seeds, roasted
    and crushed
  1.5ml/¼ tsp cayenne pepper
  5cm/2in piece of fresh root ginger
  150ml/¼ pint/⅔ cup Greek (US
    strained plain) yogurt
  2 small red (bell) peppers
  2 small yellow (bell) peppers
  300g/11oz small or baby
    (pearl) onions
  30ml/2 tbsp olive oil
  15ml/1 tbsp ground sumac
  salt and ground black pepper
To serve
  8 Lebanese flat breads
  150ml/¼ pint/⅔ cup Greek
    (US strained plain) yogurt
  5ml/1 tsp ground sumac
  1 bunch rocket (arugula),
    about 50g/2oz
  50g/2oz/2 cups fresh flat leaf parsley
  10ml/2 tsp olive oil
  juice of ½ lemon

COOK'S TIP
If you want to use a griddle on the barbecue, cook the kebabs over a high heat to begin with, then lower the heat, and turn them frequently.

1 Place the lamb pieces in a bowl and sprinkle over the crushed seeds and the cayenne pepper. Grate the ginger and squeeze it over the lamb. When all the juices have been extracted, discard the pulp. Pour over the yogurt. Mix well, then cover and marinate overnight in the refrigerator.

2 Prepare the barbecue. Stand a large sieve over a bowl and pour in the lamb mixture. Leave to drain well. Cut the peppers in half, remove the cores and seeds, then cut the flesh into rough chunks. Place in a bowl. Add the onions and the olive oil.

3 Pat the drained lamb with kitchen paper to remove excess marinade. Add the lamb to the bowl, season and toss well. Divide the lamb, peppers and onions into eight equal portions and thread on to eight long metal skewers.

4 Position a lightly oiled grill rack over the coals to heat. Grill the kebabs for about 10 minutes over medium-high heat, turning every 2 minutes to prevent the meat and vegetables from getting too charred. When cooked, transfer the kebabs to a platter, lightly sprinkle with the sumac, cover loosely with foil, and leave to rest for a few minutes.

5 Wrap the breads in foil and put them on the barbecue to warm. Place the yogurt in a small serving bowl and sprinkle the surface with sumac. Arrange the rocket and parsley in separate bowls and pour over the oil and lemon juice. Serve with the kebabs and the warmed flat bread.

COOK'S TIP
Take care not to pack the lamb pieces too tightly on the skewers because they will not brown properly.

Energy 361kcal/1515kJ; Protein 22.5g; Carbohydrate 38.4g, of which sugars 8.1g; Fat 14.1g, of which saturates 5.1g; Cholesterol 64mg; Calcium 133mg; Fibre 3g; Sodium 249mg.

LAMB CUTLETS <u>WITH</u> LAVENDER

LAVENDER IS AN UNUSUAL FLAVOUR TO USE WITH MEAT, BUT ITS HEADY, SUMMERY SCENT WORKS WELL WITH BARBECUED LAMB. AS WELL AS ADDING LAVENDER TO THE MARINADE, YOU CAN SCATTER SPRIGS ON THE COALS OR GRILL RACK TO SMOKE. IF YOU PREFER, ROSEMARY CAN TAKE ITS PLACE.

<u>SERVES FOUR</u>

INGREDIENTS
    4 racks of lamb, with 3–4 cutlets each
    1 shallot, finely chopped
    45ml/3 tbsp chopped fresh lavender
    15ml/1 tbsp balsamic vinegar
    30ml/2 tbsp olive oil
    15ml/1 tbsp lemon juice
    salt and ground black pepper
    handful of lavender sprigs

COOK'S TIP
You can ask your butcher to prepare the cutlets for you; otherwise follow the instructions given with Rosemary Scented Lamb, later in this chapter.

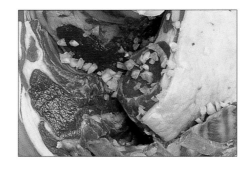

1 Prepare the barbecue. Position a lightly oiled grill rack over the hot coals. Place the racks of lamb in a wide dish and sprinkle over the chopped shallot so that each one is covered.

2 Sprinkle the chopped fresh lavender over the lamb racks.

3 Beat together the vinegar, olive oil and lemon juice, and pour them over the lamb. Season well with salt and pepper and then turn to coat evenly.

4 Scatter lavender sprigs over the grill rack or on the coals. Cook the lamb over medium-high heat for 15–20 minutes, turning once and basting with marinade, until golden brown on the outside and slightly pink in the centre.

LAMB BURGERS WITH REDCURRANT SAUCE

THESE RATHER SPECIAL BURGERS TAKE A LITTLE EXTRA TIME TO PREPARE BUT ARE WELL WORTH IT, BECAUSE EACH CONTAINS SOME MELTINGLY SOFT MOZZARELLA CHEESE. THE REDCURRANT CHUTNEY IS THE PERFECT COMPLEMENT TO THE MINTY LAMB TASTE OF THE BURGERS.

SERVES FOUR

INGREDIENTS

    500g/1¼lb/2½ cups minced
        (ground) lean lamb
    1 small onion, finely chopped
    30ml/2 tbsp finely chopped fresh mint
    30ml/2 tbsp finely chopped
        fresh parsley
    115g/4oz mozzarella cheese
    30ml/2 tbsp oil, for basting
    salt and freshly ground black pepper
For the redcurrant chutney
    115g/4oz/1½ cups fresh or
        frozen redcurrants
    10ml/2 tsp clear honey
    5ml/1 tsp balsamic vinegar
    30ml/2 tbsp finely chopped mint

1 In a large bowl, mix together the lamb, onion, mint and parsley until evenly combined. Season well with plenty of salt and pepper.

2 Roughly divide the minced meat mixture into eight equal pieces and use your hands to press each of the pieces into flat rounds.

3 Cut the mozzarella cheese into four chunks. Place one chunk of cheese on half the lamb rounds. Top each with another round of meat mixture.

4 Press each of the two rounds of meat together firmly, making four flattish burger shapes. Use your fingers to blend the edges and seal in the cheese completely.

5 Prepare the barbecue. Position a lightly oiled grill rack over the hot coals. Place all the ingredients for the chutney in a bowl and mash them together with a fork. Season well with salt and freshly ground black pepper.

6 Brush the lamb burgers with olive oil and cook them over a medium-high heat for about 15 minutes, turning once, until golden brown. Serve with the redcurrant chutney.

Energy 344kcal/1432kJ; Protein 30.1g; Carbohydrate 5g, of which sugars 4.6g; Fat 22.8g, of which saturates 11.7g; Cholesterol 113mg; Calcium 171mg; Fibre 1.9g; Sodium 206mg.

GRILLED SKEWERED LAMB

IN GREECE, THIS SKEWERED LAMB DISH IS KNOWN AS SOUVLAKIA. TENDER LAMB IS MARINATED IN HERBS, OLIVE OIL AND LEMON JUICE AND THEN BARBECUED WITH SWEET PEPPERS AND RED ONIONS. THE SOUVLAKIA ARE AT THEIR BEST SERVED WITH TZATZIKI, A LARGE TOMATO SALAD AND BARBECUED BREAD.

SERVES FOUR

INGREDIENTS
    1 small shoulder of lamb, boned and
      with most of the fat removed
    2–3 onions, preferably red onions,
      quartered
    2 red or green (bell) peppers,
      quartered and seeded
    75ml/5 tbsp extra virgin olive oil
    juice of 1 lemon
    2 garlic cloves, crushed
    5ml/1 tsp dried oregano
    2.5ml/½ tsp dried thyme or some
      sprigs of fresh thyme, chopped
    salt and ground black pepper

1 Ask your butcher to trim the meat and cut it into 4cm/1½in cubes. (A little fat is desirable with souvlakia, because it keeps them moist and succulent during cooking.) Separate the onion quarters into pieces, each composed of two or three layers, and slice each pepper quarter in half widthways.

2 Put the oil, lemon juice, garlic and herbs in a large bowl. Season with salt and pepper, and whisk well to combine. Add the meat cubes, stirring to coat them in the mixture.

3 Cover the bowl tightly and leave to marinate for 4–8 hours in the refrigerator, stirring several times.

VARIATION
If you prefer, you can use 4–5 best end neck fillets instead of shoulder.

4 Lift out the meat cubes, reserving the marinade, and thread them on to long metal skewers, alternating each piece of meat with a piece of pepper and a piece of onion. Lay them across a grill pan or baking tray and brush them with the reserved marinade.

5 Prepare the barbecue. Position a lightly oiled grill rack over the hot coals. Cook the souvlakia over medium-high heat for 10 minutes, or until they start to get scorched. Turn the skewers over, brush them again with the marinade (or a little olive oil) and cook them for 10–15 minutes more. Serve the souvlakia immediately.

COOK'S TIP
Although these souvlakia cook best with a little fat left on the meat, always be sure to trim excess fat from meats that are to be barbecued, as the fat will drip on to the coals and can cause flare-ups.

Energy 419kcal/1743kJ; Protein 32.3g; Carbohydrate 16.3g, of which sugars 13.1g; Fat 25.4g, of which saturates 8.4g; Cholesterol 138mg; Calcium 51mg; Fibre 3.4g; Sodium 89mg.

MOROCCAN SPICED LAMB

THIS MOROCCAN SPECIALITY OFTEN CONSISTS OF A WHOLE LAMB GRILLED SLOWLY OVER A CHARCOAL FIRE FOR MANY HOURS. THIS VERSION IS FOR A LARGE SHOULDER, RUBBED WITH SPICES AND CHARGRILLED. WHEN COOKED, THE MEAT IS HACKED OFF AND DIPPED IN ROASTED SALT AND CUMIN.

SERVES FOUR TO SIX

INGREDIENTS
    1 shoulder of lamb, about 1.8kg/4lb
    4 garlic cloves, crushed
    15ml/1 tbsp paprika
    15ml/1 tbsp freshly ground
      cumin seeds
    105ml/7 tbsp extra virgin olive oil
    45–60ml/3–4 tbsp finely chopped
      mint leaves
    a few sturdy thyme sprigs,
      for basting
    salt and ground black pepper
To serve
    45ml/3 tbsp cumin seeds
    25ml/1½ tbsp coarse sea salt

1 Open up the natural pockets in the lamb, and stuff with the garlic. Mix the paprika, ground cumin and seasoning, and rub all over the shoulder. Cover and leave the lamb for about 1 hour. Mix the oil and mint in a bowl for basting the meat during roasting.

2 Prepare a barbecue. Once the flames have died down, rake the hot coals to one side and insert a drip tray flat beside them. Position a lightly oiled grill rack over the hot coals.

3 Place the lamb shoulder on the grill rack over medium-high heat and directly over the drip tray. Cover with a lid or tented heavy-duty foil. For the initial 30 minutes turn the meat frequently, basting using the thyme branches and mint oil. Then roast the joint for a further 2 hours, turning and basting every 15 minutes so that it remains moist.

4 If you need to replenish the coals, do so before the heat is too low. It will take about 10 minutes to heat sufficiently to continue the cooking.

5 Dry-roast the cumin seeds and coarse salt for 2 minutes in a heavy frying pan. Do not let them burn. Tip them into a mortar and pound with the pestle until roughly ground.

6 When the meat is cooked, remove from the barbecue, wrap in double foil and rest it for 15 minutes. Serve sliced with the roasted cumin seeds and salt for dipping.

Energy 618kcal/2564kJ; Protein 42.7g; Carbohydrate 0.8g, of which sugars 0.1g; Fat 49.3g, of which saturates 21.2g; Cholesterol 183mg; Calcium 16mg; Fibre 0.2g; Sodium 150mg.

HERB-FLAVOURED LAMB

THIS BONED LEG OF LAMB IS BUTTERFLIED SO THAT IT COOKS QUICKLY ON THE BARBECUE, REMAINING TENDER AND RARE INSIDE. THE NATIVE AUSTRALIAN HERB, ANISEED MYRTLE, ADDS A SUBTLE FLAVOUR TO THE MEAT. YOU CAN BONE AND BUTTERFLY THE LAMB YOURSELF OR ASK THE BUTCHER TO DO IT FOR YOU.

2 Cover and marinate in the refrigerator overnight. Remove it from the refrigerator 1½ hours before you start cooking. After 30 minutes, rub some salt all over the lamb.

3 Prepare the barbecue. Lift the lamb out of the marinade, and reserve the marinade. Pat the lamb dry with kitchen paper to remove all the excess marinade, then skewer the lamb in three places using long metal skewers to keep it flat.

4 Once the flames have died down, rake the hot coals to one side and insert a drip tray beside them. Position a lightly oiled grill rack over the hot coals. Lay the lamb on the grill rack over high heat directly above the coals for 3–5 minutes to lightly char one side.

5 Turn the lamb over and put it back on the grill rack, this time over the drip tray. Cover with a lid or tented heavy-duty foil. Grill the lamb for 20 minutes, basting the charred side occasionally with the marinade to keep it moist.

6 Move the lamb so that it is over the coals, replace the lid and grill it for 5–8 minutes more so that it chars slightly. Lift it on to a tray and let it rest under tented foil for 10–15 minutes. Cut into thick slices and serve with the juices from the drip tray.

SERVES SIX

INGREDIENTS
    1 leg of lamb, about 1.8kg/4lb,
      boned and butterflied
    juice of 1 lemon
    15ml/1 tbsp ground Australian
      aniseed myrtle or 5ml/1 tsp fennel
      seeds ground with 10ml/2 tsp dried
      thyme
    90ml/6 tbsp extra virgin olive oil
    salt and ground black pepper

COOK'S TIP
Australian aniseed myrtle has a subtle Pernod-like flavour with a sweet aftertaste. It can be used with meat, seafood or in baking. Available from specialist suppliers.

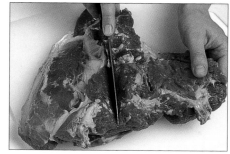

1 Cut down the length of the leg of lamb down to the bone and remove the bones. Cut into the thick parts of the meat to flatten it. Lay the lamb in a flat dish. Squeeze the lemon juice over both sides then season with ground black pepper. Rub the myrtle or fennel and thyme, and the oil, all over the meat.

Energy 302kcal/1260kJ; Protein 29.7g; Carbohydrate 0g, of which sugars 0g; Fat 20.4g, of which saturates 5.4g; Cholesterol 100mg; Calcium 7mg; Fibre 0g; Sodium 63mg.

ROSEMARY-SCENTED LAMB

THE BEST THING ABOUT THIS RECIPE IS THAT ALL THE WORK IS DONE THE NIGHT BEFORE. YOU CAN ASK YOUR BUTCHER TO FRENCH TRIM THE LAMB RACKS IF YOU WANT TO MAKE YOUR PREPARATION TIME QUICKER. ALLOW PLENTY OF TIME FOR MARINATING, ALTHOUGH THE COOKING TIME IS QUICK.

SERVES FOUR TO EIGHT

INGREDIENTS
  2 x 8-chop racks of lamb, chined
  8 large fresh rosemary sprigs
  2 garlic cloves, thinly sliced
  90ml/6 tbsp extra virgin olive oil
  30ml/2 tbsp verjuice or red wine
  salt and ground black pepper

1 Cut the fat off the ribs down the top 5cm/2in from the bone ends. Turn the joint over and score between the bones. Cut and scrape away the meat and connective tissue between the bones. Cut the racks into eight portions, each consisting of two linked chops, and tie a rosemary sprig to each one.

2 Lay the portions in a single layer in a bowl or wide dish. Mix the garlic, oil and verjuice or wine, and pour over the lamb, cover and chill overnight, turning them as often as possible.

3 Bring the marinating chops to room temperature 1 hour before cooking. Prepare the barbecue. Remove the lamb from the marinade, and discard the marinade. Season the meat 15 minutes before cooking.

4 Position a lightly oiled grill rack over the hot coals. Stand the lamb chops upright on the rack over medium-high heat, propping them against each other. Cover with a lid or tented heavy-duty foil and grill for 2 minutes.

5 Carefully turn the chops on to one side, and grill for a further 4 minutes each side for rare meat or 5 minutes if you prefer lamb medium cooked.

6 Remove the chops from the grill, transfer to serving plates, cover and rest for 5–10 minutes before serving.

COOK'S TIP
Allowing the hot chops to stand before serving will give the juices time to gather on the plate and create a light sauce.

Energy 433kcal/1788kJ; Protein 23.4g; Carbohydrate 0g, of which sugars 0g; Fat 37.6g, of which saturates 16.4g; Cholesterol 101mg; Calcium 17mg; Fibre 0g; Sodium 83mg.

MIXED GRILL SKEWERS

THIS HEARTY SELECTION OF MEATS, COOKED ON A SKEWER AND DRIZZLED WITH HORSERADISH SAUCE, MAKES A POPULAR MAIN COURSE. KEEP ALL THE PIECES OF MEAT ABOUT THE SAME THICKNESS SO THAT THEY WILL COOK EVENLY. THROW SOME BAY LEAVES ON TO THE COALS IF YOU LIKE.

SERVES FOUR

INGREDIENTS

    4 small lamb noisettes, each about
      2.5cm/1in thick
    4 lamb's kidneys
    4 streaky (fatty) bacon rashers (strips)
    8 cherry tomatoes
    8 chipolata sausages
    12–16 bay leaves
    salt and ground black pepper
For the horseradish sauce
    30ml/2 tbsp horseradish relish
    45ml/3 tbsp melted butter

1 Trim any excess fat from the lamb noisettes with a sharp knife. Halve the kidneys and remove the cores, using kitchen scissors.

2 Cut each bacon rasher in half and wrap around the tomatoes or kidneys.

3 Thread the lamb noissettes, bacon-wrapped kidneys and cherry tomatoes, chipolatas and bay leaves on to four long metal skewers. Set aside while you prepare the sauce.

4 Mix the horseradish relish with the melted butter and stir until thoroughly mixed. Put half the sauce into a serving bowl.

5 Brush a little of the horseradish sauce from the pan over the meat and sprinkle with salt and freshly ground black pepper.

6 Prepare the barbecue. Position a lightly oiled grill rack over the hot coals. Cook the skewers over medium heat for 12 minutes, turning occasionally, until the meat is golden brown and thoroughly cooked. Serve hot, drizzled with the sauce from the bowl.

Energy 422kcal/1756kJ; Protein 27.2g; Carbohydrate 7g, of which sugars 3.4g; Fat 31.9g, of which saturates 14.2g; Cholesterol 323mg; Calcium 68mg; Fibre 1g; Sodium 955mg.

BACON KOFTAS

KOFTA KEBABS CAN BE MADE WITH ANY TYPE OF MINCED MEAT, BUT BACON IS VERY SUCCESSFUL. YOU WILL NEED A FOOD PROCESSOR FOR THE BEST RESULT AS THE INGREDIENTS NEED TO BE CHOPPED FINELY. THEY GO VERY NICELY WITH A BULGUR WHEAT SALAD, WHICH IS SUBSTANTIAL AND QUICK TO MAKE.

SERVES FOUR

INGREDIENTS

   250g/9oz lean streaky (fatty) bacon
     rashers (strips), roughly chopped
   1 small onion, roughly chopped
   1 celery stick, roughly chopped
   75ml/5 tbsp fresh wholemeal
     (whole-wheat) breadcrumbs
   45ml/3 tbsp chopped fresh thyme
   30ml/2 tbsp Worcestershire sauce
   1 egg, beaten
   salt and ground black pepper
   olive oil, for brushing
For the salad
   115g/4oz/¾ cup bulgur wheat
   60ml/4 tbsp toasted sunflower seeds
   15ml/1 tbsp olive oil
   salt and freshly ground black pepper
   handful of celery leaves, chopped

1 Soak eight bamboo skewers in water for 30 minutes. Place the bacon, onion, celery and breadcrumbs in a food processor and process until chopped. Add the thyme, Worcestershire sauce and seasoning. Bind to a firm mixture with the egg.

2 Divide the mixture into eight equal portions and use your hands to shape them around eight bamboo skewers.

3 For the salad, place the bulgur wheat in a bowl and pour over boiling water to cover. Leave to stand for 30 minutes, until the grains are tender. Prepare the barbecue. Position a lightly oiled grill rack over the hot coals.

4 Drain the bulgur wheat well, then stir in the sunflower seeds, olive oil, salt and pepper. Stir in the celery leaves.

5 Cook the kofta skewers over medium-high heat for 8–10 minutes, turning occasionally, until golden brown. Serve with the salad.

Energy 340kcal/1417kJ; Protein 14g; Carbohydrate 31.7g, of which sugars 2.5g; Fat 18.2g, of which saturates 5.5g; Cholesterol 41mg; Calcium 55mg; Fibre 0.7g; Sodium 1025mg.

BASIL AND PECORINO STUFFED PORK

THIS IS A VERY EASY DISH TO MAKE AND LOOKS EXTREMELY IMPRESSIVE. IT IS GOOD FOR A BULK COOKOUT, BECAUSE YOU CAN GET SEVERAL FILLETS ON A BARBECUE GRILL, AND EACH ONE YIELDS ABOUT EIGHT CHUNKY SLICES. SERVE WITH A CHICKPEA AND ONION SALAD.

1 Make a 1cm/½in slit down the length of one of the fillets. Continue to slice, cutting along the fold of the meat, until you can open it out flat. Lay between two sheets of baking parchment and pound with a rolling pin to an even thickness of about 1cm/½in. Lift off the top sheet of parchment and brush the meat with a little oil. Press half the basil leaves on to the surface, then scatter over half the Pecorino cheese and chilli flakes. Add a little black pepper.

2 Roll up lengthways to form a sausage and tie with kitchen string (twine). Repeat with the second fillet. Put them in a shallow bowl with the remaining oil, cover and put in a cool place until ready to cook.

3 Prepare the barbecue. Twenty minutes before you are ready to cook, season the meat with salt. Wipe any excess oil off the meat. Once the flames have died down, rake the hot coals to one side and insert a drip tray beside them. Position a lightly oiled grill rack over the hot coals.

4 Put the tenderloins on to the grill rack over high heat, directly over the coals. Grill for 5 minutes over the coals, turning to sear on all sides, then move them over the drip tray and grill for 15 minutes more. Cover with a lid or tented heavy-duty foil, and turn them over from time to time. When done, remove and wrap in foil. Leave to rest for 10 minutes before slicing into rounds and serving.

SERVES SIX TO EIGHT

INGREDIENTS
   2 pork fillets (tenderloins), each
      about 350g/12oz
   45ml/3 tbsp olive oil
   40g/1½oz/1½ cups fresh basil
      leaves, chopped
   50g/2oz Pecorino cheese, grated
   2.5ml/½ tsp chilli flakes
   salt and ground black pepper

COOK'S TIP
• If you don't use a lid and drip tray, move the coals so there are less on one side than the other. Move the pork during cooking to prevent burning.
• Pork fillets are incredibly versatile and perfect for the barbecue. Not only can they be exquisitely stuffed, but the large suface area, and the fact that they are cooked on all sides, makes for exceptionally flavourful meat dishes.

Energy 174kcal/725kJ; Protein 21.3g; Carbohydrate 0.1g, of which sugars 0.1g; Fat 9.7g, of which saturates 3.1g; Cholesterol 61mg; Calcium 91mg; Fibre 0.3g; Sodium 131mg.

PORK RIBS <u>WITH</u> GINGER RELISH

THIS DISH WORKS BEST WHEN THE PORK RIBS ARE GRILLED IN WHOLE, LARGE SLABS, THEN SLICED TO SERVE. NOT ONLY DOES THIS KEEP THE MEAT SUCCULENT, BUT IT ALSO CREATES PERFECT-SIZED PORTIONS FOR GUESTS TO GRAB! MAKE THE GINGER RELISH THE DAY BEFORE IF POSSIBLE.

SERVES FOUR

INGREDIENTS
  4 pork rib slabs, each with 6 ribs,
    total weight about 2kg/4½lb
  40g/1½oz/3 tbsp light muscovado
    (brown) sugar
  3 garlic cloves, crushed
  5cm/2in piece of fresh root ginger,
    finely grated
  10ml/2 tsp Sichuan peppercorns,
    finely crushed
  2.5ml/½ tsp ground black pepper
  5ml/1 tsp finely ground star anise
  5ml/1 tsp Chinese five-spice powder
  90ml/6 tbsp dark soy sauce
  45ml/3 tbsp sunflower oil
  15ml/1 tbsp sesame oil
For the relish
  60ml/4 tbsp sunflower oil
  300g/11oz banana shallots,
    finely chopped
  9 garlic cloves, crushed
  7.5cm/3in piece of fresh root ginger,
    finely grated
  60ml/4 tbsp seasoned rice
    wine vinegar
  45ml/3 tbsp sweet chilli sauce
  105ml/7 tbsp tomato ketchup
  90ml/6 tbsp water
  60ml/4 tbsp chopped fresh coriander
    (cilantro) leaves
  salt

1 Lay the slabs of pork ribs in a large shallow dish. Mix the remaining ingredients in a bowl and pour the marinade over the ribs, making sure they are evenly coated. Cover and chill the ribs overnight.

2 To make the relish, heat the oil in a heavy pan, add the shallots and cook them gently for 5 minutes. Add the garlic and ginger and cook for about 4 minutes more. Increase the heat and add all the remaining ingredients except the coriander. Cover and simmer gently for 10 minutes until thickened. Tip into a bowl and stir in the coriander. When completely cold, chill until needed.

3 Remove the ribs from the refrigerator 1 hour before cooking. Prepare the barbecue. Remove the ribs from the marinade and pat them dry with kitchen paper. Pour the marinade into a pan. Bring it to the boil on the stove, then simmer for 3 minutes.

4 Once the flames have died down, rake the hot coals to one side and insert a large drip tray beside them. Position a lightly oiled grill rack over the hot coals. Lay the ribs over high heat directly over the coals and cook them for 3 minutes on each side, then move over the drip tray. Cover with a lid or tented heavy-duty foil and cook for a further 30–35 minutes, turning and basting occasionally with the marinade.

5 The meat should be ready when it is golden-brown in appearance. If, towards the end of the cooking time, the ribs need crisping up a bit, move them quickly back over the coals. Stop basting with the marinade 5 minutes before cooking time. Cut into single ribs to serve, with the relish.

PORK SATAY KEBABS

MACADAMIA NUTS HAVE AN UNMISTAKEABLY RICH FLAVOUR AND ARE USED HERE WITH ASIAN FLAVOURINGS AND CHILLIES TO MAKE A HOT AND SPICY MARINADE FOR BITE SIZE PIECES OF TENDER PORK. SERVE THE SATAY KEBABS WITH A REFRESHING LEAF SALAD AND A RICE SALAD OR BARBECUED VEGETABLES.

MAKES EIGHT TO TWELVE

INGREDIENTS
  450g/1lb pork fillet (tenderloin)
  15ml/1 tbsp light muscovado
    (brown) sugar
  1cm/½in cube shrimp paste
  1–2 lemon grass stalks
  30ml/2 tbsp coriander seeds, dry-fried
  6 macadamia nuts or
    blanched almonds
  2 onions, roughly chopped
  3–6 fresh red chillies, seeded and
    roughly chopped
  2.5ml/½ tsp ground turmeric
  300ml/½ pint/1¼ cups canned
    coconut milk
  30ml/2 tbsp groundnut (peanut) oil
    or sunflower oil
  salt

1 Soak 8–12 bamboo skewers in water for 30 minutes to prevent them scorching on the barbecue.

2 Cut the pork into small, bite size chunks, then spread it out in a single layer in a shallow dish. Sprinkle with the sugar, to help release the juices, and then set aside.

3 Fry the shrimp paste briefly in a foil parcel in a dry frying pan. Alternatively, warm the foil parcel on a skewer held over the gas flame.

4 Cut off the lower 5cm/2in of the lemon grass stalks and chop finely. Process the dry-fried coriander seeds to a powder in a food processor.

5 Add the nuts and chopped lemon grass, process briefly, then add the onions, chillies, shrimp paste, turmeric and a little salt; process to a fine paste.

6 Pour in the coconut milk and oil. Switch the machine on very briefly to mix. Pour the mixture over the pork and leave to marinate for 1–2 hours.

7 Prepare the barbecue. Position a lightly oiled grill rack over the hot coals. Thread three or four pieces of marinated pork on to each bamboo skewer and grill over medium heat for 8–10 minutes, or until tender, basting frequently with the remaining marinade up until the final 5 minutes. Serve the skewers immediately while hot.

Energy 103kcal/432kJ; Protein 13.1g; Carbohydrate 5.2g, of which sugars 4.4g; Fat 3.5g, of which saturates 0.8g; Cholesterol 33mg; Calcium 20mg; Fibre 0.5g; Sodium 54mg.

PORK CHOPS <u>WITH</u> FIELD MUSHROOMS

LEMON GRASS AND TYPICAL AROMATIC THAI FLAVOURINGS MAKE A SUPERB MARINADE FOR PORK CHOPS, WHICH ARE ACCOMPANIED BY A FIERY SAUCE THAT IS SIMPLY PUT TOGETHER IN A PAN ON THE BARBECUE GRILL RACK. SERVE WITH THE BARBECUED MUSHROOMS, A SALAD AND CRUSTY BREAD.

<u>SERVES FOUR</u>

INGREDIENTS
    4 pork chops
    4 large field (portabello) mushrooms
    45ml/3 tbsp vegetable oil
    4 fresh red chillies, seeded and
      thinly sliced
    45ml/3 tbsp Thai fish sauce
    90ml/6 tbsp fresh lime juice
    4 shallots, chopped
    5ml/1 tsp roasted ground rice
    30ml/2 tbsp spring onions
      (scallions), chopped, plus shredded
      spring onions to garnish
    coriander (cilantro) leaves, to garnish
For the marinade
    2 garlic cloves, chopped
    15ml/1 tbsp sugar
    15ml/1 tbsp Thai fish sauce
    30ml/2 tbsp soy sauce
    15ml/1 tbsp sesame oil
    15ml/1 tbsp whisky or dry sherry
    2 lemon grass stalks, finely chopped
    2 spring onions (scallions), chopped

1 To make the marinade, combine the garlic, sugar, sauces, oil and whisky or sherry in a large, shallow dish. Stir in the lemon grass and spring onions.

2 Add the pork chops, turning to coat them in the marinade. Cover and leave to marinate for 1–2 hours. Prepare the barbecue. Position a lightly oiled grill rack over the hot coals.

3 Lift the chops out of the marinade and place them on the grill rack. Cook over high heat for 5–7 minutes on each side. Brush with the marinade during cooking up until the final 5 minutes of cooking. Meanwhile, brush both sides of the mushrooms with 15ml/1 tbsp of the oil and cook them for about 2 minutes without turning.

4 Heat the remaining oil in a wok or small frying pan on the grill rack, then remove the pan from the heat and stir in the chillies, fish sauce, lime juice, shallots, ground rice and chopped spring onions. Put the pork chops and mushrooms on a large serving plate and spoon over the sauce. Garnish with the coriander leaves and shredded spring onion.

Energy 408kcal/1705kJ; Protein 49.7g; Carbohydrate 9.8g, of which sugars 8.3g; Fat 19.1g, of which saturates 4.9g; Cholesterol 123mg; Calcium 62mg; Fibre 2g; Sodium 1176mg.

PORK SCHNITZEL

THIN PORK ESCALOPES ARE IDEAL FOR ROLLING AROUND A RICHLY FLAVOURED STUFFING AND THEN BARBECUED IN THIS VARIATION OF A CROATIAN RECIPE. SERVE THEM WITH A CREAMY SAUCE FLAVOURED WITH MUSHROOMS AND BACON, AND SOME COUNTRY-STYLE CRUSTY BREAD FOR MOPPING UP JUICES.

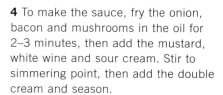

3 Divide the livers evenly between the four prepared pork steaks and roll up into neat parcels. Secure with cocktail sticks or string.

4 To make the sauce, fry the onion, bacon and mushrooms in the oil for 2–3 minutes, then add the mustard, white wine and sour cream. Stir to simmering point, then add the double cream and season.

5 Prepare the barbecue. Position a lightly oiled grill rack over the hot coals. Brush the pork rolls with oil and cook over medium heat for 8–10 minutes on each side, brushing with oil as necessary, until golden brown.

6 Reheat the sauce over the barbecue. Remove the cocktail sticks or string from the rolls. Serve the schnitzels with the sauce and garnish with a little parsley.

COOK'S TIP

Veal or chicken breast fillet would also work well with this recipe.

SERVES FOUR

INGREDIENTS
    4 pork leg steaks or escalopes (US pork scallop), about 200g/7oz each
    60ml/4 tbsp olive oil
    115g/4oz chicken livers, chopped
    1 garlic clove, crushed
    salt and ground black pepper
    15ml/1 tbsp chopped fresh parsley, to garnish
For the sauce
    1 onion, thinly sliced
    115g/4oz streaky (fatty) bacon, thinly sliced
    175g/6oz/2 cups sliced mixed wild mushrooms
    120ml/4fl oz/½ cup olive oil
    5ml/1 tsp ready-made mustard
    150ml/¼ pint/⅔ cup white wine
    120ml/4fl oz/½ cup sour cream
    250ml/8fl oz/1 cup double (heavy) cream

1 Soak 8 cocktail sticks (toothpicks) in water for 30 minutes. Place each pork steak between 2 sheets of dampened clear film (plastic wrap) or baking parchment and flatten with a meat mallet or rolling pin until about 15 x 10cm/6 x 4in. Season well.

2 Heat half the oil in a frying pan and cook the chicken livers and garlic for 1–2 minutes. Remove, drain on kitchen paper and leave to cool.

Energy 969kcal/4009kJ; Protein 50.2g; Carbohydrate 3.8g, of which sugars 3.3g; Fat 81.6g, of which saturates 33.7g; Cholesterol 248mg; Calcium 83mg; Fibre 0.7g; Sodium 532mg.

BELMONT SAUSAGE WITH MUSHROOM RELISH

NOTHING QUITE BEATS GOOD QUALITY SAUSAGE, AND THIS RECIPE ENSURES YOU GET JUST THAT. YOU CAN CHANGE THE COMBINATION OF HERBS AND SPICES OR TWIST THE SAUSAGE INTO SMALL LENGTHS. IT REALLY IS A VERY ADAPTABLE RECIPE, AND THE MUSHROOM RELISH IS PERFECT TO GO WITH IT.

SERVES SIX TO EIGHT

INGREDIENTS
    450g/1lb skinless and boneless belly
      pork, cut into large pieces
    450g/1lb pork shoulder, cut into
      large pieces
    300–400g/11–14oz back fat, cut into
      large pieces
    50g/2oz/1 cup freshly made
      breadcrumbs
    2 garlic cloves, crushed
    10ml/2 tsp salt
    10ml/2 tsp ground coriander
    5ml/1 tsp ground black pepper
    5ml/1 tsp ground cumin
    1.5ml/¼ tsp cayenne pepper
    1.5ml/¼ tsp ground cinnamon
    45ml/3 tbsp chopped fresh basil
    60ml/4 tbsp chopped fresh marjoram
    60ml/4 tbsp chopped fresh flat
      leaf parsley
    enough cleaned sausage casing for
      just over 900g/2lb sausage: about
      50g/2oz or 2.7m/9ft
    30ml/2 tbsp olive oil for brushing
    6 metal skewers
For the relish
    45ml/3 tbsp extra virgin olive oil
    2 onions, finely chopped
    2 garlic cloves, finely chopped
    150g/5oz/2 cups finely chopped
      chestnut mushrooms
    25g/1oz/3 tbsp drained sun-dried
      tomatoes in oil, finely chopped
    90ml/6 tbsp water
    20ml/4 tsp sugar
    30ml/2 tbsp chopped fresh flat
      leaf parsley
    30ml/2 tbsp sherry vinegar
    salt and ground black pepper

1 Pass both meats through the mincer (grinder) once and the back fat twice, using the plate with the widest holes. Place in a large bowl and add the breadcrumbs. Add the garlic with a pinch of the salt, and the remaining sausage ingredients except the remaining salt, the casings and the oil. Mix thoroughly. Cover and chill overnight.

2 Rinse the casing by running cold water through it. Fit the casing on to the sausage-making attachment of the mincer, or use a piping bag with a wide nozzle. Add the remaining salt to the mixture and mix well. Fill the casing in one continuous length, leaving a gap of 13cm/5in of empty casing halfway. Separate into two sausages, securing by tying the ends. Curl each sausage into a round, cover and chill.

3 To make the relish, heat the oil in a pan and fry the onions and garlic for about 10 minutes. Add the mushrooms and tomatoes and fry for 1 minute. Stir in the measured water and boil until it has evaporated. Stir in the sugar, parsley and vinegar. Season, cover and cool.

4 Prepare the barbecue. Skewer the sausages to maintain the round shape. Once the flames have died down, rake the hot coals to one side and insert a drip tray beside them. Position a lightly oiled grill rack over the hot coals. Brush the sausages with a little oil and place them on the grill rack over the drip tray. Cover with a lid or tented heavy-duty foil, and cook for 5–7 minutes on each side, or until cooked and golden. Serve with the relish.

Energy 765kcal/3159kJ; Protein 21.9g; Carbohydrate 6.1g, of which sugars 4.9g; Fat 72.7g, of which saturates 26.8g; Cholesterol 117mg; Calcium 38mg; Fibre 1.4g; Sodium 87mg.

FIVE-SPICED PORK RIBS

BARBECUED PORK SPARE RIBS MARINATED WITH CHINESE FLAVOURINGS HAVE GOT TO BE ONE OF THE ALL-TIME FAVOURITES. CHOOSE THE MEATIEST SPARE RIBS YOU CAN FIND TO MAKE THE DISH A REAL SUCCESS AND HAVE PLENTY OF NAPKINS HANDY.

SERVES FOUR

INGREDIENTS
  1kg/2¼lb Chinese-style pork
    spare ribs
  10ml/2 tsp Chinese five-spice powder
  2 garlic cloves, crushed
  15ml/1 tbsp grated fresh
    root ginger
  2.5ml/½ tsp chilli sauce
  60ml/4 tbsp dark soy sauce
  45ml/3 tbsp muscovado
    (brown) sugar
  15ml/1 tbsp sunflower oil
  4 spring onions (scallions)

1 If the spare ribs are still attached to each other, cut between them to separate them (or you could ask your butcher to do this when you buy them). Place the spare ribs in a large bowl.

2 Mix together all the remaining ingredients, except the spring onions, and pour over the ribs. Toss well to coat evenly. Cover the bowl and leave to marinate in the refrigerator overnight.

3 Prepare the barbecue. Position a lightly oiled grill rack over the hot coals. Cook the ribs over medium-high heat, turning frequently, for about 30–40 minutes. Brush occasionally with the remaining marinade up until the final 5 minutes.

4 While the ribs are cooking, finely slice the spring onions. Scatter them over the ribs and serve immediately.

Energy 562kcal/2346kJ; Protein 47.2g; Carbohydrate 12.7g, of which sugars 12.6g; Fat 36.3g, of which saturates 13.3g; Cholesterol 165mg; Calcium 46mg; Fibre 0g; Sodium 1047mg.

VEAL CHOPS <u>WITH</u> BASIL BUTTER

SUCCULENT VEAL CHOPS FROM THE LOIN ARE AN EXPENSIVE CUT AND ARE BEST COOKED QUICKLY AND SIMPLY. THE FLAVOUR OF BASIL GOES PARTICULARLY WELL WITH VEAL, BUT OTHER HERBS CAN BE USED INSTEAD IF YOU PREFER. SERVE WITH BARBECUED VEGETABLES OR A SALAD.

SERVES TWO

INGREDIENTS
  25g/1oz/2 tbsp butter, softened
  15ml/1 tbsp Dijon mustard
  15ml/1 tbsp chopped fresh basil
  olive oil, for brushing
  2 veal loin chops, 2.5cm/1in thick,
    about 225g/8oz each
  salt and ground black pepper
  fresh basil sprigs, to garnish

COOK'S TIP
Chilled herb butters make perfect impromptu sauces for cooked meats and fish. Basil butter is a firm favourite, but other fresh herbs such as chives, tarragon and parsley also work well.

1 To make the basil butter, cream the softened butter with the Dijon mustard and chopped fresh basil in a large mixing bowl, then season with plenty of freshly ground black pepper.

2 Prepare the barbecue. Position a lightly oiled grill rack over the hot coals.

3 Brush both sides of each chop with olive oil and season with a little salt. Cook the chops over high heat for 7–10 minutes, basting with oil and turning once, until done to your liking.

4 Top each chop with basil butter and serve at once, garnished with basil.

Energy 718kcal/3017kJ; Protein 113.8g; Carbohydrate 0.3g, of which sugars 0.0g; Fat 29.13g, of which saturates 16.0g; Cholesterol 3135mg; Calcium 35mg; Fibre 0.3g; Sodium 448mg.

HOME-MADE BURGERS <u>WITH</u> RELISH

MAKING YOUR OWN BURGERS MEANS YOU CONTROL WHAT GOES INTO THEM. THESE ARE FULL OF FLAVOUR AND ALWAYS PROVE POPULAR. SERVE IN BUNS WITH LETTUCE AND THE TANGY RATATOUILLE RELISH, WHICH IS VERY EASY TO MAKE.

SERVES FOUR

INGREDIENTS
2 shallots, unpeeled
450g/1lb/2 cups fresh lean minced
   (ground) beef
30ml/2 tbsp chopped parsley
30ml/2 tbsp tomato ketchup
1 garlic clove, crushed
1 fresh green chilli, seeded and
   finely chopped
15ml/1 tbsp olive oil
400g/14oz can ratatouille
4 burger buns
lettuce leaves
salt and ground black pepper

VARIATION
These burgers also taste great with spicy corn relish on the side. To make the relish, heat 30ml/2 tbsp oil in a pan and fry 1 onion, 2 crushed garlic cloves and 1 seeded and finely chopped red chilli until soft. Add 10ml/2 tsp garam masala and cook for 2 minutes, then mix in a 320g/11¼oz can of sweetcorn and the grated rind and juice of 1 lime.

1 Prepare the barbecue. Put the shallots in a bowl with boiling water to cover. Leave for 1–2 minutes, then slip off the skins and chop the shallots finely.

2 Mix 1 shallot with the beef in a bowl. Add the parsley and tomato ketchup, with salt and pepper to taste. Mix well with clean hands. Divide the mixture into four. Knead each portion into a ball, then flatten it into a burger.

3 Make a spicy relish by cooking the remaining shallot with the garlic and green chilli in the olive oil for 2–3 minutes, or until softened.

4 Add the canned ratatouille to the pan containing the vegetables. Bring to the boil, then simmer for 5 minutes. Position a lightly oiled grill rack over the hot coals.

5 Transfer the pan to the edge of the barbecue. Cook the burgers over high heat for about 5 minutes on each side, until browned and cooked through.

6 Split the burger buns. Arrange the lettuce leaves on the bun bases, add the burgers and top with warm relish and the bun tops.

Energy 487kcal/2037kJ; Protein 27.9g; Carbohydrate 31.7g, of which sugars 7.8g; Fat 28.6g, of which saturates 9g; Cholesterol 68mg; Calcium 92mg; Fibre 2g; Sodium 492mg.

STILTON BURGERS

A VARIATION ON THE TRADITIONAL BURGER, THIS TASTY RECIPE CONTAINS A DELICIOUS SURPRISE: A CREAMY FILLING OF LIGHTLY MELTED STILTON CHEESE. HOME-MADE BURGERS ARE QUITE QUICK TO MAKE AND TASTE SUPERIOR TO BOUGHT ONES. CHOOSE GOOD QUALITY BEEF FOR THE BEST FLAVOUR.

SERVES FOUR

INGREDIENTS
   450g/1lb/2 cups minced
     (ground) beef
   1 onion, chopped
   1 celery stick, chopped
   5ml/1 tsp dried mixed herbs
   5ml/1 tsp prepared mustard
   50g/2oz/½ cup crumbled
     Stilton cheese
   4 burger buns
   salt and ground black pepper

3 Shape and flatten the remaining four portions and place on top. Use your hands to mould the rounds together, encasing the crumbled cheese, and shaping them into four burgers.

4 Cook over medium-high heat for about 5 minutes on each side. Split the burger buns and place a burger inside each. Serve with salad and mustard pickle, if you like.

1 Prepare the barbecue. Position a lightly oiled grill rack over the hot coals. Mix the minced beef with the onion, celery, mixed herbs and mustard. Season well with salt and pepper, and bring together with your hands to form a firm mixture.

2 Divide the mixture into eight equal portions. Shape four portions into rounds and flatten each one slightly. Place a little of the crumbled cheese in the centre of each round.

Energy 428kcal/1789kJ; Protein 29.6g; Carbohydrate 25.9g, of which sugars 2.2g; Fat 23.5g, of which saturates 10.7g; Cholesterol 79mg; Calcium 113mg; Fibre 1.1g; Sodium 454mg.

PEPPERED STEAKS IN BEER AND GARLIC

STEAKS GO VERY WELL WITH A ROBUST MARINADE OF GARLIC, WORCESTERSHIRE SAUCE AND BEER. MARINADES HAVE A DUAL PURPOSE OF FLAVOURING AS WELL AS TENDERIZING MEAT AND SO WILL IMPROVE THE TEXTURE AS WELL AS THE TASTE. SERVE WITH A BAKED POTATO AND CRISP MIXED SALAD.

SERVES FOUR

INGREDIENTS

    4 beef sirloin or rump steaks, about
      175g/6oz each
    2 garlic cloves, crushed
    120ml/4fl oz/½ cup brown ale
      or stout
    30ml/2 tbsp muscovado
      (molasses) sugar
    30ml/2 tbsp Worcestershire sauce
    15ml/1 tbsp corn oil
    15ml/1 tbsp crushed
      black peppercorns

1 Place the steaks in a dish and add the garlic, ale or stout, sugar, Worcestershire sauce and oil. Turn to coat evenly, then leave to marinate in the refrigerator for 2–3 hours or overnight.

2 Prepare the barbecue. Position a lightly oiled grill rack over the hot coals. Remove the steaks and reserve the marinade. Sprinkle the peppercorns over the steaks and press them into the surface.

3 Cook the steaks over high heat, basting them occasionally with the reserved marinade during cooking. (Take care when basting, as the alcohol will tend to flare up: spoon or brush on just a small amount at a time and allow the final basting to cook through.)

4 Turn the steaks once during cooking, and cook them for about 3–6 minutes on each side, depending on how rare you like them.

Energy 355kcal/1480kJ; Protein 39.8g; Carbohydrate 4.7g, of which sugars 4.7g; Fat 19g, of which saturates 7.1g; Cholesterol 102mg; Calcium 13mg; Fibre 0g; Sodium 114mg.

SPICY MEATBALLS

THESE QUICK-TO-PREPARE MEATBALLS MAKE A TASTY APPETIZER OR A MAIN COURSE SERVED WITH FLAT BREAD AND SALAD OR ROASTED VEGETABLES. THEY CAN BE COOKED ON THE GRILL RACK, BUT AS THEY ARE RATHER SMALL YOU MIGHT FIND THEM EASIER TO COOK IN A HEAVY FRYING PAN ON THE BARBECUE.

SERVES SIX

INGREDIENTS
115g/4oz fresh spicy sausages
115g/4oz/½ cup minced (ground) beef
2 shallots, finely chopped
2 garlic cloves, finely chopped
75g/3oz/1½ cups fresh white
  breadcrumbs
1 egg, beaten
30ml/2 tbsp chopped fresh parsley,
  plus extra to garnish
15ml/1 tbsp olive oil
salt and ground black pepper
Tabasco or other hot chilli sauce,
  to serve

1 Use your hands to remove the skins from the spicy sausages, placing the sausagemeat in a mixing bowl and breaking it up with a fork.

2 Add the minced beef, shallots, garlic, breadcrumbs, beaten egg and parsley, with plenty of salt and pepper. Mix well, then use your hands to shape the mixture into 18 small balls. Prepare the barbecue. Heat a heavy frying pan or flat griddle over the hot coals.

3 Brush the meatballs with olive oil and cook over medium heat for about 10–15 minutes, turning regularly until evenly browned and cooked through. (Or cook them directly on the grill rack.)

4 Transfer the meatballs to a warm dish and sprinkle with parsley. Serve with chilli sauce.

Energy 175kcal/732kJ; Protein 8.6g; Carbohydrate 11.5g, of which sugars 0.9g; Fat 10.9g, of which saturates 3.6g; Cholesterol 55mg; Calcium 43mg; Fibre 0.5g; Sodium 287mg.

STEAK CIABATTA

THIS ALL-TIME FAVOURITE TASTES ALL THE BETTER WHEN ENJOYED ON A BEACH AFTER AN AFTERNOON SPENT BATTLING THE SURF.

SERVES FOUR

INGREDIENTS
 2 romaine or cos lettuces
 3 garlic cloves, crushed to a paste
  with enough salt to season
  the steaks
 30ml/2 tbsp extra virgin olive oil
 4 sirloin steaks, 2.5cm/1in thick,
  total weight about 900g/2lb
 4 small ciabatta rolls
 salt and ground black pepper
For the dressing
 10ml/2 tsp Dijon mustard
 5ml/1 tsp cider or white wine vinegar
 15ml/1 tbsp olive oil

2 Mix the garlic and oil together in a shallow dish. Add the steaks and rub the mixture into both surfaces. Cover and leave in a cool place until ready to cook.

1 Separate the lettuce leaves and clean them. Put into an airtight container until ready to use. Make a dressing for the salad by mixing the mustard and vinegar in a small jar. Gradually whisk in the oil, then season to taste.

3 Prepare the barbecue. Position a lightly oiled grill rack over the hot coals. Transfer the steaks to the grill rack. For rare meat, cook the steaks for 2 minutes on one side, without moving, then turn over and grill the other side for 3 minutes. For medium steaks, cook for 4 minutes on each side. Transfer to a plate, cover loosely and leave to rest for 2 minutes.

4 Dress the lettuce leaves. Split each ciabatta. Place the ciabatta cut-side down on the grill rack for a minute to heat. Slice the steaks and arrange on top of the ciabatta, with some of the leaves. Replace the lids and cut each filled ciabatta in half to serve.

COOK'S TIP
A steak sandwich is also delicious spread with hummus. Follow the classic hummus recipe given in the Accompaniments chapter.

Energy 665kcal/2796kJ; Protein 64g; Carbohydrate 53.5g, of which sugars 4.4g; Fat 23.2g, of which saturates 6.4g; Cholesterol 115mg; Calcium 158mg; Fibre 3g; Sodium 698mg

BARBECUE ROAST BEEF

"Mopping" is big in the Southwestern states of the USA, where the technique is often used to keep large pieces of meat moist and succulent during the long, slow cooking process. For this recipe, the technique has been adapted. Once seared, mop the meat constantly.

SERVES FOUR

INGREDIENTS
  800g/1¾lb beef fillet (tenderloin)
  30ml/2 tbsp bottled grated
  horseradish
  30ml/2 tbsp olive oil
  120ml/4fl oz/½ cup Chimay
  salt and ground black pepper

COOK'S TIP
Chimay is a naturally brewed beer from Belgium, which could be substituted with any other good-quality beer you fancy. Non-alcoholic beers are also fine, or even soda water, if you want.

1 Pat the beef dry with kitchen paper and place it in a dish. Rub it all over with 5ml/1 tsp of the horseradish and the olive oil. Cover and leave to marinate for 2 hours in a cool place.

2 If spit roasting, skewer the meat with a long spit. Prepare the barbecue. Mix the remaining horseradish with the beer in a deep bowl.

3 Season the meat well. Position a lightly oiled grill rack over the coals to heat. Cook the beef over high heat for about 2 minutes on each side, so that the outside sears and acquires a good colour.

4 Set the spit turning over the coals. Dip a large basting brush in the horseradish and beer mixture and generously mop the meat all over with it. Continue to mop, as the meat turns, for a total grilling time of 11 minutes. Use all of the basting mixture.

5 Rest the meat in a warm place under tented foil for about 10 minutes before slicing thickly. This dish is great served hot, with roasted vegetables, or left to go cold and eaten with thick slices of country-style bread and horseradish-flavoured mayonnaise.

Energy 409kcal/1701kJ; Protein 45.5g; Carbohydrate 0.8g, of which sugars 0.8g; Fat 24.1g, of which saturates 8.4g; Cholesterol 116mg; Calcium 12mg; Fibre 0g; Sodium 130mg.

SPICY BEEF KOFTAS WITH CHICKPEA PURÉE

WHEREVER YOU GO IN THE MIDDLE EAST YOU WILL ENCOUNTER THESE TASTY KEBABS, AS STREET FOOD, ON BARBECUES, AT BEACH BARS AND AT FAMILY MEALS. CHICKPEA PURÉE IS THE TRADITIONAL ACCOMPANIMENT, AND A MIXED SALAD WILL ALSO GO WELL WITH THE RICH FLAVOURS.

SERVES SIX

INGREDIENTS

500g/1¼lb/2½ cups finely minced (ground) beef
1 onion, grated
10ml/2 tsp ground cumin
10ml/2 tsp ground coriander
10ml/2 tsp paprika
4ml/¾ tsp cayenne pepper
5ml/1 tsp salt
small bunch of fresh flat leaf parsley, finely chopped
small bunch of fresh coriander (cilantro), finely chopped
For the chickpea purée
225g/8oz/1¼ cups dried chickpeas, soaked overnight, drained and cooked until soft
50ml/2fl oz/¼ cup olive oil
juice of 1 lemon
2 garlic cloves, crushed
5ml/1 tsp cumin seeds
30ml/2 tbsp light tahini paste
60ml/4 tbsp thick Greek (US strained plain) yogurt
40g/1½oz/3 tbsp butter, melted
salt and ground black pepper
salad and bread, to serve

1 Mix the minced beef with the onion, cumin, ground coriander, paprika, cayenne, salt, parsley and fresh coriander. Knead the mixture well, then pound it until smooth in a mortar with a pestle or in a blender or food processor. Place the minced beef mixture in a dish then cover and leave to stand in a cool place for 1 hour.

2 Meanwhile, make the chickpea purée. Preheat the oven to 200°C/400°F/Gas 6. In a blender or food processor, process the chickpeas with the olive oil, lemon juice, garlic, cumin seeds, tahini and yogurt until well mixed. Season with salt and pepper, tip the purée into an ovenproof dish, cover with foil and heat through in the oven for 20 minutes. Prepare the barbecue. Position a lightly oiled grill rack over the hot coals.

3 Divide the meat mixture into six portions. Gently squeeze and pat the meat mixture into shape along each of six skewers so that it is quite thick and resembles a fat sausage. Cook the koftas over high heat for 4–5 minutes on each side.

4 Melt the butter in a small pan on the barbecue and pour it over the hot chickpea purée. Serve the koftas with the hot chickpea purée, a mixed salad and bread.

Energy 449kcal/1870kJ; Protein 26.3g; Carbohydrate 20.5g, of which sugars 2.5g; Fat 29.7g, of which saturates 10.7g; Cholesterol 64mg; Calcium 141mg; Fibre 5g; Sodium 134mg.

HOME-MADE VENISON SAUSAGES

VENISON SAUSAGES HAVE AN EXCELLENT FLAVOUR, A MUCH LOWER FAT CONTENT THAN MOST SAUSAGES AND THEY'RE EASY TO MAKE IF YOU FORGET ABOUT SAUSAGE SKINS AND JUST SHAPE THE MIXTURE. GRIDDLED ONIONS AND TOMATOES AND BARBECUED MUSHROOMS GO VERY NICELY WITH THE SAUSAGES.

MAKES 1.4KG/3LB

INGREDIENTS
  900g/2lb/4 cups finely minced
    (ground) venison
  450g/1lb/2 cups finely minced
    (ground) belly of pork
  15ml/1 tbsp salt
  10ml/2 tsp ground black pepper
  1 garlic clove, crushed
  5ml/1 tsp dried thyme
  1 egg, beaten
  plain (all-purpose) flour, for dusting
  oil, for brushing
  griddled onions and tomatoes, and
    barbecued field (portabello)
    mushrooms, to serve

1 Combine all the sausage ingredients, except the flour and oil, in a bowl. Take a small piece of the mixture and fry it in a little oil in a heavy frying pan, then taste to check the seasoning for the batch. Adjust if necessary.

2 Form the mixture into chipolata-size sausages using floured hands.

3 Prepare the barbecue. Position a lightly oiled grill rack over the hot coals. Brush the sausages with oil and cook over high heat for 10 minutes or until they are golden brown and cooked right through.

4 If you use a large pan, you'll be able to fry some onion rings alongside the sausages. At the same time, cook some mushrooms and halved tomatoes on a griddle to serve on the side.

COOK'S TIP
As these sausages are made without casings you may find them rather awkward to turn on the grill rack. A hinged wire basket is useful for cooking delicate items over the barbecue.

Per Sausage: Energy 156kcal/652kJ; Protein 15.3g; Carbohydrate 0g, of which sugars 0g; Fat 10.9g, of which saturates 3.9g; Cholesterol 54mg; Calcium 6mg; Fibre 0g; Sodium 377mg

VENISON CHOPS WITH ROMESCO SAUCE

ROMESCO IS THE CATALAN WORD FOR THE ÑORA CHILLI. IT LENDS A SPICY ROUNDNESS TO ONE OF SPAIN'S GREATEST SAUCES, FROM TARRAGONA. THE SAUCE ALSO CONTAINS GROUND TOASTED NUTS AND OFTEN ANOTHER FIERCER CHILLI. IT CAN BE SERVED HOT, AS HERE, OR COLD AS A DIP FOR VEGETABLES.

SERVES FOUR

INGREDIENTS

4 venison chops, cut 2cm/¾in thick
   and about 175–200g/6–7oz each
30ml/2 tbsp olive oil
50g/2oz/¼ cup butter
For the *romesco* sauce
   3 *ñora* chillies
   1 hot dried chilli
   25g/1oz/¼ cup almonds
   150ml/¼ pint/⅔ cup olive oil
   1 slice stale bread, crusts removed
   3 garlic cloves, chopped
   3 tomatoes, peeled, seeded and
      roughly chopped
   60ml/4 tbsp sherry vinegar
   60ml/4 tbsp red wine vinegar
   salt and ground black pepper

1 To make the *romesco* sauce, slit both types of chilli and remove the seeds, then leave the chillies to soak in warm water for about 30 minutes until soft. Drain the chillies, dry them on kitchen paper and chop finely.

2 Dry-fry the almonds in a frying pan over a medium heat, shaking the pan occasionally, until the nuts are toasted evenly. Transfer the nuts to a food processor or blender.

3 Add 45ml/3 tbsp of the oil to the frying pan and fry the bread slice until golden on both sides. Lift it out with a slotted spoon and drain on kitchen paper. Tear the bread and add to the food processor or blender. Fry the chopped garlic in the oil remaining in the pan.

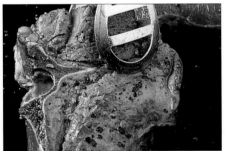

COOK'S TIP
Always be careful when preparing chillies, as the juice can irritate cuts or the eyes if it touches them. Wear rubber gloves during preparation or rub olive oil over the fingers before preparation and then scrub hands thoroughly afterwards.

4 Add the soaked chillies and tomatoes to the processor or blender. Tip in the garlic, with the oil from the pan, and blend the mixture to form a smooth paste.

5 With the motor running, gradually add the remaining olive oil and then the vinegars. When the sauce is smooth and well blended, scrape it into a bowl and season with salt and ground black pepper to taste. Cover with clear film (plastic wrap) and chill for 2 hours. Transfer to a small pan.

6 Prepare the barbecue. Position a lightly oiled grill rack over the hot coals. Melt the butter with the oil in a small pan on the grill rack and use to brush over the chops. Cook the chops for 5–6 minutes on each side until golden brown and cooked through.

7 Meanwhile, heat the *romesco* sauce gently. If it is too thick, stir in a little boiling water. Serve the sauce with the chops, accompanied by vegetables or salad.

Energy 531kcal/2206kJ; Protein 30.3g; Carbohydrate 6g, of which sugars 2.9g; Fat 43.9g, of which saturates 11.8g; Cholesterol 89mg; Calcium 43mg; Fibre 1.5g; Sodium 185mg.

INDONESIAN BEEF BURGERS

THIS UNUSUAL INDONESIAN RECIPE CONTAINS COCONUT, WHICH GIVES THE BURGERS A RICH AND SUCCULENT FLAVOUR. THEY TASTE GREAT WITH A SHARP YET SWEET MANGO CHUTNEY AND CAN BE EATEN IN MINI NAAN OR PITTA BREADS.

MAKES EIGHT

INGREDIENTS
  500g/1¼lb/2½ cups minced
    (ground) beef
  5ml/1 tsp anchovy paste
  10ml/2 tsp tomato purée (paste)
  10ml/2 tsp ground coriander
  5ml/1 tsp ground cumin
  7.5ml/1½ tsp finely grated fresh
    root ginger
  2 garlic cloves, crushed
  1 egg white
  75g/3oz solid creamed coconut,
    grated or 40g/1½oz desiccated (dry
    unsweetened shredded) coconut
  45ml/3 tbsp chopped fresh
    coriander (cilantro)
  salt and ground black pepper
  8 fresh vine leaves (optional),
    to serve

1 Mix the minced beef, anchovy paste, tomato purée, coriander, cumin, ginger and garlic in a bowl. Add the egg white, with salt and pepper to taste. Mix well using your hands. Add the grated coconut and work it gently into the meat mixture so that it doesn't melt, or stir in the desiccated coconut. Add the fresh coriander.

2 Divide into eight pieces and form chunky burgers, about 7.5cm/3in in diameter. Chill for 30 minutes.

3 Prepare the barbecue. Once the flames have died down, rake the hot coals to one side and insert a drip tray beside them. Position a lightly oiled grill rack over the hot coals. Cook the chilled burgers over medium-high heat directly over the drip tray for 10–15 minutes, turning them over once or twice. Check they are cooked by breaking off a piece of one of the burgers.

4 If you are using the vine leaves, wash them and pat dry with kitchen paper. Wrap one around each burger. Serve with mango chutney and mini naan or pitta breads.

Energy 177kcal/734kJ; Protein 13.4g; Carbohydrate 0.8g, of which sugars 0.7g; Fat 13.4g, of which saturates 7g; Cholesterol 38mg; Calcium 22mg; Fibre 1.1g; Sodium 90mg.

BARBECUED MARINATED BEEF

THIS DISH OF THINLY SLICED BEEF, MARINATED WITH SUGAR, SOY SAUCE AND GARLIC, IS IDEAL FOR FLASH-FRYING IN A GRIDDLE OR FOR BARBECUING OVER A CLOSE-MESHED BARBECUE. SERVE IT WITH A QUICK VERSION OF THE TRADITIONAL KOREAN FERMENTED-CABBAGE DISH, KIMCHI.

SERVES FOUR

INGREDIENTS
- 500g/1¼lb beef fillet (tenderloin)
- 15ml/1 tbsp sugar
- 30ml/2 tbsp light soy sauce
- 30ml/2 tbsp sesame oil
- 2 garlic cloves, mashed to a paste with a further 5ml/1 tsp sugar
- 2.5ml/½ tsp finely ground black pepper

For the *kimchi*
- 500g/1¼lb Chinese leaves (Chinese cabbage), sliced across into 2.5cm/1in pieces
- 60ml/4 tbsp sunflower oil
- 15ml/1 tbsp sesame oil
- 50g/2oz/¼ cup sugar
- 105ml/7 tbsp white rice vinegar
- 2.5cm/1in piece of fresh root ginger, finely chopped
- 3 garlic cloves, finely chopped
- 1 fresh fat medium-hot red chilli
- 2 spring onions (scallions), thinly sliced

For the *sigumchi namul*
- 350g/12oz baby spinach leaves
- 10ml/2 tsp sesame oil
- 30ml/2 tbsp light soy sauce
- 15ml/1 tbsp mirin
- 10ml/2 tsp sesame seeds, finely toasted

COOK'S TIP
This meat dish will cook very successfully on a close-meshed disposable barbecue but the meat may fall through the gaps in grill racks of other barbecues, so a griddle is preferable if you are cooking on most kinds of barbecue.

1 Freeze the beef for 1 hour to make it easier to slice. Remove it from the freezer and slice it as thinly as possible. Layer in a shallow dish, sprinkling each layer with sugar. Cover and chill for 30 minutes. Mix the soy sauce, sesame oil, garlic paste and pepper together in a bowl and pour over the beef, ensuring all the pieces are thoroughly coated in the mixture. Cover and chill overnight.

2 To make the *kimchi*, blanch the Chinese leaves in plenty of boiling water for 5 seconds, drain and refresh under cold running water. Drain again and pat with kitchen paper to remove excess water. Put the Chinese leaves in a bowl. Mix the remaining ingredients together and add to the leaves. Toss to mix, cover and chill. The mixture can be made up to 2 days ahead, but tastes best if eaten within 2 hours.

3 To make the *sigumchi namul*, blanch the spinach in boiling water for 1 minute, drain it and refresh under cold water. Drain again, pat with kitchen paper to remove any excess water and put into a serving bowl. Mix the oil, soy sauce and mirin together. Fold into the spinach with the sesame seeds. Cover and keep in a cool place (not the refrigerator). Serve within 2 hours.

4 Prepare the barbecue. Heat a griddle on the grill rack over hot coals. Flash-fry the meat in batches for 15–20 seconds on each side. Serve immediately with the *sigumchi namul* and the *kimchi*.

Energy 500kcal/2080kJ; Protein 31.4g; Carbohydrate 25.8g, of which sugars 25.5g; Fat 30.6g, of which saturates 6.5g; Cholesterol 76mg; Calcium 231mg; Fibre 4.7g; Sodium 900mg.

THE GAUCHO BARBECUE

THIS DELICIOUS TRADITIONAL PAMPAS BEEF DISH CONSISTS OF SHORT RIBS AND RUMP STEAK ACCOMPANIED BY PORK SAUSAGES. IT INVOLVES NO MARINATING, BUT THE MEAT IS BRUSHED WITH BRINE DURING COOKING TO KEEP IT MOIST. SERVE EACH MEAT AS IT IS COOKED, ACCOMPANIED BY A SELECTION OF SALADS AND SALSAS.

SERVES SIX

INGREDIENTS
  50g/2oz/¼ cup coarse sea salt
  200ml/7fl oz/scant 1 cup
    warm water
  6 pork sausages
  1kg/2¼lb beef short ribs
  1kg/2¼lb rump (round) steak, in
    one piece
  salads, salsas and breads, to serve

1 Dissolve the sea salt in the measured water in a bowl. Leave to cool.

2 Prepare the barbecue. Position a lightly oiled grill rack over the hot coals.

3 Start by cooking the sausages, which should take 15–20 minutes over medium heat, depending on their size. Once cooked on all sides, slice the sausages thickly and arrange them on a plate. Let guests help themselves while you cook the remaining meats.

4 Place the short ribs bony side down on the grill rack. Cook for 15 minutes, turn, brush the cooked side of each rib with brine and grill for a further 25–30 minutes and continue basting. Slice the meat and transfer to a plate for guests to help themselves.

5 Place the whole rump steak on the grill rack and cook for 5 minutes, then turn over and baste the browned side with brine.

6 Continue turning and basting in this way for 20–25 minutes in total, until the meat is cooked to your liking. Allow the meat to rest for 5 minutes under tented heavy-duty foil, then slice thinly and serve with salads, salsa and bread.

COOK'S TIPS
• This dish is quick to cook over the barbecue, but don't be tempted to partially precook any meat and then to finish it off on the barbecue, as this will encourage bacteria to grow.
• Remember that if you are not cooking at home you will need to transport meat in a cooler bag or box and take out what you need as and when you need it to avoid it becoming warm before it is cooked.
• Always pack the cooler with the foods you are going to cook first on the top and close the cooler completely each time you take an item of food out.

VARIATION
A selection of meat cuts can be used, from sirloin to flank steak or chuck steak. Sweetbreads, skewered chicken hearts and kidneys are popular additions to the Gaucho barbecue, as well as chicken, lamb and pork. The star of the show, however, will always be the beef.

Energy 873kcal/3637kJ; Protein 84.4g; Carbohydrate 6.3g, of which sugars 0.9g; Fat 56.7g, of which saturates 23.8g; Cholesterol 246mg; Calcium 46mg; Fibre 0.3g; Sodium 1333mg.

THE VEGETARIAN BARBECUE

Barbecuing vegetables gives them a delicious flavour and they can be combined with cheese, nuts, beans and tofu to make some exciting main courses that will appeal to everyone.

The smoky flavours created by chargrilling really lifts vegetable fruits and roots such as aubergines (eggplants), squashes, peppers and asparagus, which can then be served with dips and sauces, such as a peanut satay sauce or a yogurt pesto. Halloumi cheese is a super ingredient for the vegetarian barbecue because it has a firm texture that does not melt in the same way as other cheeses and so is useful to cook as an accompaniment to a melange of grilled vegetables.

You can also make rolls or parcels from the vegetables themselves, such as sliced aubergines, and cook these on the barbecue, as well as filling vegetables with aromatic stuffings and cooking them over the coals or inside foil parcels.

With so many fantastic, flavourful combinations, it's easy to plan a vegetarian barbecue feast.

THAI VEGETABLE CAKES

HERE, NUTTY-TASTING TEMPEH, WHICH IS MADE FROM SOYBEANS, IS COMBINED WITH A FRAGRANT BLEND OF LEMON GRASS, FRESH CORIANDER AND GINGER, AND FORMED INTO SMALL PATTIES BEFORE BEING GRILLED. SERVE WITH THE DIPPING SAUCE, ACCOMPANIED BY A SWEET SAKE OR RICE WINE.

MAKES EIGHT

INGREDIENTS
  1 lemon grass stalk, outer leaves
    removed and inside chopped
  2 garlic cloves, chopped
  2 spring onions (scallions), chopped
  2 shallots, chopped
  2 chillies, seeded and chopped
  2.5cm/1in piece fresh root
    ginger, chopped
  60ml/4 tbsp chopped fresh coriander
    (cilantro), plus extra to garnish
  250g/9oz tempeh, thawed if
    frozen, sliced
  15ml/1 tbsp lime juice
  5ml/1 tsp sugar
  45ml/3 tbsp plain (all-purpose) flour
  1 large (US extra large) egg,
    lightly beaten
  vegetable oil, for frying
  salt and ground black pepper
For the dipping sauce
  45ml/3 tbsp mirin
  45ml/3 tbsp white wine vinegar
  2 spring onions (scallions),
    thinly sliced
  15ml/1 tbsp sugar
  2 chillies, finely chopped
  30ml/2 tbsp chopped fresh
    coriander (cilantro)
  large pinch of salt

1 Prepare the barbecue. To make the dipping sauce, mix all the ingredients together in a small bowl and set aside.

2 Place the lemon grass, garlic, spring onions, shallots, chillies, ginger and coriander in a food processor or blender and process to a coarse paste. Add the tempeh, lime juice and sugar, then process to combine. Add the salt and pepper, flour and egg. Process again until the mixture forms a coarse, sticky paste. Position a lightly oiled grill rack over the hot coals.

3 Take one-eighth of the tempeh mixture at a time and form into balls with your hands – the mixture will be quite sticky, so it may help to dampen your palms. Gently flatten the balls.

4 Brush the tempeh cakes with oil. Cook over high heat for 5–6 minutes, turning once, until golden. Drain on kitchen paper. Garnish and serve warm with the dipping sauce.

Energy 119kcal/494kJ; Protein 4.5g; Carbohydrate 8.2g, of which sugars 3.6g; Fat 7.8g, of which saturates 1g; Cholesterol 24mg; Calcium 202mg; Fibre 1g; Sodium 15mg.

RED BEAN AND MUSHROOM BURGERS

VEGETARIANS, VEGANS AND MEAT-EATERS ALIKE WILL ENJOY THESE HEALTHY, LOW-FAT VEGGIE BURGERS. WITH SALAD, PITTA BREAD AND GREEK-STYLE YOGURT, THEY MAKE A SUBSTANTIAL MEAL. YOU MAY FIND A HINGED WIRE GRILL USEFUL FOR COOKING THESE BURGERS.

SERVES FOUR

INGREDIENTS

  15ml/1 tbsp olive oil
  1 small onion, finely chopped
  1 garlic clove, crushed
  5ml/1 tsp ground cumin
  5ml/1 tsp ground coriander
  2.5ml/½ tsp ground turmeric
  115g/4oz/1½ cups finely
    chopped mushrooms
  400g/14oz can red kidney beans
  30ml/2 tbsp chopped fresh
    coriander (cilantro)
  wholemeal (whole-wheat)
    flour (optional)
  olive oil, for brushing
  salt and ground black pepper
  Greek (US strained plain) yogurt,
    to serve

COOK'S TIP
Bean burgers are not quite as firm as meat burgers, and will need careful handling on the barbecue.

1 Heat the olive oil in a frying pan and fry the onion and garlic over a medium heat, stirring, until softened. Add the spices and cook for a further minute, stirring continuously.

2 Add the mushrooms and cook, stirring, until softened and dry. Remove the pan from the heat and empty the contents into a large bowl.

3 Drain the red kidney beans thoroughly, place them in a bowl and mash them roughly with a fork.

4 Stir the kidney beans into the frying pan, with the fresh coriander, and mix thoroughly. Season the mixture well with plenty of salt and pepper. Prepare the barbecue. Position a lightly oiled grill rack over the hot coals.

5 Using floured hands, form the mixture into four flat burger shapes. If the mixture is too sticky to handle, mix in a little wholemeal flour.

6 Lightly brush the burgers with olive oil and cook on a hot barbecue for 8–10 minutes, turning once, until golden brown. Serve with a spoonful of yogurt and a mixed salad, if you like.

Energy 159kcal/666kJ; Protein 7.6g; Carbohydrate 19.1g, of which sugars 4.5g; Fat 6.3g, of which saturates 0.9g; Cholesterol 0mg; Calcium 77mg; Fibre 6.7g; Sodium 392mg.

ROASTED VEGETABLE QUESADILLAS

THIS RECIPE IS A WONDERFUL EXAMPLE OF HOW THE GRIDDLE AND GRILL RACK CAN BE USED SIMULTANEOUSLY TO COPE WITH A RANGE OF INGREDIENTS. HAVE A LONG GRIDDLE ON ONE SIDE OF THE GRILL RACK FOR THE ONIONS AND PEPPERS; THE AUBERGINES CAN COOK ON THE GRILL RACK.

SERVES SIX TO EIGHT

INGREDIENTS
    1 yellow and 1 orange (bell) pepper,
      each quartered and seeded
    2 red (bell) peppers, quartered
      and seeded
    2 red onions, cut into wedges with
      root intact
    8 long baby aubergines (eggplants),
      total weight about 175g/6oz,
      halved lengthways
    30ml/2 tbsp olive oil
    400g/14oz mozzarella
    2 fresh green chillies, seeded and
      sliced into rounds
    15ml/1 tbsp Mexican tomato sauce
    8 corn or wheat flour tortillas
    handful of fresh basil leaves
    salt and ground black pepper

1 Prepare the barbecue. Position a lightly oiled grill rack over the hot coals. Heat a griddle on the grill rack.

COOK'S TIPS
• The quesadillas can be cut into wedges and eaten as they come off the griddle or wrapped in foil to keep warm while the rest are cooked.
• When cooking for vegetarians as well as non-vegetarians, always remember to keep one side of the barbecue for cooking the vegetarian dishes only so that they do not come in contact with meat.

2 Toss the peppers, onions and aubergines in the oil on a large baking tray. Place the peppers, skin-side down, on the griddle or directly on the grill rack over medium-high heat and cook until seared and browned underneath. If the food starts to char, remove the griddle until the coals cool down. Put the peppers under an upturned bowl and set aside to cool slightly so that the skins will loosen.

3 Grill the onions and aubergines until they have softened slightly and are branded with brown grill marks, then set them aside. Rub the skins off the peppers with your fingers, cut each piece of pepper in half and add to the other vegetables.

4 Cut the mozzarella into 20 slices. Place them, along with the roasted vegetables, in a large bowl and add the chillies and tomato sauce. Stir well to mix, and season with salt and pepper to taste. Place the griddle over a medium heat and cook all the tortillas on one side only.

5 Lay a tortilla on the griddle, cooked-side up, and pile about a quarter of the vegetable mixture into the centre of the tortilla. Scatter over some basil leaves. When the tortilla browns underneath, put another tortilla on top, cooked side down. Carefully turn the quesadilla over using a wide pizza server with a tubular handle and continue to cook until the underside has browned and the cheese just starts to melt. Remove from the pan with the pizza server and either serve immediately or wrap in foil to keep warm while you cook the remaining three quesadillas.

VARIATION
Thinly sliced courgettes (zucchini) are also delicious when griddled and can be added to the mixture here or used instead of the aubergines.

Energy 233kcal/971kJ; Protein 11.8g; Carbohydrate 17g, of which sugars 8.5g; Fat 13.5g, of which saturates 7.4g; Cholesterol 29mg; Calcium 214mg; Fibre 2.7g; Sodium 268mg.

POTATO AND CHEESE POLPETTES

THESE LITTLE MORSELS OF POTATO AND GREEK FETA CHEESE, FLAVOURED WITH DILL AND LEMON JUICE, ARE EXCELLENT WHEN GRILLED ON THE BARBECUE. THEY CAN BE ACCOMPANIED WITH A TOMATO SAUCE, IF YOU LIKE, OR A NICELY DRESSED SALAD OF TOMATOES, SALAD LEAVES AND ONIONS.

SERVES FOUR

INGREDIENTS
500g/1¼lb potatoes
115g/4oz feta cheese
4 spring onions (scallions),
  chopped
45ml/3 tbsp chopped fresh dill
1 egg, beaten
15ml/1 tbsp lemon juice
15ml/1 tbsp olive oil
salt and ground black pepper

1 Boil the potatoes in their skins in salted water until soft. Drain, then peel while still warm.

2 Place the cooked potatotes in a bowl and mash. Crumble the feta cheese into the potatoes and add the spring onions, dill, egg and lemon juice, and season with pepper and a little salt. Stir well, then cover and chill until firm.

3 Divide the mixture into walnut-size balls, then flatten them slightly. Brush lightly with olive oil. Prepare the barbecue. Position a lightly oiled grill rack over the hot coals. Arrange the polpettes on the grill rack and cook over medium heat, turning once, until golden brown. Serve at once.

Energy 230kcal/960kJ; Protein 8.4g; Carbohydrate 20.9g, of which sugars 2.3g; Fat 13.1g, of which saturates 5.3g; Cholesterol 68mg; Calcium 122mg; Fibre 1.4g; Sodium 446mg.

MOROCCAN-STYLE CHARGRILLED VEGETABLES

CHARGRILLED VEGETABLES ARE GIVEN EXTRA FLAVOUR BY ADDING GARLIC, GINGER, ROSEMARY AND HONEY, AND TASTE DELICIOUS WITH COUSCOUS. YOGURT OR HARISSA GO VERY WELL WITH THE DISH. SERVE WITH A SALAD OF MOZZARELLA TOSSED WITH DRESSED SALAD LEAVES.

SERVES SIX

INGREDIENTS
- 75ml/5 tbsp olive oil
- 6 garlic cloves, crushed
- 25g/1oz fresh root ginger, grated
- a few large fresh rosemary sprigs
- 10ml/2 tsp clear honey
- 3 red onions, peeled and quartered
- 2–3 courgettes (zucchini), halved lengthways and cut across into 2–3 pieces
- 2–3 red, green or yellow (bell) peppers, seeded and quartered
- 2 aubergines (eggplants), cut into 6–8 long segments
- 2–3 leeks, trimmed and cut into long strips
- 2–3 sweet potatoes, peeled, halved lengthways and cut into long strips
- 4–6 tomatoes, quartered
- salt and ground black pepper
- natural (plain) yogurt or harissa, to serve

For the couscous
- 500g/1¼lb/2¾ cups couscous
- 5ml/1 tsp salt
- 600ml/1 pint/2½ cups warm water
- 45ml/3 tbsp sunflower oil
- about 25g/1oz/2 tbsp butter, diced

1 Preheat the oven to 200°C/400°F/ Gas 6. Put the couscous in a bowl. Stir the salt into the water, then pour it over the couscous, stirring to make sure it is absorbed evenly. Leave to stand for 10 minutes to plump up then, using your fingers, rub the sunflower oil into the grains to air them and break up any lumps. Tip the couscous into an ovenproof dish, arrange the butter over the top, cover with foil and heat in the oven for about 20 minutes.

2 Meanwhile, prepare the barbecue. Position a lightly oiled grill rack over the hot coals and heat a griddle on the grill rack.

3 Pour the oil into a large baking tray and add the garlic, ginger, rosemary and honey. Season with salt and pepper. Toss the vegetables in the flavoured oil to coat evenly. Cook the larger pieces of vegetables directly on the grill rack over medium-high heat and the smaller pieces, such as the tomatoes and onions, on the griddle, brushing with oil as required. As the vegetables cook, transfer them to a dish, cover and keep warm.

4 To serve, use your fingers to work the melted butter into the grains of couscous and fluff it up, then pile it on a large dish and shape into a mound with a little pit at the top. Spoon some vegetables into the pit and arrange the rest around the dish. Serve immediately with yogurt, or harissa if you prefer.

Energy 337kcal/1416kJ; Protein 11.5g; Carbohydrate 43.5g, of which sugars 7.1g; Fat 14.2g, of which saturates 5.9g; Cholesterol 23mg; Calcium 206mg; Fibre 5.3g; Sodium 613mg.

GRILLED GOAT'S CHEESE PIZZA

A PIZZA WITH A THIN CRUST CAN BE COOKED ON THE BARBECUE, AND IT PRODUCES A GOOD, CRISPY AND GOLDEN BASE. A FINE WIRE MESH RACK IS USEFUL FOR GRILLING THE BASE.

SERVES FOUR

INGREDIENTS
150g/5oz packet pizza-base mix
olive oil, for brushing
150ml/¼ pint/⅔ cup passata
30ml/2 tbsp red pesto
1 small red onion, thinly sliced
8 cherry tomatoes, halved
115g/4oz firm goat's cheese,
  thinly sliced
1 handful shredded fresh basil leaves
salt and ground black pepper

1 Prepare the barbecue. Position a lightly oiled grill rack over the hot coals. Make up the pizza dough according to the directions on the packet. Roll out the dough on a lightly floured surface to a round of about 25cm/10in diameter.

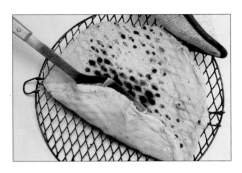

2 Brush the dough round with olive oil and place, oiled side down, on the grill rack over medium heat. Cook for about 6–8 minutes until firm and golden underneath. Brush the uncooked side with olive oil and turn the pizza over.

3 Mix together the passata and red pesto, and quickly spread over the cooked side of the pizza, to within about 1cm/½in of the edge. Arrange the onion, tomatoes and cheese on top, and sprinkle with salt and pepper.

4 Cook the pizza for 10 minutes more, until golden brown and crisp. Sprinkle with fresh basil and serve.

COOK'S TIP
For home-made pizza dough, sift 175g/ 6oz/1½ cups strong white bread flour and 1.5ml/¼ tsp salt in a bowl. Stir in 5ml/1 tsp easy-blend (rapid-rise) dried yeast. Pour in about 120ml/4fl oz/½ cup lukewarm water and 15ml/1 tbsp olive oil. Mix to form a dough. Knead until smooth. Place in a greased bowl, cover and leave to rise for 1 hour. Knock back (punch down) the dough and use as required.

Energy 338kcal/1420kJ; Protein 11g; Carbohydrate 46g, of which sugars 5g; Fat 13.5g, of which saturates 3.5g; Cholesterol 13mg; Calcium 218mg; Fibre 1.9g; Sodium 327mg.

SQUASH STUFFED WITH GOAT'S CHEESE

GEM SQUASH HAS A SWEET, SUBTLE FLAVOUR THAT CONTRASTS WELL WITH OLIVES AND SUN-DRIED TOMATOES IN THIS RECIPE. THE RICE ADDS SUBSTANCE WITHOUT CHANGING ANY OF THE FLAVOURS.

SERVES TWO

INGREDIENTS
    4 whole gem squashes
    225g/8oz/2 cups cooked white
      long grain rice
    75g/3oz/1½ cups sun-dried
      tomatoes, chopped
    40g/1½ oz/⅓ cup pitted black
      olives, chopped
    50g/2oz/¼ cup soft goat's cheese
    10ml/2 tsp olive oil
    15ml/1 tbsp chopped fresh basil
      leaves, plus basil sprigs,
      to serve
    green salad, to serve (optional)

1 Prepare the barbecue. Trim away the base of each squash, slice off the top and scoop out and discard the seeds.

2 Mix together the rice, tomatoes, olives, goat's cheese, olive oil and basil in a bowl.

3 Divide the rice mixture evenly between the squashes and place them individually on pieces of oiled, double thickness heavy-duty foil. Wrap the foil around the squashes and place them in among the coals of a medium-hot barbecue.

4 Bake for 45 minutes–1 hour, or until the squashes are tender when pierced with a skewer. Garnish with basil sprigs and serve with a green salad, if you like.

COOK'S TIP
The amount of time required to cook these vegetable parcels depends on the size of the squashes, and the heat of the coals. To maintain a medium-to-high temperature throughout the cooking time, keep rearranging the coals so that the hotter ones are nearest to the vegetable parcels. You can gauge the heat by the layer of ash that gathers on the coals.

Energy 337kcal/1416kJ; Protein 11.5g; Carbohydrate 43.5g, of which sugars 7.1g; Fat 14.2g, of which saturates 5.9g; Cholesterol 23mg; Calcium 206mg; Fibre 5.3g; Sodium 613mg.

GRILLED VEGETABLES WITH YOGURT PESTO

CHARGRILLED SUMMER VEGETABLES MAKE A MEAL ON THEIR OWN, OR ARE DELICIOUS SERVED AS A MEDITERRANEAN-STYLE SIDE DISH WITH GRILLED MEATS AND FISH. THE YOGURT PESTO MAKES A CREAMY ACCOMPANIMENT TO THE RICH FLAVOURS OF THE GRILLED VEGETABLES.

3 Slice the fennel bulbs and the red onions into thick wedges, using a sharp kitchen knife.

4 Prepare the barbecue. Position a lightly oiled grill rack over the hot coals. Stir the yogurt and pesto lightly together in a bowl, to make a marbled sauce. Spoon into a serving bowl and set aside.

5 Arrange the vegetables on the grill rack over high heat. Brush generously with olive oil and sprinkle with plenty of salt and ground black pepper.

6 Cook the vegetables until golden brown and tender, turning occasionally. The aubergines and peppers will take 6–8 minutes to cook, the courgettes, onion and fennel 4–5 minutes. Serve the vegetables as soon as they are cooked, with the yogurt pesto.

SERVES EIGHT

INGREDIENTS
    4 small aubergines (eggplants)
    4 large courgettes (zucchini)
    2 red and 2 yellow (bell) peppers
    2 fennel bulbs
    2 red onions
    300ml½ pint/1¼ cups Greek
      (US strained plain) yogurt
    90ml/6 tbsp pesto
    olive oil, for brushing
    salt and ground black pepper

1 Cut the aubergines into 1cm/½in slices. Sprinkle with salt and leave to drain for about 30 minutes. Rinse well in cold running water and pat dry.

2 Use a sharp kitchen knife to cut the courgettes in half lengthways. Cut the peppers in half, removing the seeds but leaving the stalks in place.

VARIATION
Barbecue some halloumi cheese, sliced and brushed with oil to serve with the vegetables, if you like.

COOK'S TIP
Baby vegetables are excellent for grilling whole on the barbecue, so look out for baby aubergines and peppers, in particular. There's no need to salt the aubergines if they are small.

Energy 146kcal/606kJ; Protein 6.9g; Carbohydrate 12.3g, of which sugars 11.8g; Fat 8g, of which saturates 1.9g; Cholesterol 4mg; Calcium 163mg; Fibre 5.1g; Sodium 86mg.

GRILLED VEGETABLES <u>WITH</u> SAFFRON DIP

A CREAMY DIP GOES VERY WELL WITH SIMPLY GRILLED VEGETABLES, AND HERE A DELICATELY FLAVOURED SAFFRON DIP IS SERVED WITH SLICED ROOT VEGETABLES AND ASPARAGUS SPEARS, MAKING AN UNUSUAL COMBINATION. SLICING THE VEGETABLES MEANS THAT THEY COOK MORE QUICKLY.

SERVES FOUR TO SIX

INGREDIENTS
- 4 small sweet potatoes, total weight about 675g/1½lb
- 4 carrots, total weight about 375g/13oz
- parsnips, total weight about 400g/14oz
- 4 raw beetroot (beets), total weight about 400g/14oz
- 450g/1lb asparagus, trimmed
- 60ml/4 tbsp extra virgin olive oil
- salt and ground black pepper

For the saffron dip
- 15ml/1 tbsp boiling water
- small pinch of saffron threads
- 200ml/7fl oz/scant 1 cup fromage frais or crème fraîche
- 10 fresh chives, chopped
- 10 fresh basil leaves, torn

1 To make the saffron dip, pour the measured boiling water into a small bowl and add the saffron strands. Leave to infuse for 3 minutes. Beat the fromage frais or crème fraîche until smooth, then stir in the infused saffron liquid.

2 Add the chopped chives and basil leaves. Season and stir to combine. Transfer to a serving bowl.

3 Prepare the barbecue. Cutting lengthways, slice each sweet potato and carrot into 8 pieces, each parsnip into 7 and each beetroot into 10. Toss all the vegetables except the beetroot in most of the oil in a large tray. Put the beetroot on a separate tray, because it might otherwise bleed over all the other vegetables. Gently toss the beetroot in the remaining oil and season all the vegetables well.

4 Position a lightly oiled grill rack over the hot coals. Arrange the vegetables on the grill rack over medium heat.

5 Lightly grill the vegetables for 3 minutes on each side, or until tender and branded with grill lines. Remove them as they cook and serve hot or warm with the saffron dip.

Energy 397kcal/1660kJ; Protein 7g; Carbohydrate 44.6g, of which sugars 21.6g; Fat 22.4g, of which saturates 10.5g; Cholesterol 38mg; Calcium 123mg; Fibre 9.8g; Sodium 119mg.

GRIDDLED HALLOUMI AND BEAN SALAD

HALLOUMI IS THAT HARD, WHITE, SALTY GOAT'S MILK CHEESE THAT SQUEAKS WHEN YOU BITE IT. IT GRILLS REALLY WELL AND IS THE PERFECT COMPLEMENT TO THE LOVELY FRESH-TASTING FLAVOURS OF THE VEGETABLES. THIS SALAD CAN BE GRILLED DIRECTLY ON THE GRILL RACK OVER MEDIUM HEAT.

SERVES FOUR

INGREDIENTS

20 baby new potatoes, total weight about 300g/11oz
200g/7oz extra-fine green beans, trimmed
675g/1½lb broad (fava) beans, shelled (shelled weight about 225g/8oz)
200g/7oz halloumi cheese, cut into 5mm/¼in slices
1 garlic clove, crushed to a paste with a large pinch of salt
90ml/6 tbsp olive oil
5ml/1 tsp cider vinegar or white wine vinegar
15g/½oz/½ cup fresh basil leaves, shredded
45ml/3 tbsp chopped fresh savory
2 spring onions (scallions), finely sliced
salt and ground black pepper
4 metal or wooden skewers

1 Thread five potatoes on to each skewer, and cook in a large pan of salted boiling water for about 7 minutes, or until almost tender. Add the green beans and cook for 3 minutes more. Tip in the broad beans and cook for just 2 minutes. Drain all the vegetables in a large colander.

2 Remove the potatoes, still on their skewers, from the colander, then refresh the cooked broad beans under plenty of cold running water. Pop each broad bean out of its skin to reveal the bright green inner bean. Place the beans in a bowl, cover and set aside.

3 Place the halloumi slices and the potato skewers in a wide dish. Whisk the garlic and oil together with a generous grinding of black pepper. Add to the dish and toss the halloumi and potato skewers until they are coated in the mixture.

4 Prepare the barbecue and rake the hot coals to one side. Place the cheese and potato skewers in the griddle and cook over the coals for about 2 minutes on each side. If they over-char, move the griddle to the cooler side of the grill rack.

5 Add the vinegar to the oil and garlic remaining in the dish and whisk to mix. Toss in the broad beans, herbs and spring onions, with the cooked halloumi. Serve, with the potato skewers laid alongside.

Energy 238kcal/996kJ; Protein 14.7g; Carbohydrate 21.3g, of which sugars 3.9g; Fat 11g, of which saturates 7g; Cholesterol 35mg; Calcium 244mg; Fibre 5.8g; Sodium 735mg.

GRILLED FENNEL SALAD

THIS IS SO TYPICALLY ITALIAN THAT IF YOU CLOSE YOUR EYES YOU COULD BE ON A TUSCAN HILLSIDE,
SITTING UNDER A SHADY TREE AND ENJOYING AN ELEGANT LUNCH. FENNEL HAS MANY FANS, BUT IS
OFTEN USED RAW OR LIGHTLY BRAISED, MAKING THIS GRIDDLE RECIPE A DELIGHTFUL DISCOVERY.

SERVES SIX

INGREDIENTS
   3 sweet baby orange (bell) peppers
   5 fennel bulbs with green tops, total
     weight about 900g/2lb
   30ml/2 tbsp olive oil
   15ml/1 tbsp cider or white wine
     vinegar
   45ml/3 tbsp extra virgin olive oil
   24 small niçoise olives
   2 long sprigs of fresh savory, leaves
     removed
   salt and ground black pepper

COOK'S TIP
If cooking directly on the barbecue, char
the peppers when the coals are hot, then
cool them ready for peeling. Grill the
fennel over medium-hot coals and turn
frequently once stripes have formed.

1 Prepare the barbecue. Heat a griddle
on the grill rack over hot coals. Roast
the baby peppers, turning them every
few minutes until charred all over.
Remove the pan from the heat, place
the peppers under an upturned bowl
and leave to cool a little and for the
skins to loosen.

2 Remove the green fronds from the
fennel and reserve. Slice the fennel
lengthways into five roughly equal
pieces. If the root looks a little tough,
cut it out.

3 Place the fennel pieces in a flat dish,
coat with the olive oil and season. Rub
off the charred skin from the grilled
peppers – it should come away easily –
remove the seeds and cut the flesh
into small dice.

4 Re-heat the griddle and test the
temperature again, then lower the heat
slightly and grill the fennel slices in
batches for about 8–10 minutes, turning
frequently, until they are branded with
golden grill marks. Monitor the heat so
they cook through without over-charring.
As each batch cooks, transfer it to a flat
serving dish.

5 Whisk the vinegar and olive oil
together until thoroughly combined,
then pour the dressing over the fennel.
Gently fold in the diced baby orange
peppers and the niçoise olives. Tear
the savory leaves and fennel fronds
and scatter them over the salad. Serve
either warm or cold.

Energy 96kcal/397kJ; Protein 2.5g; Carbohydrate 9.1g, of which sugars 8.7g; Fat 5.7g, of which saturates 0.8g; Cholesterol 0mg; Calcium 52mg; Fibre 5.6g; Sodium 302mg.

PASTA SALAD WITH CHARGRILLED PEPPERS

ONE OF THE MANY WONDERFUL THINGS ABOUT SUMMER IS THE ABUNDANCE OF FRESH HERBS. LOTS OF BASIL AND CORIANDER MAKE THIS SALAD ESPECIALLY TASTY. LEAVE THE PASTA TO SOAK UP THE DRESSING AND THEN ADD THE HERBS JUST BEFORE YOU ARE READY TO BARBECUE THE PEPPERS.

SERVES FOUR

INGREDIENTS
  250g/9oz/2¼ cups dried
    fusilli tricolore
  1 handful fresh basil leaves, chopped
  1 handful fresh coriander (cilantro)
    leaves, chopped
  1 garlic clove, chopped
  1 large red and 1 large green
    (bell) pepper
  salt and ground black pepper
For the dressing
  30ml/2 tbsp pesto
  juice of ½ lemon
  60ml/4 tbsp extra virgin olive oil

VARIATION
Dry-roast some pine nuts over the
barbecue to add crunch to the salad.

1 Bring a large pan of salted water to the boil. Add the pasta and cook for 10–12 minutes or according to the instructions on the packet.

2 Whisk the dressing ingredients together in a large mixing bowl. Drain the cooked pasta and tip it into the bowl of dressing. Toss well to mix and set aside to cool. Add the basil, coriander and garlic to the pasta and toss well to mix.

3 Prepare the barbecue. Position a lightly oiled grill rack over the hot coals. Put the peppers on the grill rack over high heat for about 10 minutes, turning frequently until they are charred on all sides. Put the hot peppers under an upturned bowl and leave to cool a little and for the skins to loosen.

4 Peel off the skins with your fingers, split the peppers open and pull out the cores. Remove all the seeds.

5 Chop the peppers and add them to the pasta. Taste and adjust the seasoning, if necessary, and serve.

Energy 402kcal/1688kJ; Protein 10.1g; Carbohydrate 51.6g, of which sugars 7.1g; Fat 18.7g, of which saturates 2.9g; Cholesterol 3mg; Calcium 75mg; Fibre 3.7g; Sodium 36mg.

AUBERGINE AND BUTTERNUT SALAD

BEAUTIFULLY GOLDEN BUTTERNUT SQUASH MAKES A SUBSTANTIAL SALAD WITH GRIDDLED AUBERGINE AND FETA CHEESE. LIKE ALL RECIPES FOR GRIDDLED FOOD, THIS SALAD CAN BE COOKED INDOORS AT ANY TIME OF THE YEAR AND IS JUST AS DELICIOUS IN THE WINTER AS IN THE SUMMER.

SERVES FOUR

INGREDIENTS
  2 aubergines (eggplants)
  1 butternut squash, about 1kg/2¼lb,
    peeled
  120ml/4fl oz/½ cup extra virgin
    olive oil
  5ml/1 tsp paprika
  150g/5oz feta cheese
  50g/2oz/⅓ cup pistachio nuts,
    roughly chopped
  salt and ground black pepper

1 Slice the aubergines widthways into 5mm/¼in rounds. Spread them out on a tray and sprinkle with a little salt. Leave for 30 minutes. Slice the squash in the same way, scooping out any seeds with a spoon. Place the butternut squash slices in a bowl, season lightly and toss with 30ml/2 tbsp of the oil.

2 Prepare the barbecue. Heat a griddle on the grill rack over hot coals. Lower the heat a little and grill the butternut squash slices in batches. Sear for about 3 minutes on each side, then put them on a tray. Continue until all the slices have been cooked, then dust with a little of the paprika.

3 Pat the aubergine slices dry. Toss with the remaining oil and season lightly. Cook in the same way as the squash. When all the slices are cooked, mix the aubergine and squash together in a bowl. Crumble the feta cheese over the warm salad, scatter the pistachio nuts over the top and dust with the remaining paprika.

VARIATION
Instead of aubergines try (bell) peppers or thinly sliced courgettes (zucchini) or add a few small onions or quartered onions with the root attached. Add a few raisins as well, if you like.

Energy 393kcal/1626kJ; Protein 11.2g; Carbohydrate 10.4g, of which sugars 8.5g; Fat 34.3g, of which saturates 9.2g; Cholesterol 26mg; Calcium 236mg; Fibre 6.3g; Sodium 609mg.

AUBERGINE ROLLS IN TOMATO SAUCE

THIS IS A USEFUL AND TASTY VEGETARIAN DISH THAT CAN BE PREPARED IN ADVANCE AND SIMPLY FINISHED OVER THE BARBECUE. LITTLE AUBERGINE ROLLS CONTAIN A FILLING OF RICOTTA AND GOAT'S CHEESE WITH RICE, FLAVOURED WITH BASIL AND MINT, AND THEY GO VERY WELL WITH A TOMATO SAUCE.

SERVES FOUR

INGREDIENTS
    2 aubergines (eggplants)
    olive oil, or sunflower oil for
      shallow frying
    75g/3oz/scant ½ cup ricotta cheese
    75g/3oz/scant ½ cup soft
      goat's cheese
    225g/8oz/2 cups cooked long
      grain rice
    15ml/1 tbsp chopped fresh basil
    5ml/1 tsp chopped fresh mint, plus
      mint sprigs, to garnish
    salt and ground black pepper
For the tomato sauce
    15ml/1 tbsp olive oil
    1 red onion, finely chopped
    1 garlic clove, crushed
    400g/14oz can chopped tomatoes
    120ml/4fl oz/½ cup vegetable stock
      or white wine, or a mixture
    15ml/1 tbsp chopped fresh parsley

COOK'S TIP
If you would prefer to use less oil for the aubergines, brush each slice with just a little oil, then barbecue until evenly browned.

1 To make the tomato sauce, heat the oil in a small pan and fry the onion and garlic for 3–4 minutes until softened. Add the tomatoes, vegetable stock and/or wine, and parsley. Season well. Bring to the boil, then lower the heat and simmer for 10–12 minutes, or until slightly thickened, stirring.

2 Cut each aubergine into 4–5 slices, discarding the two outer slices, which consist largely of skin. Heat the oil in a large frying pan and fry the aubergine slices until they are golden brown on both sides. Drain on kitchen paper. Mix the ricotta, goat's cheese, rice, basil and mint in a bowl. Season well with salt and pepper.

3 Prepare the barbecue. Position a lightly oiled grill rack over the hot coals. Place a generous spoonful of the cheese and rice mixture at one end of each aubergine slice and roll up. Wrap the aubergine rolls in four foil parcels and place on the grill rack. Cook for 15 minutes over medium heat. Reheat the tomato sauce on the barbecue until thoroughly bubbling. Garnish with the mint sprigs and serve with the sauce.

Energy 233kcal/980kJ; Protein 8.9g; Carbohydrate 24.6g, of which sugars 6.7g; Fat 11.8g, of which saturates 5.8g; Cholesterol 25mg; Calcium 56mg; Fibre 3.3g; Sodium 125mg.

GRILLED AUBERGINE PARCELS

AUBERGINES ARE VERSATILE VEGETABLE FRUITS WITH SOFT FLESH THAT ABSORBS OTHER FLAVOURS. PREPARE THEM IN ADVANCE, BARBECUE THEM QUICKLY TO GET THAT LOVELY SMOKY FLAVOUR AND THEN ENJOY THEM WITH A BALSAMIC VINEGAR AND TOMATO DRESSING FOR A REAL TASTE OF ITALY.

SERVES FOUR

INGREDIENTS

2 large, long aubergines (eggplants)
225g/8oz mozzarella
2 plum tomatoes
16 large fresh basil leaves
30ml/2 tbsp olive oil
salt and ground black pepper

For the dressing
60ml/4 tbsp olive oil
5ml/1 tsp balsamic vinegar
15ml/1 tbsp sun-dried tomato paste
15ml/1 tbsp lemon juice

For the garnish
30ml/2 tbsp toasted pine nuts
torn fresh basil leaves

COOK'S TIP
The best cheese to use in these delectable little parcels is undoubtedly mozzarella. Look for the authentic moist cheese, made from buffalo's milk, which is sold packed in whey. If you can find it, lightly smoked mozzarella would also work well, and would add additional flavour to the dish. It is labelled mozzarella affumicata. Alternatively, you could use a plain or smoked goat's cheese. Look for one with a similar texture to mozzarella.

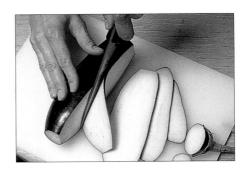

1 Remove the stalks from the aubergines and cut the aubergines lengthways into thin slices – the aim is to get 16 slices in total, disregarding the outer two slices, which consist largely of skin. (If you have a mandolin, it will cut perfect, even slices for you – otherwise, use a sharp, long-bladed cook's knife).

2 Bring a large pan of salted water to the boil and cook the aubergine slices for about 2 minutes. Drain the slices thoroughly, then dry on kitchen paper. Cut the mozzarella cheese into eight slices. Cut each tomato into eight slices, not counting the first and last slices.

3 Take two aubergine slices and place on a tray, in a cross. Place a slice of tomato in the centre, season with salt and pepper, then add a basil leaf, followed by a slice of mozzarella, another basil leaf, a slice of tomato and more seasoning.

4 Fold the ends of the aubergine slices around the mozzarella and tomato filling. Repeat to make eight parcels. Chill for about 20 minutes.

5 To make the tomato dressing, whisk together the oil, vinegar, tomato paste and lemon juice. Season to taste.

6 Prepare the barbecue. Position a lightly oiled grill rack over the hot coals. Brush the parcels with olive oil and cook over high heat for about 5 minutes on each side until golden. Garnish and serve hot, with the dressing.

Energy 350kcal/1449kJ; Protein 12.7g; Carbohydrate 5g, of which sugars 4.7g; Fat 31.2g, of which saturates 10.5g; Cholesterol 33mg; Calcium 223mg; Fibre 3.6g; Sodium 230mg.

TOFU AND PEPPER KEBABS

A CRUNCHY COATING OF GROUND, DRY-ROASTED PEANUTS PRESSED ON TO CUBED TOFU PROVIDES PLENTY OF ADDITIONAL TEXTURE AND COLOUR. ALONG WITH THE CHARGRILLED, SUCCULENT CHUNKS OF RED AND GREEN PEPPERS, THESE SIMPLE ADDITIONS GIVE THE KEBABS A SUBTLE FLAVOUR.

SERVES TWO

INGREDIENTS
250g/9oz firm tofu
50g/2oz/½ cup dry-roasted peanuts
45ml/3 tbsp olive oil
2 red and 2 green (bell) peppers
60ml/4 tbsp sweet chilli
  dipping sauce
salt and ground black pepper

1 Soak four long wooden skewers in water for 30 minutes. Pat the tofu dry on kitchen paper and then cut it into small cubes.

2 Grind the peanuts in a blender or food processor and transfer to a plate. Put the oil in a bowl and add the tofu cubes. Toss in the oil until well coated. Lift the tofu cubes out of the oil and turn them in the ground nuts to coat.

3 Prepare the barbecue. Position a lightly oiled grill rack over the hot coals. Halve and seed the peppers, and cut them into large chunks.

4 Brush the chunks of pepper with the oil from the bowl and thread them on to the skewers, alternating with the tofu cubes. Season with salt and pepper. Place on the grill rack.

5 Cook the kebabs over medium heat, turning frequently, for 10–12 minutes, or until the peppers and peanuts are beginning to brown. Transfer the kebabs to warmed plates and serve immediately with the dipping sauce.

COOK'S TIP
Chilli sauces vary from fairly mild to searingly hot, while some are quite sweet. The hot ones go particularly well with these kebabs.

Energy 516kcal/2143kJ; Protein 20.3g; Carbohydrate 30.2g, of which sugars 26.8g; Fat 35.6g, of which saturates 5.6g; Cholesterol 0mg; Calcium 681mg; Fibre 7.4g; Sodium 461mg.

SUMMER VEGETABLE KEBABS

THERE'S NOTHING NEW ABOUT THREADING VEGETABLE CHUNKS ON SKEWERS, BUT THIS METHOD OF TOSSING THEM IN A SPICY OIL AND LEMON JUICE MARINADE MAKES ALL THE DIFFERENCE. SERVE THEM WITH THE HOT AND CREAMY DIP AND YOU'LL HAVE VEGETARIAN GUESTS ASKING FOR MORE.

SERVES FOUR

INGREDIENTS
   2 aubergines (eggplants), part peeled
     and cut into chunks
   2 courgettes (zucchini), cut
     into chunks
   2–3 red or green (bell) peppers,
     seeded and cut into chunks
   12–16 cherry tomatoes
   4 small red onions, quartered
   60ml/4 tbsp olive oil
   juice of ½ lemon
   1 garlic clove, crushed
   5ml/1 tsp ground coriander
   5ml/1 tsp ground cinnamon
   10ml/2 tsp clear honey
   5ml/1 tsp salt
For the harissa and yogurt dip
   450g/1lb/2 cups Greek (US strained
     plain) yogurt
   30–60ml/2–4 tbsp harissa
   small bunch of fresh coriander
     (cilantro), finely chopped
   small bunch of mint, finely chopped
   salt and ground black pepper

COOK'S TIP
Make sure you cut the aubergines, courgettes and peppers into fairly even-size chunks, so that they will all cook at the same rate.

1 Prepare the barbecue. Position a lightly oiled grill rack over the hot coals. Put all the vegetables in a bowl. Mix together the olive oil, lemon juice, garlic, ground coriander, cinnamon, honey and salt, and pour over the vegetables.

2 Using your hands, turn the vegetables gently in the marinade, then thread them on to metal skewers. Cook the kebabs over high heat, turning them occasionally, until the vegetables are nicely browned all over.

3 Meanwhile, make the dip. Put the yogurt in a bowl and beat in the harissa, making it as fiery in taste as you like by adding more harissa. Add most of the chopped coriander and mint, reserving a little to garnish, and season well with salt and pepper.

4 While they are still hot, slide the vegetables off the skewers and dip them into the yogurt dip before eating. Garnish with the reserved herbs.

Energy 392kcal/1630kJ; Protein 9.2g; Carbohydrate 25.4g, of which sugars 17.9g; Fat 28.8g, of which saturates 3.2g; Cholesterol 0mg; Calcium 110mg; Fibre 5.5g; Sodium 19mg.

STUFFED PEPPERS

ALMONDS, DRIED FRUIT, RICE AND GARLIC MAKE A RICH AND TASTY FILLING FOR PEPPERS, WHICH CAN BE COOKED IN FOIL PARCELS ON THE GRILL RACK. PREPARE THEM JUST AS YOU ARE READY TO COOK THEM SO THAT THE FILLING IS STILL HOT WHEN THE PEPPERS GO ON THE BARBECUE.

SERVES FOUR

INGREDIENTS

  1 ripe tomato, peeled
  2 yellow or orange and 2 green
    (bell) peppers
  60ml/4 tbsp olive oil, plus extra
    for sprinkling
  2 onions, chopped
  2 garlic cloves, crushed
  75g/3oz/½ cup blanched
    almonds, chopped
  75g/3oz/scant ½ cup long grain rice,
    boiled and drained
  30ml/2 tbsp fresh mint,
    roughly chopped
  30ml/2 tbsp fresh parsley,
    roughly chopped
  30ml/2 tbsp sultanas (golden raisins)
  45ml/3 tbsp ground almonds
  salt and ground black pepper
  chopped mixed fresh herbs,
    to garnish

1 Prepare the barbecue. Position a grill rack over the hot coals. Roughly chop the tomato and set it aside.

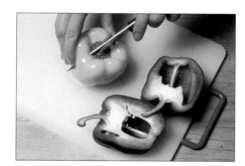

2 Halve the peppers, leaving the cores intact. Scoop out the seeds. Brush the peppers with 15ml/1 tbsp of the olive oil and cook over a medium heat for 15 minutes. Place each pair of peppers on a piece of double-thickness foil and season well with salt and pepper.

3 Fry the onions in the remaining olive oil for 5 minutes. Add the garlic and almonds to the pan and fry for a further minute.

4 Remove the pan from the heat and stir in the rice, tomato, mint, parsley and sultanas. Season well with salt and pepper and spoon the mixture into the peppers.

5 Scatter with the ground almonds and sprinkle with a little extra olive oil. Wrap the peppers in the foil and place on the grill rack. Cook over medium-high heat for 20–25 minutes. Serve garnished with fresh herbs.

VARIATION
Add a few stuffed tomatoes to the recipe to complement the peppers. Simply halve and scoop out the seeds and pulp; reserve the latter to add to the stuffing.

Energy 392kcal/1630kJ; Protein 9.2g; Carbohydrate 25.4g, of which sugars 17.9g; Fat 28.8g, of which saturates 3.2g; Cholesterol 0mg; Calcium 110mg; Fibre 5.5g; Sodium 19mg.

STUFFED ARTICHOKE HALVES

THE DISTINCTIVE FLAVOUR OF GLOBE ARTICHOKES IS ACCENTUATED WHEN THEY ARE CHARGRILLED, AND IN THIS RECIPE THEY ARE TOPPED WITH AN INTENSELY SAVOURY STUFFING OF MUSHROOMS, GRUYÈRE CHEESE AND WALNUTS, MAKING THEM RICH AND FLAVOURSOME.

SERVES FOUR

INGREDIENTS

225g/8oz/3 cups mushrooms
15g/½oz/1 tbsp butter
2 shallots, finely chopped
50g/2oz/¼ cup full- or medium-fat
 soft cheese
30ml/2 tbsp chopped walnuts
45ml/3 tbsp grated Gruyère cheese
4 large or 6 small artichoke bottoms
 (from cooked artichokes, leaves and
 choke removed, or cooked frozen or
 canned artichoke hearts)
salt and ground black pepper
fresh parsley sprigs, to garnish

3 In a large bowl, combine the soft cheese and cooked mushrooms. Add the walnuts and half the Gruyère cheese, and stir well to combine the mixture.

4 Divide the mixture among the artichoke bottoms and sprinkle over the remaining cheese. Cook over medium heat for 12 minutes covered with a lid or tented foil. Garnish and serve.

1 To make the duxelles for the stuffing, put the mushrooms in a food processor or blender and pulse until they are finely chopped.

2 Melt the butter in a frying pan and cook the shallots over a medium heat for about 2–3 minutes, or until just softened. Add the mushrooms, raise the heat slightly, and cook for 5–7 minutes more, stirring frequently, until all the liquid from the mushrooms has been driven off and they are almost dry. Season with plenty of salt and freshly ground black pepper. Prepare the barbecue. Position a lightly oiled grill rack over the hot coals.

COOK'S TIP
To cook fresh artichokes, trim the stalk and boil for 40–45 minutes. Trim away the leaves down to the base. Scrape away the hairy choke.

Energy 162kcal/672kJ; Protein 6.4g; Carbohydrate 2.2g, of which sugars 1.7g; Fat 14.1g, of which saturates 6g; Cholesterol 24mg; Calcium 103mg; Fibre 1.2g; Sodium 115mg.

ONIONS STUFFED WITH GOAT'S CHEESE

CHARGRILLED ONIONS HAVE A SWEET TASTE AND GO VERY WELL WITH A GOAT'S CHEESE, SUN-DRIED TOMATO AND PINE NUT FILLING. COOK THEM OVER INDIRECT HEAT TO ENSURE THEY COOK THROUGH WITHOUT BURNING. SERVE THEM WITH A SELECTION OF SALADS AND BREADS.

SERVES FOUR

INGREDIENTS

4 large onions
150g/5oz goat's cheese, crumbled
   or cubed
50g/2oz/1 cup fresh breadcrumbs
8 sun-dried tomatoes in olive oil,
   drained and chopped
1–2 garlic cloves, finely chopped
2.5ml/½ tsp chopped fresh
   thyme leaves
30ml/2 tbsp chopped fresh parsley
1 small egg, beaten
45ml/3 tbsp pine nuts, toasted
45ml/3 tbsp olive oil (from the jar of
   sun-dried tomatoes)
salt and ground black pepper

1 Bring a large pan of lightly salted water to the boil. Add the whole onions in their skins and boil them for about 10 minutes. Drain and cool, then cut each onion in half horizontally and slip off the skins, taking care to keep the onion halves from unravelling.

2 Using a teaspoon to scoop out the flesh, remove the centre of each onion, leaving a thick shell.

3 Chop the scooped-out onion flesh and place it in a bowl. Add the goat's cheese, breadcrumbs, sun-dried tomatoes, garlic, thyme, half the parsley and the egg. Mix well, then season to taste with salt and pepper, and add the toasted pine nuts.

4 Brush the outside of the onion shells with oil and divide the stuffing among the onions. Drizzle a little oil over the top.

5 Prepare the barbecue. Part the coals in the centre and insert a drip tray. Position a lightly oiled grill rack over the coals and drip tray. Cook over medium heat over the drip tray for 45 minutes–1 hour, covered with a lid or tented heavy-duty foil. Brush with oil occasionally during cooking. When cooked, sprinkle with the remaining parsley to garnish.

VARIATIONS
• Omit the goat's cheese and add 115g/4oz finely chopped mushrooms and 1 grated carrot.
• Substitute feta cheese for the goat's cheese and raisins for the pine nuts.
• Substitute smoked mozzarella for the goat's cheese and substitute pistachio nuts for the pine nuts.
• Use red and yellow (bell) peppers preserved in olive oil instead of sun-dried tomatoes.

Energy 400kcal/1659kJ; Protein 14g; Carbohydrate 19g, of which sugars 7.3g; Fat 30.4g, of which saturates 9.2g; Cholesterol 82mg; Calcium 115mg; Fibre 2.4g; Sodium 345mg.

BEAN- AND LEMON-STUFFED MUSHROOMS

LARGE FIELD MUSHROOMS HAVE A RICH FLAVOUR AND A MEATY TEXTURE THAT GO WELL WITH THIS FRAGRANT HERB, BEAN AND LEMON STUFFING. THE GARLIC AND PINE NUT ACCOMPANIMENT IS A TRADITIONAL MIDDLE EASTERN DISH WITH A SMOOTH, CREAMY CONSISTENCY.

SERVES FOUR

INGREDIENTS
  200g/7oz/1 cup dried or 400g/14oz/
    2 cups drained, canned aduki beans
  45ml/3 tbsp olive oil, plus extra
    for brushing
  1 onion, finely chopped
  2 garlic cloves, crushed
  30ml/2 tbsp fresh chopped or 5ml/
    1 tsp dried thyme
  8 large field (portabello) mushrooms,
    stalks finely chopped
  50g/2oz/1 cup fresh wholemeal
    (whole-wheat) breadcrumbs
  juice of 1 lemon
  185g/6½oz/generous ¾ cup
    crumbled goat's cheese
  salt and ground black pepper
For the pine nut paste
  50g/2oz/½ cup pine nuts,
    lightly toasted
  50g/2oz/1 cup cubed white bread
  2 garlic cloves, chopped
  about 200ml/7fl oz/scant 1 cup milk
  45ml/3 tbsp olive oil
  15ml/1 tbsp chopped fresh parsley,
    to garnish (optional)

1 If using dried beans, soak them overnight, then drain and rinse well. Place in a pan, add enough water to cover and bring to the boil. Boil rapidly for 10 minutes, then reduce the heat, cook for 30 minutes, or until tender, then drain. If using canned beans, drain, rinse under cold running water, then drain well again, and set aside.

2 Heat the oil in a large, heavy frying pan, add the onion and garlic and cook over a low heat, stirring frequently, for 5 minutes, or until softened.

3 Add the thyme and the mushroom stalks and cook for a further 3 minutes, stirring occasionally, until tender.

4 Stir in the aduki beans, breadcrumbs and lemon juice, season to taste then cook gently for 2–3 minutes, or until heated through. Mash about two-thirds of the beans with a fork or potato masher, leaving the remaining beans whole, then mix thoroughly together. Prepare the barbecue. Position a lightly oiled grill rack over the hot coals.

5 To make the pine nut paste, place all the ingredients in a food processor or blender and process until smooth and creamy. Add a little more milk if the mixture appears too thick. Sprinkle with parsley, if using.

6 Brush the base and sides of the mushrooms with oil. Top each with a spoonful of the bean mixture. Cook over medium heat for 20 minutes covered with a lid or tented heavy-duty foil.

7 Top each mushroom with cheese and grill for 5 minutes more, or until the cheese is melted. Serve with a green leaf salad, if you like, or wilted spinach.

Energy 604kcal/2520kJ; Protein 25.5g; Carbohydrate 38.8g, of which sugars 8.7g; Fat 39.7g, of which saturates 12g; Cholesterol 46mg; Calcium 237mg; Fibre 8.8g; Sodium 858mg.

CASSAVA AND VEGETABLE KEBABS

SO MANY VEGETABLES ARE SUITABLE FOR COOKING ON THE BARBECUE AND THIS RECIPE INCLUDES AN ATTRACTIVE AND DELICIOUS ASSORTMENT OF AFRICAN VEGETABLES THAT ARE MARINATED IN A SPICY GARLIC SAUCE. SERVE THE VEGETABLES ACCOMPANIED BY A CREAMY BEAN DIP, SUCH AS HUMMUS.

SERVES FOUR

INGREDIENTS
175g/6oz cassava
1 onion, cut into wedges
1 aubergine (eggplant), cut into bite
  size pieces
1 courgette (zucchini), sliced
1 ripe plantain, sliced
½ red (bell) pepper and ½ green
  (bell) pepper, seeded and sliced
16 cherry tomatoes
rice or couscous, to serve
For the marinade
60ml/4 tbsp lemon juice
60ml/4 tbsp olive oil
45–60ml/3–4 tbsp soy sauce
15ml/1 tbsp tomato purée (paste)
1 green chilli, seeded and
  finely chopped
½ onion, grated
2 garlic cloves, crushed
5ml/1 tsp mixed (apple pie) spice
pinch of dried thyme

1 If using wooden skewers, soak eight in water for 30 minutes. Peel the cassava and cut into bite size pieces. Place in a large bowl, cover with boiling water and leave to blanch for about 5 minutes. Drain well.

2 Place all the prepared vegetables, including the cassava, in a large bowl and mix with your hands so that all the vegetables are evenly distributed.

3 Blend the marinade ingredients in a jug (pitcher) and pour over the vegetables. Cover and leave to marinate for 1–2 hours.

4 Prepare the barbecue. Position a lightly oiled grill rack over the hot coals. Thread the vegetables, with the cherry tomatoes, on to the wooden or metal skewers and cook over high heat for about 15 minutes until tender and browned. Turn the skewers frequently and baste them occasionally with the marinade.

5 Meanwhile, pour the remaining marinade into a small pan and simmer on the grill rack for about 10 minutes to reduce. Strain the reduced marinade into a jug. Serve the kebabs on a bed of rice or couscous, with the sauce on the side.

Energy 167kcal/702kJ; Protein 3g; Carbohydrate 26.1g, of which sugars 7.6g; Fat 6.3g, of which saturates 1g; Cholesterol 0mg; Calcium 34mg; Fibre 3.3g; Sodium 7mg.

ROASTED RED PEPPERS WITH COUSCOUS

COUSCOUS MAKES A GOOD BASIS FOR A STUFFING, AND IN THIS RECIPE IT IS STUDDED WITH RAISINS AND FLAVOURED WITH FRESH MINT. CHARRED PEPPERS MAKE THE COMBINATION OF FLAVOURS TRULY SPECIAL AND THE PEPPERS ARE SIMPLE TO COOK IN THEIR FOIL PARCELS.

SERVES FOUR

INGREDIENTS
  6 (bell) peppers
  25g/1oz/2 tbsp butter
  1 onion, finely chopped
  5ml/1 tsp olive oil
  2.5ml/½ tsp salt
  175g/6oz/1 cup couscous
  25g/1oz/2 tbsp raisins
  30ml/2 tbsp chopped fresh mint
  1 egg yolk
  salt and ground black pepper
  mint leaves, to garnish

1 Carefully slit each pepper with a sharp knife and remove the core and seeds. Melt the butter in a small pan and add the chopped onion. Cook until soft but not browned.

2 To cook the couscous, bring 250ml/8fl oz/1 cup water to the boil. Add the oil and salt, then remove from the heat and add the couscous. Stir and leave to stand, covered, for 5 minutes. Stir in the onion, raisins and mint. Season well and stir in the egg yolk. Prepare the barbecue. Position a grill rack over the hot coals.

3 Use a teaspoon to fill the peppers with the couscous mixture to about three-quarters full (the couscous will swell while cooking). Wrap each pepper in a piece of oiled baking foil.

4 Cook over medium heat for 20 minutes, or until tender. Serve hot or cold, garnished with fresh mint leaves.

Energy 262kcal/1094kJ; Protein 5.8g; Carbohydrate 42.4g, of which sugars 18.9g; Fat 8.7g, of which saturates 4g; Cholesterol 64mg; Calcium 40mg; Fibre 3.9g; Sodium 53mg.

TOFU SATAY

SMOKED TOFU IS MARINATED WITH GARLIC AND SOY SAUCE BEFORE IT IS GRILLED WITH PEPPERS AND SERVED WITH A CRUNCHY PEANUT SAUCE. TOFU READILY SOAKS UP THE FLAVOURS OF A MARINADE OR FOODS IT IS COOKED WITH, SO YOU COULD ALSO SPREAD SOME MOISTENED HERBS ON TO THE COALS.

2 Beat all the peanut sauce ingredients together in a large bowl, using a wooden spoon, until well blended. Avoid using a food processor to blend the ingredients, as the texture should be slightly chunky. Prepare the barbecue. Position a lightly oiled grill rack over the hot coals.

3 Drain the tofu and thread the cubes on to the satay sticks, alternating the tofu with the pepper squares and bay leaves. (Larger bay leaves may need to be halved before threading.)

4 Brush the satays with sunflower oil and cook over high heat, turning the sticks occasionally, until the tofu and peppers are browned and crisp. Serve hot with the peanut sauce.

COOK'S TIP

If you can only find plain tofu, leave it to marinate for 30 minutes to 1 hour for the best flavour.

VARIATION

Add mushrooms, cherry tomatoes and onion segments to the skewers if you like.

SERVES FOUR TO SIX

INGREDIENTS
    2 x 200g/7oz packs smoked tofu
    45ml/3 tbsp light soy sauce
    10ml/2 tsp sesame oil
    1 garlic clove, crushed
    1 yellow and 1 red (bell) pepper,
        cut into squares
    8–12 fresh bay leaves
    sunflower oil, for brushing
For the peanut sauce
    2 spring onions (scallions),
        finely chopped
    2 garlic cloves, crushed
    good pinch of chilli powder, or a few
        drops of hot chilli sauce
    5ml/1 tsp sugar
    15ml/1 tbsp white wine vinegar
    30ml/2 tbsp light soy sauce
    45ml/3 tbsp crunchy peanut butter

1 Soak 8–12 satay sticks in water for 30 minutes. Cut the tofu into bite size cubes and place in a large bowl. Add the soy sauce, sesame oil and crushed garlic and mix well. Cover with clear film (plastic wrap) and marinate for at least 20 minutes.

Energy 143kcal/593kJ; Protein 7.8g; Carbohydrate 6.2g, of which sugars 5.2g; Fat 9.8g, of which saturates 1.7g; Cholesterol 0mg; Calcium 350mg; Fibre 1.4g; Sodium 210mg.

ROASTED PUMPKIN WITH SPICES

ROASTED PUMPKIN HAS A WONDERFUL, RICH FLAVOUR ESPECIALLY WHEN CHARGRILLED WITH SPICES. EAT IT STRAIGHT FROM THE SKIN, EAT THE SKIN, TOO, OR SCOOP OUT THE COOKED FLESH, ADD A SPOONFUL OF SALSA AND CRÈME FRAÎCHE, AND WRAP IT IN A WARM TORTILLA.

SERVES SIX

INGREDIENTS
1kg/2¼lb pumpkin
60ml/4 tbsp oil
10ml/2 tsp hot chilli sauce
2.5ml/½ tsp salt
2.5ml/½ tsp ground allspice
5ml/1 tsp ground cinnamon
chopped fresh herbs, to garnish
salsa and crème fraîche, to serve

COOK'S TIPS
• Green-, grey- or orange-skinned pumpkins all roast well. The orange-fleshed varieties are the most colourful when it comes to cooking.
• It's worth scoring the flesh of the pumpkin slices in several places to get them to cook more quickly.

1 Cut the pumpkin into large pieces. Scoop out and discard the fibre and seeds.

2 Mix the oil and chilli sauce and drizzle most of the mixture evenly over the pumpkin pieces. Prepare the barbecue. Position a lightly oiled grill rack over the hot coals.

3 Put the salt in a small bowl and add the ground allspice and cinnamon. Sprinkle the mixture over the pumpkin.

4 Cook over medium-high heat for 25 minutes, basting occasionally and turning regularly until the pumpkin flesh is tender. Serve with the salsa and crème fraîche separately.

Energy 90kcal/371kJ; Protein 1.2g; Carbohydrate 4.2g, of which sugars 3.3g; Fat 7.7g, of which saturates 1.2g; Cholesterol 0mg; Calcium 49mg; Fibre 1.7g; Sodium 27mg.

ON THE SIDE

*Many of the side dishes for barbecued main dishes can be
cooked on (or even in) the barbecue itself. Vegetables can be
simply roasted wrapped in foil nestling between the coals
while you grill the main course on the grill rack above. Serve
them with a smoky salsa or a richly flavoured butter and you
will have side dishes that taste just as exciting as the main
dish. You can also grill vegetables directly on the grill rack
and they will have that wonderful smoky flavour — try
buttery Husk-grilled Corn on the Cob or Grilled Potatoes
with Chive Flowers. Probably the most useful side dishes are
the salads that you can prepare in advance and bring out
while everything is cooking. This chapter also includes cold
salads that will contrast well with your barbecued meat, fish,
poultry or vegetarian feast: refreshing and crisp or deliciously
creamy — side orders to tempt every palate.*

SEARED MIXED ONION SALAD

THIS IS A FINE MIX OF FLAVOURS. ON ITS OWN, IT MAKES A GOOD VEGETARIAN SALAD, BUT IT IS ALSO DELICIOUS SERVED WITH GRILLED MEAT SUCH AS BEEF. COMBINE AS MANY DIFFERENT ONIONS AS YOU WISH; LOOK IN ETHNIC MARKETS TO FIND A DIVERSE SELECTION

SERVES FOUR TO SIX

INGREDIENTS
6 red spring onions (scallions), trimmed
6 green spring onions (scallions), trimmed and split lengthways
250g/9oz small or baby (pearl) onions, peeled and left whole
2 pink onions, sliced horizontally into 5mm/¼in rounds
2 red onions, sliced into wedges
2 small yellow onions, sliced into wedges
4 banana shallots, halved lengthways
200g/7oz shallots, preferably Thai
45ml/3 tbsp olive oil, plus extra for drizzling
juice of 1 lemon
45ml/3 tbsp chopped fresh flat leaf parsley
30ml/2 tbsp balsamic vinegar
salt and ground black pepper
kuchai flowers (optional), to garnish

1 Prepare the barbecue. Spread out the onions and shallots in a large flat dish. Whisk the oil and lemon juice together and pour over the mixture. Turn the onions and shallots in the dressing to coat them evenly. Season to taste.

2 Position a grill rack over the coals to heat. Place a griddle or perforated metal vegetable basket on the grill rack over medium-high heat, rather than cook directly on the rack and risk losing onions through the gaps in the rack. Grill the onions in batches, for 5–7 minutes, turning them occasionally.

3 As each batch of onions is cooked, lift them on to a platter and keep hot. Just before serving, add the parsley and gently toss to mix, then drizzle over the balsamic vinegar and extra olive oil.

4 Garnish with a few kuchai flowers, if you like, and serve with warmed pitta bread and grilled halloumi for a vegetarian starter or with grilled meat or fish as a main course.

COOK'S TIP
When available, scatter the whole salad with a few kuchai flowers. These are the lovely blossoms of the evil-smelling Chinese chive. They are available all year round and are sold in Thai food stores.

Energy 117kcal/485kJ; Protein 2.7g; Carbohydrate 14g, of which sugars 10.1g; Fat 6g, of which saturates 0.8g; Cholesterol 0mg; Calcium 66mg; Fibre 3.1g; Sodium 9mg.

BAKED SWEET POTATO SALAD

WHILE YOU ARE BARBECUING YOUR MAIN DISH, BAKE SWEET POTATOES IN FOIL PARCELS AMONG THE COALS OF THE BARBECUE AND THEN CUBE AND TOSS THE FLESH INTO A CHILLI-SPICED SALAD FOR A WARM SALAD WITH A DIFFERENCE. IT MAKES A FILLING PARTNER TO BARBECUED MEATS AND FISH.

SERVES FOUR TO SIX

INGREDIENTS
  1kg/2¼lb sweet potatoes
For the dressing
  45ml/3 tbsp chopped fresh
    coriander (cilantro)
  juice of 1 lime
  150ml/¼ pint/⅔ cup natural
    (plain) yogurt
For the salad
  1 red (bell) pepper, seeded and
    finely diced
  3 celery sticks, finely diced
  ¼ red-skinned onion, finely chopped
  1 red chilli, finely chopped
  salt and ground black pepper
  coriander leaves, to garnish

1 Pierce the potatoes all over and rub the outside with plenty of salt and olive oil and then wrap each one tightly in a triple thickness of heavy-duty foil. Prepare the barbecue. Push the potatoes in between the coals heated to medium-high. Cook for 1 hour.

2 Combine the dressing ingredients in a bowl, season and chill.

3 In a large bowl mix the red pepper, celery, onion and chilli together. When the sweet potatoes are cooked, remove them from the foil packets and allow to cool for a few minutes. When just cool enough to handle, carefully remove the skin using a small, sharp knife.

4 Cut the peeled potatoes into cubes and add them to the bowl. Remove the dressing from the refrigerator, drizzle over the potato cubes and toss carefully so that vegetables are combined with the dressing. Season again to taste and serve, garnished with fresh coriander.

Energy 176kcal/749kJ; Protein 4g; Carbohydrate 40.4g, of which sugars 14g; Fat 1g, of which saturates 0.3g; Cholesterol 0mg; Calcium 115mg; Fibre 5.2g; Sodium 101mg.

GRILLED POTATOES <u>WITH</u> CHIVE FLOWERS

THERE IS SOMETHING VERY ENJOYABLE ABOUT USING EDIBLE FLOWERING PLANTS AND HERBS FROM THE GARDEN. GRABBING A HANDFUL OF THIS HERB OR THAT FLOWER IS ALL PART OF THE CREATIVITY OF COOKING AND EATING OUTDOORS, AND IT CAN PRODUCE REALLY EXCITING AND UNEXPECTED RESULTS.

SERVES FOUR TO SIX

INGREDIENTS

  900g/2lb salad potatoes, such as
    charlottes, Jersey royals or
    French ratte
  15ml/1 tbsp champagne vinegar
  105ml/7 tbsp olive oil
  45ml/3 tbsp chopped chives
  about 10 chive flowers
  4–6 small bunches yellow cherry
    tomatoes on the vine
  salt and ground black pepper

COOK'S TIP
If well established in the garden, chives
will usually blossom in early spring.

1 Prepare the barbecue. Boil the potatoes in a large pan of lightly salted water for about 10 minutes, or until just tender. Meanwhile, make the dressing by whisking the vinegar with 75ml/ 5 tbsp of the oil, then stirring in the chives and flowers. Drain the potatoes and cut them in half. Season to taste.

2 Position a lightly oiled grill rack over the hot coals. Toss the potatoes in the remaining oil and lay them on the grill rack over medium-high heat, cut-side down. Leave for about 5 minutes, then press down a little so that they are imprinted with the marks of the grill.

3 Turn the potatoes over and cook the second side for about 3 minutes. Place the potatoes in a bowl, pour over the dressing and toss lightly to mix.

4 Grill the tomatoes for 3 minutes, or until they are just beginning to blister. Serve with the potatoes, which can be hot, warm or cold.

Energy 232kcal/970kJ; Protein 3g; Carbohydrate 26.2g, of which sugars 4g; Fat 13.5g, of which saturates 2.1g; Cholesterol 0mg; Calcium 14mg; Fibre 2.2g; Sodium 23mg.

HUSK-GRILLED CORN <u>ON THE</u> COB

KEEPING THE HUSKS ON THE CORN PROTECTS THE KERNELS AND ENCLOSES THE BUTTER, SO THE FLAVOURS ARE CONTAINED. FRESH CORN WITH HUSKS INTACT ARE PERFECT, BUT BANANA LEAVES OR A DOUBLE LAYER OF FOIL ARE ALSO SUITABLE.

<u>SERVES SIX</u>

INGREDIENTS
  3 dried chipotle chillies
  250g/9oz/generous 1 cup butter,
    softened
  7.5ml/1½ tsp lemon juice
  45ml/3 tbsp chopped fresh flat
    leaf parsley
  6 corn on the cob, with husks intact
  salt and ground black pepper

1 Heat a heavy frying pan. Add the dried chillies and roast them by stirring them continuously for 1 minute without letting them scorch. Put them in a bowl with almost boiling water to cover. Use a saucer to keep them submerged, and leave them to rehydrate for up to 1 hour. Drain, remove the seeds and chop the chillies finely. Place the butter in a bowl and add the chillies, lemon juice and parsley. Season and mix well.

2 Peel back the husks from each cob without tearing them. Remove the silk. Smear about 30ml/2 tbsp of the chilli butter over each cob. Pull the husks back over the cobs, ensuring that the butter is well hidden. Put the rest of the butter in a pot, smooth the top and chill to use later. Place the cobs in a bowl of cold water and leave in a cool place for 1–3 hours; longer if that suits your work plan better.

3 Prepare the barbecue. Remove the corn cobs from the water and wrap in pairs in foil. Position a lightly oiled grill rack over the hot coals. Grill the corn over medium-high heat for 15–20 minutes until softened.

4 Remove the foil and cook them for about 5 minutes more, turning them often to char the husks a little. Serve hot, with the rest of the chilli butter.

Energy 435kcal/1805kJ; Protein 3.4g; Carbohydrate 27.1g, of which sugars 10.1g; Fat 35.6g, of which saturates 21.9g; Cholesterol 89mg; Calcium 28mg; Fibre 1.8g; Sodium 525mg.

CHARGRILLED AUBERGINE <u>AND</u> LEMON SALAD

LEMON SUBTLY UNDERLINES THE FLAVOUR OF MELTINGLY SOFT AUBERGINE IN THIS CLASSIC SICILIAN DISH. IT IS DELICIOUS SERVED AS AN ACCOMPANIMENT TO A PLATTER OF COLD MEATS, WITH PASTA OR SIMPLY ON ITS OWN WITH SOME GOOD CRUSTY BREAD.

SERVES FOUR

INGREDIENTS

　1 large aubergine (eggplant),
　　about 675g/1½lb
　60ml/4 tbsp olive oil
　grated rind and juice of 1 lemon
　30ml/2 tbsp capers, rinsed
　12 pitted green olives
　30ml/2 tbsp chopped fresh flat
　　leaf parsley
　salt and ground black pepper

COOK'S TIP
This salad will taste even better when made the day before. It will keep well, covered in the refrigerator, for up to 4 days. Return the salad to room temperature before serving.

1 Prepare the barbecue. Heat a griddle on the grill rack over the hot coals. Cut the aubergine into 2.5cm/1in cubes. Place in a bowl and pour in the oil. Toss well so that the cubes are well coated. Griddle the aubergine cubes in batches over medium heat for about 10 minutes, tossing frequently, until golden and softened. Remove with a slotted spoon, drain on kitchen paper and sprinkle with a little salt.

2 Place the aubergine cubes in a large serving bowl, toss with the lemon rind and juice, capers, olives and chopped parsley, and season well with salt and pepper. Serve at room temperature.

VARIATION
Add toasted pine nuts and shavings of Parmesan cheese for a main course dish.

Energy 140kcal/580kJ; Protein 1.9g; Carbohydrate 4g, of which sugars 3.6g; Fat 13.2g, of which saturates 2g; Cholesterol 0mg; Calcium 42mg; Fibre 4.2g; Sodium 288mg.

STUFFED VEGETABLE CUPS

THE SPICY, TOMATO-RED FILLING OF THESE VEGETABLES CARRIES AN IRRESISTABLY TART CITRUS TANG. THESE VERSATILE VEGETARIAN TREATS ARE EQUALLY DELICIOUS HOT OR COLD AND ARE IDEAL SERVED AS AN APPETIZER OR AS A LIGHT MAIN COURSE.

SERVES FOUR

INGREDIENTS

4 potatoes, peeled
4 onions, skinned
4 courgettes (zucchini),
 halved widthways
2–4 garlic cloves, chopped
45–60ml/3–4 tbsp olive oil
45–60ml/3–4 tbsp tomato
 purée (paste)
1.5ml/¼ tsp ras al hanout or
 curry powder
large pinch of ground allspice
seeds of 2–3 cardamom pods
juice of ½ lemon
30–45ml/2–3 tbsp chopped
 fresh parsley
90–120ml/6–8 tbsp vegetable stock
salt and ground black pepper
salad, to serve (optional)

1 Bring a large pan of salted water to the boil. Starting with the potatoes, then the onions and finally the courgettes, add to the boiling water and cook until they become almost tender but not cooked through. Allow about 10 minutes for the potatoes, 8 minutes for the onions and 4–6 minutes for the courgettes. Remove the vegetables from the pan and leave to cool.

COOK'S TIP

If possible, use a small melon baller or apple corer to hollow out the vegetables. It will be much easier and neater than using a teaspoon.

2 When the vegetables are cool enough to handle, hollow them out, retaining the flesh. Prepare the barbecue. Position a grill rack over the hot coals.

3 Finely chop the scooped-out vegetable flesh and put in a bowl. Add the garlic, half the olive oil, the tomato purée, ras al hanout or curry powder, allspice, cardamom seeds, lemon juice, parsley and salt and pepper, and mix well together. Use the stuffing mixture to fill the hollowed out vegetables.

4 Place each vegetable in a double thickness of foil and drizzle with the stock and the remaining oil. Wrap the foil tightly around the vegetables. Cook over medium-high heat for 35–40 minutes or until tender. Serve warm with a salad, if you like.

Energy 225kcal/937kJ; Protein 6.4g; Carbohydrate 30.2g, of which sugars 12.3g; Fat 9.5g, of which saturates 1.4g; Cholesterol 0mg; Calcium 98mg; Fibre 4.8g; Sodium 47mg.

BARBECUED VEGETABLES <u>WITH</u> SMOKED TOMATO SALSA

USE A DOUBLE LAYER OF COALS TO START THE BARBECUE SO THAT THEY WILL BE DEEP ENOUGH TO MAKE A BED FOR THE FOIL-WRAPPED VEGETABLES, THEN GRILL THE TOMATOES ABOVE.

SERVES FOUR TO SIX

INGREDIENTS
  2 small whole heads of garlic
  2 butternut squash, about 450g/1lb
    each, halved lengthways and seeded
  4–6 onions, about 115g/4oz each,
    with a cross cut in the top of each
  4–6 baking potatoes, about
    175g/6oz each
  4–6 sweet potatoes, about
    175g/6oz each
  45ml/3 tbsp olive oil
  fresh thyme, bay leaf and
    rosemary sprigs
  salt and ground black pepper
  2 handfuls of hickory wood chips
    soaked in cold water for at least
    30 minutes
For the tomato salsa
  500g/1¼lb tomatoes, quartered
    and seeded
  2.5ml/½ tsp sugar
  a pinch of chilli flakes
  1.5ml/¼ tsp smoky sweet
    chilli powder
  30ml/2 tbsp good quality
    tomato chutney

1 Prepare a barbecue with plenty of coals. Wrap the garlic, squash and onions separately in a double layer of heavy-duty foil, leaving them open. Pair up the potatoes: one sweet, one ordinary. Drizzle a little oil over the contents of each packet, season well with salt and pepper and pop in a herb sprig. Spray with a little water and scrunch up the foil to secure the parcels.

2 Place the parcels on top of the coals heated to medium-high, noting what goes where, if possible. The garlic will take 20 minutes to cook, the squash 30 minutes, the onions 45 minutes and the potatoes 1 hour. As each vegetable cooks, remove the parcel and wrap it in an extra layer of foil to keep warm. Set aside. Shortly before serving, loosen the tops of all the parcels, except the garlic, and put them all back on the coals so that the vegetables dry out a little before being served.

3 Meanwhile, make the tomato salsa. Put a lightly oiled grill rack in place to heat. Sprinkle the tomatoes with sugar, chilli flakes and seasoning. Place them on the grill rack above the vegetables and cook, covered, for 5 minutes.

4 Drain the hickory chips and place a handful on the coals, replace the cover and leave to smoke for 5 minutes. Add some more wood chips and grill for 10 minutes more, or until the tomatoes have dried a little. Remove the tomatoes from the rack and spoon the flesh from the charred skins into a bowl, crush with a fork and mix in the other ingredients. Serve with the vegetables.

COOK'S TIP
The vegetables taste wonderful with grilled marinated sirloin steaks, or with Parmesan cheese shaved on top.

Energy 244kcal/1029kJ; Protein 6.2g; Carbohydrate 42.4g, of which sugars 13g; Fat 6.7g, of which saturates 1.1g; Cholesterol 0mg; Calcium 65mg; Fibre 5.4g; Sodium 54mg.

VEGETABLES IN COCONUT AND GINGER PASTE

SWEET POTATOES AND BEETROOT TAKE ON A WONDERFUL SWEETNESS WHEN CHARGRILLED, AND THEY ARE DELICIOUS WITH THE SAVOURY ONIONS. ALL THE VEGETABLES ARE COATED IN AN AROMATIC COCONUT, GINGER AND GARLIC PASTE. SERVE THEM TO ACCOMPANY SIMPLY GRILLED MEAT.

SERVES FOUR

INGREDIENTS
  30ml/2 tbsp groundnut (peanut) oil
    or mild olive oil
  450g/1lb sweet potatoes, peeled and
    cut into thick strips or chunks
  4 beetroot (beets), cooked, peeled
    and cut into wedges
  450g/1lb small red or yellow
    onions, halved
  5ml/1 tsp coriander seeds,
    lightly crushed
  3–4 small fresh red chillies, chopped
  salt and ground black pepper
  chopped fresh coriander (cilantro),
    to garnish
For the paste
  2 large garlic cloves, chopped
  1–2 green chillies, seeded
    and chopped
  15ml/1 tbsp chopped fresh
    root ginger
  45ml/3 tbsp chopped fresh
    coriander (cilantro)
  75ml/5 tbsp coconut milk
  30ml/2 tbsp groundnut (peanut) oil
    or mild olive oil
  grated rind of ½ lime
  2.5ml/½ tsp light muscovado
    (brown) sugar

1 First make the paste. Process the garlic, chillies, ginger, coriander and coconut milk in a food processor, blender or coffee grinder.

2 Turn the paste into a small bowl and beat in the oil, lime rind and muscovado sugar.

3 Prepare the barbecue. Position a lightly oiled grill rack over the hot coals and place a wire vegetable basket on the grill rack to heat.

COOK'S TIP
Orange-fleshed sweet potatoes look more attractive than white-fleshed ones in this dish – and they are more nutritious.

4 Put the oil in a large roasting tin and add the vegetables and coriander seeds. Toss to mix. Transfer to the wire basket and cook over medium-high heat for 15 minutes.

5 Return the vegetables to the roasting tin, add the paste and toss to coat thoroughly. Add the chillies and season well with salt and pepper.

6 Grill the vegetables for a further 25–35 minutes, or until the sweet potatoes and onions are fully cooked and tender. Shake the basket regularly. Serve immediately, sprinkled with a little chopped fresh coriander.

Energy 284kcal/1194kJ; Protein 4.8g; Carbohydrate 42.4g, of which sugars 21.6g; Fat 11.9g, of which saturates 1.7g; Cholesterol 0mg; Calcium 106mg; Fibre 6.8g; Sodium 139mg.

ROASTED ONIONS WITH SUN-DRIED TOMATOES

ONIONS ROAST TO A WONDERFUL SWEET CREAMINESS WHEN COOKED IN THEIR SKINS. THEY NEED BUTTER, LOTS OF BLACK PEPPER AND SALTY FOOD TO SET OFF THEIR SWEETNESS. LET THEM COOK AWAY NEXT TO THE COALS WHILE YOU USE THE GRILL RACK TO COOK YOUR ACCOMPANYING DISH.

<u>SERVES SIX</u>

INGREDIENTS
    6 even-sized red onions, unpeeled
    olive oil, for drizzling
    175–225g/6–8oz crumbly cheese
      (such as Lancashire, Caerphilly or
      Cheshire), thinly sliced
    a few snipped chives
    salt and ground black pepper
For the sun-dried tomato butter
    115g/4oz/½ cup butter, softened
    65g/2½oz sun-dried tomatoes in
      olive oil, drained and finely chopped
    30ml/2 tbsp chopped fresh basil
      or parsley

VARIATIONS
• Use goat's cheese instead of
Lancashire, Caerphilly or Cheshire.
• Fry fresh white breadcrumbs in butter
with a little garlic until crisp and then
mix with lots of chopped fresh parsley.
Scatter the crisp crumb mixture over the
onions before serving.

1 To make the sun-dried tomato butter,
cream the butter and then beat in the
tomatoes and basil or parsley. Season to
taste with salt and pepper and shape
into a roll, then wrap in foil and chill.

2 Prepare the barbecue. Wrap the
unpeeled onions separately in a double
thickness of heavy-duty foil, leaving the
top open. Drizzle in a little oil then
close. Place the parcels among the
coals heated to medium-high and cook
for 1 hour, or until they are tender and
feel soft when lightly squeezed.

3 Slit the tops of the onions and open
them up. Season with plenty of black
pepper and add chunks of the sun-
dried tomato butter. Scatter the cheese
and chives over the top and eat
immediately, mashing the butter and
cheese into the soft, sweet onion.

COOK'S TIP
If you only have dry sun-dried tomatoes,
you will need to soften them in boiling
water beforehand.

Energy 304kcal/1258kJ; Protein 9g; Carbohydrate 8.6g, of which sugars 6.3g; Fat 25.6g, of which saturates 16.3g; Cholesterol 69mg; Calcium 260mg; Fibre 1.9g; Sodium 334mg.

ROASTED BEETROOT WITH GARLIC SAUCE

BEETROOT HAS A LOVELY SWEET AND EARTHY FLAVOUR THAT IS MOST PRONOUNCED WHEN IT IS ROASTED. IN GREECE IT IS OFTEN SERVED WITH A GARLIC SAUCE CALLED SKORTHALIA, WHICH CONTRASTS BEAUTIFULLY WITH THE SWEETNESS OF THE BEETROOT.

2 While the blender or processor is running, drizzle in the olive oil through the lid or feeder tube. The sauce should be runny. Spoon it into a serving bowl and set it aside.

3 Prepare the barbecue. Rinse the beetroot under running water to remove any grit, but be careful not to pierce the skin or the colour will run.

4 Wrap the beetroot in groups of 3 or 4 in a double thickness of heavy-duty foil and leave the tops open. Drizzle over a little of the oil and sprinkle lightly with salt.

5 Close up the parcels and arrange them among the coals heated to medium-high. Bake for about 1½ hours until perfectly soft.

6 Remove the beetroot from the foil parcels. When they are just cool enough to handle, peel them. Slice them in thin round slices and serve with the remaining oil drizzled all over.

7 To serve, either spread a thin layer of garlic sauce on top, or hand it around separately. Serve with fresh bread, if you like.

SERVES FOUR

INGREDIENTS
　675g/1½lb medium or small
　　beetroot (beets)
　75–90ml/5–6 tbsp extra virgin
　　olive oil
　salt
For the garlic sauce
　4 medium slices of bread, crusts
　　removed, soaked in water for
　　10 minutes
　2–3 garlic cloves, chopped
　15ml/1 tbsp white wine vinegar
　60ml/4 tbsp extra virgin olive oil

1 To make the garlic sauce, squeeze most of the water out of the bread, but leave it quite moist. Place it in a blender or food processor. Add the garlic and vinegar, with salt to taste, and blend until smooth.

Energy 344kcal/1435kJ; Protein 5.1g; Carbohydrate 25.7g, of which sugars 12.5g; Fat 25.4g, of which saturates 3.6g; Cholesterol 0mg; Calcium 62mg; Fibre 3.6g; Sodium 247mg.

BEETROOT WITH FRESH MINT

BARBECUED FOOD TASTES GOOD WITH SALADS, AND THIS BRIGHT AND DECORATIVE BEETROOT SALAD WITH A BALSAMIC DRESSING IS QUICK TO PREPARE AS WELL AS MAKING A GOOD ACCOMPANIMENT TO LEAFY SALADS. IT CAN BE PREPARED IN ADVANCE, WHICH IS ALWAYS USEFUL WHEN YOU ARE ENTERTAINING.

SERVES FOUR

INGREDIENTS

4–6 cooked beetroot (beets)
5–10ml/1–2 tsp sugar
15–30ml/1–2 tbsp balsamic vinegar
juice of ½ lemon
30ml/2 tbsp extra virgin olive oil
1 bunch fresh mint, leaves stripped
  and thinly sliced
salt

VARIATIONS
• Add a chopped onion and some dill instead of the mint.
• To make spicy beetroot, add harissa to taste and substitute fresh coriander (cilantro) for the mint.

1 Slice the beetroot or cut into even-size dice with a sharp knife. Put the beetroot in a bowl. Add the sugar, balsamic vinegar, lemon juice, olive oil and a pinch of salt and toss together to combine.

2 Add half the thinly sliced fresh mint to the salad and toss lightly until well combined. Place the salad in the refrigerator and chill for about 1 hour. Serve garnished with the remaining mint leaves.

Energy 95kcal/399kJ; Protein 1.7g; Carbohydrate 10.2g, of which sugars 9.6g; Fat 5.6g, of which saturates 0.8g; Cholesterol 0mg; Calcium 21mg; Fibre 1.9g; Sodium 66mg.

LEMONY COUSCOUS SALAD

THIS IS A POPULAR SALAD OF OLIVES, ALMONDS AND COURGETTES MIXED WITH FLUFFY COUSCOUS AND DRESSED WITH HERBS, LEMON JUICE AND OLIVE OIL. IT HAS A DELICATE FLAVOUR AND MAKES AN EXCELLENT ACCOMPANIMENT TO GRILLED CHICKEN OR KEBABS.

SERVES FOUR

INGREDIENTS
275g/10oz/1⅔ cups couscous
550ml/18fl oz/2½ cups boiling
    vegetable stock
2 small courgettes (zucchini)
16–20 black olives
25g/1oz/¼ cup flaked (sliced)
    almonds, toasted
60ml/4 tbsp olive oil
15ml/1 tbsp lemon juice
15ml/1 tbsp chopped fresh
    coriander (cilantro)
15ml/1 tbsp chopped fresh parsley
good pinch of ground cumin
good pinch of cayenne pepper

1 Place the couscous in a bowl and pour over the boiling vegetable stock. Stir with a fork and then set aside for 10 minutes for the stock to be absorbed into the grains. Fluff up the couscous using a fork to separate the grains.

2 Trim the courgettes at both ends then cut into pieces about 2.5cm/1in long. Slice thinly and then cut into fine julienne strips with a sharp knife. Halve the black olives, discarding the stones (pits).

3 Carefully mix the courgettes, olives and almonds into the couscous so that they are well incorporated.

4 Blend together the olive oil, lemon juice, coriander, parsley, cumin and cayenne in a small bowl. Stir into the salad, tossing gently to mix the dressing thoroughly through the couscous and vegetables. Transfer to a large serving dish and serve immediately.

Energy 327kcal/1358kJ; Protein 6.9g; Carbohydrate 37.2g, of which sugars 1.6g; Fat 17.6g, of which saturates 2.3g; Cholesterol 0mg; Calcium 66mg; Fibre 1.9g; Sodium 425mg.

TABBOULEH

THIS IS A WONDERFULLY REFRESHING, TANGY SALAD OF SOAKED BULGUR WHEAT AND MASSES OF FRESH MINT, PARSLEY AND SPRING ONIONS. FEEL FREE TO INCREASE THE AMOUNT OF HERBS FOR A GREENER SALAD. IT CAN BE SERVED AS AN APPETIZER OR AS AN ACCOMPANIMENT TO A MAIN COURSE.

SERVES FOUR TO SIX

INGREDIENTS
  250g/9oz/1½ cups bulgur wheat
  1 large bunch spring onions
    (scallions), thinly sliced
  1 cucumber, finely chopped or diced
  3 tomatoes, chopped
  1.5–2.5ml/¼–½ tsp ground cumin
  1 large bunch fresh parsley, chopped
  1 large bunch fresh mint, chopped
  juice of 2 lemons, or to taste
  60ml/4 tbsp extra virgin olive oil
  salt
  olives, lemon wedges, tomato wedges,
    cucumber slices and mint sprigs,
    to garnish (optional)
  cos or romaine lettuce and natural
    (plain) yogurt, to serve (optional)

1 Pick over the bulgur wheat to remove any dirt. Place it in a bowl, cover with cold water and leave to soak for about 30 minutes.

2 Tip the bulgur wheat into a sieve and drain well, shaking to remove any excess water, then return it to the bowl.

3 Add the spring onions to the bulgur wheat, then mix and squeeze together with your hands to combine.

4 Add the cucumber, tomatoes, cumin, parsley, mint, lemon juice, oil and salt to the bulgur wheat and toss to combine.

5 Heap the tabbouleh on to a bed of lettuce and garnish with olives, lemon and tomato wedges, cucumber and mint sprigs and serve with a bowl of natural yogurt, if you like.

VARIATIONS
Use couscous soaked in boiling water in place of the bulgur wheat and use chopped fresh coriander (cilantro) instead of parsley.

Energy 180kcal/748kJ; Protein 3.6g; Carbohydrate 24.3g, of which sugars 2.8g; Fat 8.1g, of which saturates 1.1g; Cholesterol 0mg; Calcium 42mg; Fibre 1.4g; Sodium 10mg.

SALAD WITH WATERMELON AND FETA CHEESE

THE COMBINATION OF SWEET AND JUICY WATERMELON WITH SALTY FETA CHEESE IS AN ISRAELI ORIGINAL AND WAS INSPIRED BY THE TURKISH TRADITION OF EATING WATERMELON WITH SALTY WHITE CHEESE IN THE HOT SUMMER MONTHS. IT'S JUST GREAT WITH BARBECUED FOOD.

SERVES FOUR

INGREDIENTS
   30–45ml/2–3 tbsp extra virgin
     olive oil
   juice of ½ lemon
   5ml/1 tsp vinegar to taste
   sprinkling of fresh thyme
   pinch of ground cumin
   4 large slices of watermelon, chilled
   1 frisée lettuce, core removed
   130g/4½oz feta cheese,
     preferably sheep's milk feta,
     cut into bite size pieces
   handful of lightly toasted
     pumpkin seeds
   handful of sunflower seeds
   10–15 black olives

1 Pour the extra virgin olive oil, lemon juice and vinegar into a bowl or jug (pitcher). Add the fresh thyme and ground cumin, and whisk until well combined. Cover the dressing and set aside until you are ready to serve the salad, but do not chill.

2 Cut the rind off the watermelon and remove as many seeds as possible. Cut the flesh into triangular-shaped chunks.

3 Put the lettuce leaves in a bowl, pour over the dressing and toss together. Arrange the leaves on a serving dish or individual plates and add the watermelon, feta cheese, pumpkin and sunflower seeds, and the black olives. Serve the salad immediately.

COOK'S TIP
The best choice of olives for this recipe are plump black Mediterranean olives such as Kalamata, and other shiny, brined varieties or dry-cured black olives such as Italian varieties.

Energy 242kcal/1006kJ; Protein 7.9g; Carbohydrate 11.4g, of which sugars 9.7g; Fat 18.6g, of which saturates 6g; Cholesterol 23mg; Calcium 147mg; Fibre 1.2g; Sodium 752mg.

WILD GREEN SALAD

A MIXTURE OF SALAD LEAVES MAKES A REFRESHING ACCOMPANIMENT TO A MEAL, ESPECIALLY WHEN YOU CHOOSE THOSE THAT HAVE CONTRASTING FLAVOURS, LIKE THE ONES USED HERE. THE SALAD IS LIGHTLY DRESSED AND GOES WELL WITH A YOGURT AND FETA CHEESE ACCOMPANIMENT.

SERVES FOUR

INGREDIENTS

   1 large bunch wild rocket (arugula),
     about 115g/4oz
   1 packet mixed salad leaves
   ¼ white cabbage, thinly sliced
   1 cucumber, sliced
   1 small red onion, chopped
   2–3 garlic cloves, chopped
   3–5 tomatoes, cut into wedges
   1 green (bell) pepper, seeded
     and sliced
   2–3 mint sprigs, sliced or torn
   15–30ml/1–2 tbsp chopped fresh
     parsley and/or tarragon or dill
   pinch of dried oregano or thyme
   45ml/3 tbsp extra virgin olive oil
   juice of ½ lemon
   15ml/1 tbsp red wine vinegar
   15–20 black olives
   salt and ground black pepper

1 In a large salad bowl, put the rocket, mixed salad leaves, white cabbage, cucumber, onion and garlic. Toss gently with your fingers to combine the leaves and vegetables.

COOK'S TIP
If you like, accompany this salad with 50g/2oz of crumbled feta cheese mixed into 115g/4oz natural (plain) yogurt and sprinkled with paprika.

2 Arrange the tomatoes, pepper, mint, fresh and dried herbs, salt and pepper on top of the greens and vegetables. Drizzle over the oil, lemon juice and vinegar, stud with the olives and serve.

VARIATION
For a tomato salad, omit the cabbage, use fewer salad leaves and substitute 450g/1lb ripe cherry tomatoes for the tomatoes in the recipe.

Energy 146kcal/605kJ; Protein 3.1g; Carbohydrate 10g, of which sugars 9.4g; Fat 10.6g, of which saturates 1.6g; Cholesterol 0mg; Calcium 99mg; Fibre 3.9g; Sodium 337mg.

CARROT AND ORANGE SALAD

THIS IS A WONDERFUL, FRESH-TASTING SALAD WITH SUCH A FABULOUS COMBINATION OF CITRUS FRUIT AND VEGETABLES THAT IT IS DIFFICULT TO KNOW WHETHER IT IS A SALAD OR A DESSERT. IT MAKES A REFRESHING ACCOMPANIMENT TO GRILLED MEAT, CHICKEN OR FISH.

2 Cut a thin slice of peel and pith from each end of the oranges. Place cut-side down on a plate and cut off the peel and pith in strips. Holding the oranges over a bowl and using a sharp knife, carefully cut out each segment leaving the membrane behind. Squeeze the juice from the membrane into the bowl.

3 Blend the oil, lemon juice and orange juice in a small bowl to make a light dressing. Season with salt and freshly ground black pepper, and a little sugar, if you like.

SERVES FOUR

INGREDIENTS
  450g/1lb carrots
  2 large navel oranges
  15ml/1 tbsp extra virgin olive oil
  30ml/2 tbsp freshly squeezed
    lemon juice
  pinch of sugar (optional)
  30ml/2 tbsp chopped pistachio nuts
    or toasted pine nuts
  salt and ground black pepper

1 Peel the carrots and coarsely grate them into a large bowl.

4 Toss the oranges with the carrots and pour the dressing over. Sprinkle over the pistachios or pine nuts and serve.

Energy 131kcal/547kJ; Protein 2.7g; Carbohydrate 14.6g, of which sugars 13.9g; Fat 7.3g, of which saturates 1.1g; Cholesterol 0mg; Calcium 65mg; Fibre 4.2g; Sodium 71mg.

POTATO AND OLIVE SALAD

THIS DELICIOUS SALAD COMES FROM NORTH AFRICA. THE COMBINATION OF GARLIC, CUMIN AND LOTS OF FRESH CORIANDER MAKES IT PARTICULARLY TASTY AND YET IT IS QUICK AND SIMPLE TO PREPARE. IDEAL AS PART OF A SALAD SELECTION TO ACCOMPANY GRILLED MEAT, FISH OR POULTRY.

SERVES FOUR

INGREDIENTS

8 large new potatoes
large pinch of salt
large pinch of sugar
3 garlic cloves, chopped
15ml/1 tbsp vinegar of your choice,
  such as a fruit variety
large pinch of ground cumin or whole
  cumin seeds
pinch of cayenne pepper or hot
  paprika, to taste
30–45ml/2–3 tbsp extra virgin
  olive oil
30–45ml/2–3 tbsp chopped fresh
  coriander (cilantro) leaves
10–15 dry-fleshed black
  Mediterranean olives

1 Peel and chop the new potatoes into chunks. Put them in a pan, pour in water to cover and add the salt and sugar. Bring to the boil, then reduce the heat and boil gently for about 8–10 minutes, or until the potatoes are just tender. Drain well and leave in a colander to cool completely.

2 When cool enough to handle, cut the potatoes into thick slices and put them in a bowl.

3 Sprinkle the garlic, vinegar, cumin and cayenne or paprika over the salad. Drizzle with olive oil and sprinkle with coriander and olives. Chill before serving.

Energy 196kcal/822kJ; Protein 3g; Carbohydrate 24.5g, of which sugars 2.2g; Fat 10.2g, of which saturates 1.6g; Cholesterol 0mg; Calcium 42mg; Fibre 2.5g; Sodium 302mg.

TRADITIONAL COLESLAW

EVERY DELI SELLS COLESLAW BUT THERE IS BORING COLESLAW AND EXCITING COLESLAW. THE KEY TO GOOD COLESLAW IS A ZESTY DRESSING AND AN INTERESTING SELECTION OF VEGETABLES. THINLY SLICED CABBAGE IS ALSO ESSENTIAL AND IS BEST DONE USING A MANDOLIN, IF YOU HAVE ONE.

SERVES SIX TO EIGHT

INGREDIENTS
    1 large white or green cabbage, very
        thinly sliced
    3–4 carrots, coarsely grated
    ½ red and ½ green (bell) pepper,
        chopped
    1–2 celery sticks, finely chopped or
        5–10ml/1–2 tsp celery seeds
    1 onion, chopped
    2–3 handfuls of raisins or sultanas
        (golden raisins)
    45ml/3 tbsp white wine vinegar or
        cider vinegar
    60–90ml/4–6 tbsp sugar, to taste
    175–250ml/6–8fl oz/¾–1 cup
        mayonnaise, to bind
    salt and ground black pepper

1 Put the cabbage, carrots, peppers, celery or celery seeds, onion, and raisins or sultanas in a salad bowl and mix to combine well. Add the vinegar, sugar, salt and ground black pepper and toss together well until thoroughly combined. Leave to stand for about 1 hour.

2 Stir enough mayonnaise into the salad to bind the ingredients together lightly. Taste the salad for seasoning and sweet-and-sour flavour, adding more sugar, salt and pepper if needed. Chill. Drain off any excess liquid from the salad before serving.

Energy 222kcal/921kJ; Protein 2g; Carbohydrate 16.1g, of which sugars 15.4g; Fat 17g, of which saturates 2.6g; Cholesterol 16mg; Calcium 55mg; Fibre 3.4g; Sodium 120mg.

THE ULTIMATE DELI-STYLE SALAD

A LOVELY CHUNKY SALAD, TOSSED IN A LIGHT, CREAMY DRESSING AND FRESH WITH PIQUANT FLAVOURS, IS A MUST-HAVE FOR ANY BARBECUE SPREAD. IT IS TEMPTING TO POP ALONG TO YOUR LOCAL DELI FOR SOMETHING READY-PREPARED, BUT YOU CAN MAKE THIS VERY ONE EASILY AT HOME.

SERVES SIX TO EIGHT

INGREDIENTS
    1kg/2¼lb waxy salad
        potatoes, scrubbed
    1 red or white onion, finely chopped
    2–3 celery sticks, finely chopped
    60–90ml/4–6 tbsp chopped
        fresh parsley
    15–20 pimiento-stuffed olives, halved
    3 hard-boiled eggs, chopped
    60ml/4 tbsp extra virgin olive oil
    60ml/4 tbsp white wine vinegar
    15–30ml/1–2 tbsp mild or
        wholegrain mustard
    celery seeds, to taste (optional)
    175–250ml/6–8fl oz/
        ¾–1 cup mayonnaise
    salt and ground black pepper
    paprika, to garnish

1 Cook the potatoes in a pan of salted boiling water until tender. Drain, return to the pan and leave for 2–3 minutes to cool and dry a little.

2 When the potatoes are cool enough to handle but still very warm, cut them into chunks or slices and place in a salad bowl.

3 Sprinkle the potatoes with salt and pepper, then add the onion, celery, parsley, olives and the chopped eggs. In a jug (pitcher), combine the olive oil, vinegar, mustard and celery seeds, if using, pour over the salad and toss to combine. Add enough mayonnaise to bind the salad together. Chill before serving, sprinkled with a little paprika.

Energy 331kcal/1375kJ; Protein 5.1g; Carbohydrate 21.4g, of which sugars 2.6g; Fat 25.6g, of which saturates 4.2g; Cholesterol 88mg; Calcium 45mg; Fibre 2.1g; Sodium 358mg.

CANNELLINI BEAN SALAD

TENDER WHITE BEANS ARE DELICIOUS IN THIS SPICY DRESSING WITH THE BITE OF FRESH, CRUNCHY GREEN PEPPER IN THIS DISH FROM ISRAEL. IT IS PERFECT FOR PREPARING AHEAD OF TIME AND TASTES GREAT AS A FIRST COURSE WITH PITTA BREAD AS WELL AS ACCOMPANYING MAIN COURSE DISHES.

SERVES FOUR

INGREDIENTS

750g/1lb 10oz tomatoes, diced
1 onion, finely chopped
½–1 mild fresh chilli, finely chopped
1 green (bell) pepper, seeded
  and chopped
pinch of sugar
4 garlic cloves, chopped
400g/14oz can cannellini beans, drained
45–60ml/3–4 tbsp olive oil
grated rind and juice of 1 lemon
15ml/1 tbsp cider vinegar or
  wine vinegar
salt and ground black pepper
chopped fresh parsley, to garnish

1 Put the tomatoes, onion, chilli, green pepper, sugar, garlic, cannellini beans, salt and plenty of ground black pepper in a large bowl and toss together until well combined.

2 Add the olive oil, lemon rind and juice and vinegar to the salad and toss lightly to combine. Chill before serving, garnished with chopped parsley.

Energy 226kcal/947kJ; Protein 8.8g; Carbohydrate 27.6g, of which sugars 12.9g; Fat 9.6g, of which saturates 1.5g; Cholesterol 0mg; Calcium 92mg; Fibre 9g; Sodium 409mg.

CLASSIC PASTA SALAD

PASTA SALAD IS A POPULAR AND SUSTAINING ACCOMPANIMENT TO ALL KINDS OF DISHES. THIS VERSION CONTAINS BRIGHT GREEN BEANS AND CHERRY TOMATOES ON THE VINE, WITH PARMESAN, OLIVES AND CAPERS TO GIVE IT PIQUANCY. COOK THE PASTA AL DENTE FOR THE BEST TEXTURE.

SERVES SIX

INGREDIENTS
   300g/11oz/2¾ cups dried fusilli
   150g/5oz green beans, topped and
      tailed and cut into 5cm/2in lengths
   1 potato, about 150g/5oz, diced
   200g/7oz cherry tomatoes on the
      vine, hulled and halved
   2 spring onions (scallions),
      finely chopped
   90g/3½oz Parmesan cheese, diced or
      coarsely shaved
   6–8 pitted black olives, cut into rings
   15–30ml/1–2 tbsp capers, to taste
For the dressing
   90ml/6 tbsp extra virgin olive oil
   15ml/1 tbsp balsamic vinegar
   15ml/1 tbsp chopped fresh flat
      leaf parsley
   salt and ground black pepper

1 Cook the pasta according to the instructions on the packet. Drain it into a colander, rinse under cold running water until cold, then shake the colander to remove as much water as possible. Leave to drain and dry, shaking the colander occasionally.

2 Cook the green beans and diced potato in a pan of salted boiling water for 5–6 minutes or until tender. Drain in a colander and leave to cool.

3 To make the dressing, put all the ingredients in a large bowl with salt and pepper to taste, and whisk well to mix.

4 Add the tomatoes, spring onions, Parmesan, olive rings and capers to the dressing, then add the cold pasta, beans and potato. Toss well to mix. Cover and leave to stand for about 30 minutes. Taste for seasoning before serving.

COOK'S TIP
To round off the soft textures of this superb salad, buy a piece of fresh Parmesan from the delicatessen to shave into wafer-thin slices. This version of the cheese is a mature, softer version of the harder cheese used for grating and sprinkling over hot dishes.

Energy 376kcal/1579kJ; Protein 13.2g; Carbohydrate 43g, of which sugars 3.7g; Fat 18g, of which saturates 5g; Cholesterol 15mg; Calcium 212mg; Fibre 2.9g; Sodium 359mg.

DESSERTS AND DRINKS

The main course is ready, the coals are still hot, so why not use the barbecue to grill or bake some mouthwatering desserts? Firm-fleshed fruits such as melons, pineapples and mangoes can easily be cooked on the grill rack or griddle and then served with a sauce or ice cream, but soft fruits can also be cooked on the barbecue. Try the recipe for strawberries cooked on cherry wood skewers with toasted marshmallows — a heavenly combination that adults as well as children will love. You can also wrap fruits in foil and bake them on the grill; to make them extra special, serve them with a sauce or stuff them with nuts or amaretti. If you want to prepare the dessert completely in advance, a simple salad of exotic fruits will make an excellent end to a satisfying barbecued meal. Also included in this chapter are some alcoholic and non-alcoholic drinks that are just right for a warm summer's day socializing with friends or enjoying a relaxing time outdoors with the family around the barbecue.

GRILLED STRAWBERRIES AND MARSHMALLOWS

It is always a treat to have permission to eat marshmallows. After cooking, dredge these little kebabs with loads of icing sugar, some of which will melt into the strawberry juice. The grill has to be very hot to sear the marshmallows quickly before they melt.

SERVES FOUR

INGREDIENTS

16 mixed pink and white
    marshmallows, chilled
16 strawberries
icing (confectioners') sugar
    for dusting
8 short lengths of cherry wood or
    metal skewers

COOK'S TIP
By chilling the marshmallows for at least half an hour, they will be firmer and easier to thread on to the skewers.

1 Prepare the barbecue. If you are using cherry wood skewers, soak them in water for 30 minutes. Position a lightly oiled grill rack just above the hot coals to heat.

2 Spike 2 marshmallows and 2 strawberries on each drained cherry wood or metal skewer and grill over the hot coals for 20 seconds on each side. If nice grill marks don't appear easily, don't persist for too long or the marshmallows may burn – cook until they are warm to the touch and only just beginning to melt.

3 Transfer the skewered strawberries and marshmallows to individual dessert plates or a large platter, dust generously with icing sugar and serve.

Energy 110kcal/466kJ; Protein 1.4g; Carbohydrate 27.6g, of which sugars 22.9g; Fat 0.1g, of which saturates 0g; Cholesterol 0mg; Calcium 11mg; Fibre 0.5g; Sodium 10mg

HONEY-SEARED MELON

THIS FABULOUSLY SIMPLE DESSERT CAN BE MADE WITH MELON THAT IS SLIGHTLY UNDERRIPE, BECAUSE THE HONEYCOMB WILL SWEETEN IT UP BEAUTIFULLY. IT'S IDEAL TO MAKE DURING THE SUMMER WHEN RASPBERRIES ARE IN SEASON AND LAVENDER IN FLOWER.

SERVES SIX

INGREDIENTS
1.3kg/3lb melon, preferably
  Charentais
200g/7oz honeycomb
5ml/1 tsp water
a bunch of lavender, plus extra
  flowers for decoration
300g/11oz/2 cups raspberries

COOK'S TIP
Make sure that the lavender you use in
this recipe is fresh.

1 Prepare the barbecue. Cut the melon in half, scoop out the seeds then cut each half into three slices. Put a third of the honeycomb in a bowl and dilute by stirring in the water. Make a brush with the lavender and dip it into the honey.

2 Heat a griddle on the grill rack over hot coals. Lightly brush the melon with the honey mixture. Grill for 30 seconds on each side. Serve hot, sprinkled with the raspberries and remaining lavender flowers, and topped with the remaining honeycomb.

Energy 113kcal/480kJ; Protein 1.9g; Carbohydrate 27.2g, of which sugars 27.2g; Fat 0.4g, of which saturates 0.1g; Cholesterol 0mg; Calcium 42mg; Fibre 2.1g; Sodium 71mg.

NECTARINES WITH PISTACHIO NUTS

FRESH, RIPE NECTARINES STUFFED WITH A GROUND ALMOND AND PISTACHIO NUT FILLING ARE SIMPLE TO COOK IN FOIL PARCELS ON THE BARBECUE. MAKE THE PARCELS AHEAD AND GRILL THEM WHILE YOU EAT YOUR MAIN COURSE. WHEN OPENED, THE NECTARINES ARE IMMERSED IN A FRUITY LIQUEUR SAUCE.

SERVES FOUR

INGREDIENTS
50g/2oz/½ cup ground almonds
15ml/1 tbsp caster (superfine) sugar
1 egg yolk
50g/2oz/½ cup shelled pistachio
  nuts, chopped
4 nectarines
200ml/7fl oz/scant 1 cup orange juice
2 ripe passion fruit
45ml/3 tbsp Cointreau or other
  orange liqueur

1 Prepare the barbecue. Position a grill rack over the hot coals. Mix the ground almonds, sugar and egg yolk to a paste, then stir in the pistachio nuts.

2 Cut the nectarines in half and carefully remove the stones (pits). Pile the ground almond and pistachio filling into the nectarine halves, packing in plenty of filling, and then place them in pairs on pieces of double-thickness foil. Wrap them up, leaving a space at the top.

3 Pour the orange juice around the nectarines, then close the tops. Place on the grill rack over medium-high heat and cook for 25 minutes.

4 Cut the passion fruit in half and scoop out the seeds. Open the foil tops and add a little of the passion fruit to each parcel. Sprinkle over the liqueur. Cook for a further 5 minutes. Place the nectarines on serving plates and spoon the sauce over and around them.

COOK'S TIP
The sugar in the nutty stuffing should caramelize over the heat, creating a lovely golden-brown crumble effect.

Energy 272kcal/1135kJ; Protein 7.6g; Carbohydrate 20.7g, of which sugars 20g; Fat 15.4g, of which saturates 1.9g; Cholesterol 50mg; Calcium 62mg; Fibre 3.5g; Sodium 74mg.

HONEY-BAKED FIGS

*TWO WILD INGREDIENTS — FIGS AND HAZELNUTS — ARE USED TO MAKE THIS DELECTABLE DESSERT.
FRESH FIGS ARE BAKED IN FOIL PARCELS WITH A LIGHTLY SPICED LEMON AND HONEY SYRUP AND ARE
SERVED WITH HOME-MADE ROASTED HAZELNUT ICE CREAM.*

SERVES FOUR

INGREDIENTS
   finely pared rind of 1 lemon
   1 cinnamon stick, roughly broken
   60ml/4 tbsp clear honey
   8 large figs
For the hazelnut ice cream
   450ml/¾ pint/scant 2 cups double
     (heavy) cream
   50g/2oz/¼ cup caster
     (superfine) sugar
   3 large (US extra large) egg yolks
   1.5ml/¼ tsp vanilla extract
   75g/3oz/¾ cup hazelnuts

1 To make the ice cream, gently heat the cream in a pan until almost boiling. Meanwhile, beat the sugar and egg yolks in a bowl until creamy.

2 Pour a little hot cream into the egg yolk mixture and stir with a wooden spoon. Pour back into the pan and mix well. Cook over a low heat, stirring constantly, until the mixture thickens slightly and lightly coats the back of the spoon – do not allow it to boil. Pour the custard into a bowl, stir in the vanilla extract and leave to cool.

3 Preheat the oven to 180°C/350°F/Gas 4. Place the hazelnuts on a baking sheet and roast for 10–12 minutes, or until golden. Leave the nuts to cool, then grind them in a food processor.

4 If you have an ice cream maker, pour in the cold custard and churn until half-set. Add the ground hazelnuts and continue to churn until the ice cream is thick. Freeze until firm.

5 To make by hand, pour the custard into a freezerproof container and freeze for 2 hours. Turn into a bowl and beat with an electric whisk or turn into a food processor and beat until smooth. Stir in the hazelnuts and freeze until half-set. Beat once more, then freeze until firm.

6 Prepare the barbecue. Position a grill rack over the hot coals. Remove the ice cream from the freezer and allow to soften slightly.

VARIATION
Use pecans instead of hazelnuts.

7 Put the lemon rind, cinnamon stick, honey and 200ml/7fl oz/scant 1 cup water in a small pan and heat slowly until boiling. Simmer the mixture for 5 minutes, then leave to stand for 15 minutes.

8 Using a sharp knife, cut the figs almost into quarters but leaving them attached at the base. Place them in pairs on pieces of double-thickness foil. Wrap them up, leaving a space at the top. Pour the honey syrup around and over the figs, then close the tops. Place on the grill rack over medium-high heat and cook for 15 minutes.

9 Arrange the figs on small serving plates, with the cooking syrup poured around them. Serve accompanied by a scoop or two of the ice cream.

Energy 909kcal/3770kJ; Protein 8.2g; Carbohydrate 48.7g, of which sugars 48.4g; Fat 77.1g, of which saturates 39.6g; Cholesterol 305mg; Calcium 206mg; Fibre 4.2g; Sodium 60mg.

GRILLED MANGO SLICES WITH LIME SORBET

IF YOU CAN LOCATE THEM, USE ALPHONSO MANGOES FOR THIS DISH. MAINLY CULTIVATED IN INDIA, THEY HAVE A HEADY SCENT AND GLORIOUSLY SENSUAL, SILKY TEXTURE. THE SCORED FLESH AND DIAMOND BRANDING MAKE A VISUALLY APPEALING DESSERT.

SERVES SIX

INGREDIENTS
  250g/9oz/1¼ cups sugar
  juice of 6 limes
  3 star anise
  6 small or 3 medium to large
    mangoes
  groundnut (peanut) oil, for brushing

1 Place the sugar in a heavy pan and add 250ml/8fl oz/1 cup water. Heat gently until the sugar has dissolved. Increase the heat and boil for 5 minutes. Cool completely. Add the lime juice and any pulp that has collected in the squeezer. Strain the mixture and reserve 200ml/7fl oz/scant 1 cup in a bowl with the star anise.

2 Pour the remaining liquid into a measuring jug or cup and make up to 600ml/1 pint/2½ cups with cold water. Mix well and pour into a freezerproof container. Freeze for 1½ hours, stir well and return to the freezer until set.

3 Transfer the sorbet mixture to a processor and pulse to a smooth icy purée. Freeze for another hour. Alternatively, make the sorbet in an ice cream maker; it will take about 20 minutes, and should then be frozen for at least 30 minutes before serving.

4 Prepare the barbecue. Pour the reserved syrup into a pan and boil for 2–3 minutes, or until thickened a little. Leave to cool. Cut the cheeks from either side of the stone (pit) on each unpeeled mango, and score the flesh on each in a diamond pattern. Brush with a little oil. Heat a griddle on the grill rack over hot coals. Lower the heat a little and grill the mango halves, cut-side down, for 30–60 seconds until branded with golden grill marks.

5 Invert the mango cheeks on individual plates and serve hot or cold with the syrup drizzled over and a scoop or two of the sorbet. Decorate with star anise.

COOK'S TIP
If this dessert is part of a larger barbecue meal, cook the mangoes in advance using a griddle set over the first red hot coals. Set aside until ready, and serve cold.

Energy 250kcal/1068kJ; Protein 1.3g; Carbohydrate 64.7g, of which sugars 64.2g; Fat 0.3g, of which saturates 0.2g; Cholesterol 0mg; Calcium 40mg; Fibre 3.9g; Sodium 6mg.

FRUIT SKEWERS <u>WITH</u> LIME CHEESE

GRILLED FRUITS MAKE A FINE FINALE TO A BARBECUE, AND ARE ESPECIALLY GOOD COOKED ON LEMON GRASS SKEWERS, WHICH GIVE THE FRUIT A SUBTLE LEMON TANG. THE FRUITS USED HERE MAKE AN IDEAL EXOTIC MIX, BUT ALMOST ANY SOFT FRUIT CAN BE SUBSTITUTED.

SERVES FOUR

INGREDIENTS

    4 long fresh lemon grass stalks
    1 mango, peeled, stoned (pitted) and
      cut into chunks
    1 papaya, peeled, seeded and cut
      into chunks
    1 star fruit (carambola), cut into
      thick slices and halved
    8 fresh bay leaves
    freshly grated nutmeg
    60ml/4 tbsp maple syrup
    50g/2oz/¼ cup demerara (raw) sugar
For the lime cheese
    150g/5oz/⅔ cup curd cheese or
      low-fat soft cheese
    120ml/4fl oz/½ cup double
      (heavy) cream
    grated rind and juice of ½ lime
    30ml/2 tbsp icing (confectioners') sugar

1 Prepare the barbecue. Position a lightly oiled grill rack over the hot coals. Cut the top of each lemon grass stalk into a point with a sharp knife. Discard the outer leaves, then use the back of the knife to bruise the length of each stalk to release the aromatic oils. Thread each stalk, skewer-style, with the fruit pieces, alternating one or two chunks with the bay leaves.

2 To make the lime cheese, mix all the ingredients together in a bowl.

3 Place a piece of foil on a baking sheet. Lay the kebabs on top and sprinkle a little nutmeg over each. Drizzle the maple syrup over and dust liberally with the demerara sugar. Grill for 5 minutes, until lightly charred, basting with the maple syrup from the foil, if necessary. Serve the lightly charred fruit kebabs with the lime cheese.

COOK'S TIP
Only fresh lemon grass will work as skewers for this recipe. It is now possible to buy lemon grass stalks in jars. These are handy for curries and similar dishes, but are too soft to use as skewers.

Energy 360kcal/1508kJ; Protein 7.1g; Carbohydrate 43.4g, of which sugars 43.3g; Fat 19.3g, of which saturates 12g; Cholesterol 50mg; Calcium 98mg; Fibre 3.7g; Sodium 219mg.

CHARGRILLED PINEAPPLE

THIS IS A BOLD DESSERT, ATTRACTIVE TOO, IF YOU LEAVE THE GREEN TOPS ON THE PINEAPPLE. HEATING PINEAPPLE REALLY BRINGS THE FLAVOUR TO THE FORE AND, WITH THE ICE-COLD GRANITA, IT'S THE IDEAL FINISH TO A GLAMOROUS BARBECUE.

SERVES EIGHT

INGREDIENTS
    2 medium pineapples
    15ml/1 tbsp caster (superfine) sugar
      mixed with 15ml/1 tbsp water
For the granita
    15ml/1 tbsp sugar
    1 fresh long mild red chilli, seeded
      and finely chopped
    900ml/1½ pints/3¾ cups pineapple
      juice or fresh purée

COOK'S TIP
Chilli is a regular ingredient in fruit and citrus granitas, because it counters the sharp taste of the fruit.

1 To make the granita, place the sugar and chilli in a small heavy pan with 30ml/2 tbsp of the pineapple juice. Heat gently until the sugar has dissolved, then bring to a fast boil for 30 seconds. Pour the remaining pineapple juice into a large, shallow freezerproof container. The ideal size is about 25 x 14cm/10 x 5½in. Stir in the chilli mixture and freeze for 2 hours.

2 Fork the frozen edges of the sorbet mixture into the centre and freeze for a further 1½ hours until crunchy. Give it another fork over. Return it to the freezer, where it can stay for up to 1 week.

3 Prepare the barbecue. Thaw the granita for about 10 minutes in the refrigerator before serving, and fork it over to break up the ice crystals.

4 Cut each pineapple lengthways into four equal wedges, slicing right through the leafy crown. Remove the core from each wedge.

5 Heat a griddle on the grill rack over hot coals. Lower the heat slightly. Brush the cut sides of the pineapple wedges with the sugar mixture and grill for about 1 minute on each side, or until branded. Serve warm with the granita.

Energy 112kcal/482kJ; Protein 0.9g; Carbohydrate 28.4g, of which sugars 28.4g; Fat 0.4g, of which saturates 0g; Cholesterol 0mg; Calcium 34mg; Fibre 1.5g; Sodium 12mg.

CALVADOS-FLAMED BANANAS

SOFT AND CREAMY BAKED BANANAS, FLAMED WITH CALVADOS, ARE DELICIOUS SERVED WITH A RICH BUTTERSCOTCH SAUCE. THE SAUCE CAN BE MADE IN ADVANCE AND THE BANANAS ARE QUICKLY COOKED. HAVE A SENSIBLE PERSON IGNITE THE CALVADOS, WHICH MAKES A SPECTACULAR END TO A MEAL.

SERVES SIX

INGREDIENTS
115g/4oz/generous ½ cup sugar
150ml/¼ pint/⅔ cup water
25g/1oz/2 tbsp butter
150ml/¼ pint/⅔ cup double
  (heavy) cream
6 large slightly underripe bananas
90ml/6 tbsp Calvados

1 Place the sugar and measured water in a large pan and heat gently until the sugar has dissolved. Increase the heat and boil until the mixture turns a rich golden caramel colour. Remove from the heat and carefully add the butter and cream; the mixture will foam up in the pan. Replace it over a gentle heat and stir to a smooth sauce, then pour into a bowl and leave to cool. Cover and chill until needed.

2 Prepare the barbecue. Wrap the bananas individually in foil. Position a grill rack over the hot coals. Grill the wrapped bananas over high heat for 10 minutes.

3 Transfer the bananas to a tray, open up the parcels and slit the upper side of each banana skin.

4 Meanwhile, gently warm the Calvados in a small pan, then pour some into each banana. Put them back on the barbecue and wait for a few seconds before carefully igniting the Calvados with a long match. Serve with the sauce as soon as the flames die down.

Energy 359kcal/1501kJ; Protein 1.7g; Carbohydrate 43.7g, of which sugars 41.4g; Fat 17.2g, of which saturates 10.6g; Cholesterol 43mg; Calcium 29mg; Fibre 1.1g; Sodium 33mg.

GRILLED PAPAYA WITH GINGER

AMARETTI AND STEM GINGER MAKE A TASTY FILLING FOR PAPAYA, AND THE WARM FLAVOUR OF GINGER ENHANCES THE SWEETNESS OF THE FRUIT. THE DISH TAKES NO MORE THAN TEN MINUTES TO PREPARE. DON'T OVERCOOK PAPAYA OR THE FLESH WILL BECOME VERY WATERY.

SERVES FOUR

INGREDIENTS

2 ripe papayas
2 pieces of stem ginger in syrup,
    drained, plus 15ml/1 tbsp syrup
    from the jar
8 amaretti or other dessert biscuits,
    coarsely crushed
45ml/3 tbsp raisins
shredded, finely pared rind and juice
    of 1 lime
25g/1oz/¼ cup pistachio
    nuts, chopped
15ml/1 tbsp light muscovado
    (brown) sugar
60ml/4 tbsp crème fraîche, plus
    extra to serve

VARIATION
For a subtle change to the filling, use
Greek yogurt and almonds instead of
crème fraîche and pistachio nuts.

1 Prepare the barbecue. Position a grill rack over the hot coals. Cut the papayas in half, scoop out their seeds and discard. Using a sharp knife, slice the stem ginger into fine pieces the size of matchsticks.

2 Tip the crushed amaretti biscuits into a bowl, add the stem ginger matchsticks and the raisins, and use your fingers to rub the contents together into a rough, dry crumble.

3 Stir in the lime rind and juice, and two-thirds of the nuts, then add the sugar and the crème fraîche. Mix well.

4 Place each papaya half on a piece of double-thickness foil. Fill the halves with the amaretti mixture and drizzle with the ginger syrup. Sprinkle with the remaining nuts and close up the foil. Place on the grill rack over hot coals and cook for about 25 minutes, or until tender. Serve with extra crème fraîche.

Energy 292kcal/1228kJ; Protein 3.6g; Carbohydrate 44.6g, of which sugars 35.7g; Fat 12.3g, of which saturates 5.7g; Cholesterol 17mg; Calcium 84mg; Fibre 4.2g; Sodium 127mg.

FRUIT WEDGES WITH GRANITAS

THESE WATERMELON AND ORANGE GRANITAS ARE PERFECT FOR A HOT SUMMER'S DAY AND IDEAL TO FINISH A MEAL. PREPARE THEM IN ADVANCE BUT MAKE SURE THEY ARE NICE AND SLUSHY WHEN READY TO SERVE. FRESH PINEAPPLE, MANGO AND BANANA GRILL QUICKLY AND MAKE A GREAT CONTRAST.

SERVES SIX TO EIGHT

INGREDIENTS
  1 pineapple
  1 mango
  2 bananas
  45–60ml/3–4 tbsp icing
    (confectioners') sugar
For the watermelon granita
  1kg/2¼lb watermelon, seeds removed
  250g/9oz/1¼ cups caster
    (superfine) sugar
  150ml/¼ pint/⅔ cup water
  juice of ½ lemon
  15ml/1 tbsp orange flower water
  2.5ml/½ tsp ground cinnamon
For the spiced orange granita
  900ml/1½ pints/3¾ cups water
  350g/12oz/1¾ cups sugar
  5–6 cloves
  5ml/1 tsp ground ginger
  2.5ml/½ tsp ground cinnamon
  600ml/1 pint/2½ cups fresh
    orange juice
  15ml/1 tbsp orange flower water

1 To make the watermelon granita, purée the watermelon flesh in a blender. Put the sugar and water in a pan and stir until dissolved. Bring to the boil, simmer for 5 minutes, then cool.

2 Stir in the lemon juice, orange flower water and cinnamon, then beat in the watermelon purée. Pour the mixture into a bowl; place in the freezer. Stir every 15 minutes for 2 hours and then at one-hour intervals so that the mixture freezes but remains slushy.

3 To make the spiced orange granita, heat the water and sugar together in a pan with the cloves, stirring until the sugar has dissolved, then bring to the boil and boil for about 5 minutes. Leave to cool and stir in the ginger, cinnamon, orange juice and orange flower water.

4 Remove the cloves, then pour the mixture into a bowl and cover. Freeze in the same way as the granita, above.

5 Prepare the barbecue. Position a lightly oiled grill rack over the hot coals. Peel, core and slice the pineapple. Peel the mango and cut the flesh off the stone (pit) in thick slices. Peel and halve the bananas. Sprinkle the fruit with icing sugar and grill for 3–4 minutes over high heat until slightly softened and lightly browned. Arrange the fruit on a serving platter and scoop the granitas into dishes. Serve immediately.

Energy 433kcal/1848kJ; Protein 2g; Carbohydrate 111.8g, of which sugars 111.2g; Fat 0.7g, of which saturates 0.2g; Cholesterol 0mg; Calcium 71mg; Fibre 1.6g; Sodium 16mg.

MELON WITH GRILLED STRAWBERRIES

SPRINKLING THE STRAWBERRIES WITH A LITTLE SUGAR, THEN GRILLING THEM, HELPS BRING OUT THEIR FLAVOUR. SERVE THIS DELICIOUS FAT-FREE DESSERT ON ITS OWN OR WITH A SCOOP OF THE TANGY, VIRTUOUS LEMON SORBET FEATURED A LITTLE LATER IN THIS CHAPTER.

SERVES FOUR

INGREDIENTS
    115g/4oz/1 cup strawberries
    15ml/1 tbsp icing
      (confectioners') sugar, plus extra
      for dusting
    ½ cantaloupe melon

1 Soak four wooden skewers for 40 minutes. Meanwhile, scoop out the seeds from the half melon using a spoon, and discard them. Using a sharp knife, remove and discard the skin, then cut the flesh into wedges and arrange on a serving plate.

2 Prepare the barbecue. Hull the strawberries and cut them in half. Arrange the fruit in a single layer, cut-side up, on a baking sheet and dust with the icing sugar.

3 Thread the strawberry halves onto skewers and place on a grill rack over a high heat. Grill for 3–4 minutes or until the sugar starts to bubble and turn golden. Remove from the skewers and scatter over the melon slices, dusting with the remaining icing sugar.

COOK'S TIPS
• If possible, place the skewered strawberry halves in a wire basket over the grill rack.
• Remove the strawberries from the heat as soon as the sugar starts to bubble. If left to burn, it will ruin the flavour.

Energy 46kcal/197kJ; Protein 1g; Carbohydrate 10.9g, of which sugars 10.9g; Fat 0.2g, of which saturates 0g; Cholesterol 0mg; Calcium 32mg; Fibre 1.6g; Sodium 12mg.

BAKED BANANAS <u>WITH</u> ICE CREAM

BANANAS, BAKED UNTIL SOFT, MAKE THE PERFECT PARTNER FOR DELICIOUS VANILLA ICE CREAM TOPPED WITH A TOASTED HAZELNUT SAUCE. THIS IS A QUICK AND EASY DESSERT, WHICH IS SURE TO BE ESPECIALLY POPULAR WITH CHILDREN.

<u>SERVES FOUR</u>

INGREDIENTS
   4 large bananas
   15ml/1 tbsp lemon juice
   4 large scoops of vanilla ice cream
For the sauce
   25g/1oz/2 tbsp unsalted
   (sweet) butter
   50g/2oz/½ cup hazelnuts, toasted
   and roughly chopped
   45ml/3 tbsp golden (light corn) syrup
   30ml/2 tbsp lemon juice

1 Prepare the barbecue. Position a grill rack over the hot coals. Brush the bananas with the lemon juice and wrap each banana individually in a double thickness of foil. Grill the bananas for 20 minutes.

2 Meanwhile, make the sauce. Melt the butter in a small pan on the grill rack. Add the hazelnuts and cook gently for 1 minute. Add the syrup and lemon juice and heat, stirring, for 1 minute more.

3 To serve, slit each banana open with a knife and open out the skins to reveal the tender flesh. Transfer to serving plates and serve with scoops of ice cream. Pour the sauce over.

Energy 413kcal/1729kJ; Protein 6g; Carbohydrate 53.5g, of which sugars 49.6g; Fat 19.9g, of which saturates 8.6g; Cholesterol 32mg; Calcium 103mg; Fibre 2.2g; Sodium 115mg.

TOASTED BRIOCHE SLICES WITH ICE CREAM

WARM AND SYRUPY-SWEET BRIOCHE SLICES FLAVOURED WITH ORANGE AND CINNAMON MAKE A DELECTABLE CONTRAST TO VANILLA ICE CREAM IN THIS UNUSUAL VARIATION ON THE TOASTED BUN THEME. FINELY GRATED LEMON RIND AND JUICE INSTEAD WILL WORK JUST AS WELL THE ORANGE.

SERVES FOUR

INGREDIENTS
butter, for greasing
finely grated rind and juice of
    1 orange, such as navel or
    blood orange
50g/2oz/¼ cup caster
    (superfine) sugar
90ml/6 tbsp water
1.5ml/¼ tsp ground cinnamon
4 brioche buns
15ml/1 tbsp icing
    (confectioners') sugar
vanilla ice cream, to serve

1 Put the orange rind and juice, sugar, measured water and cinnamon in a heavy pan. Heat gently, stirring constantly, until the sugar has dissolved, then boil rapidly, without stirring, for 2 minutes, until thickened and syrupy.

COOK'S TIP
You could also use slices of a larger brioche, rather than buns, or madeleines, sliced horizontally in half. These are traditionally flavoured with lemon or orange flower water, making them especially tasty.

2 Remove the orange syrup from the heat and pour into a shallow heatproof dish. Prepare the barbecue. Position a lightly oiled grill rack over the hot coals. Cut each brioche into three thick slices. Grill over high heat until lightly toasted on both sides.

3 Working quickly and using tongs, lift each hot brioche slice from the grill and dip one side into the syrup. Turn it syrup-side up on to a tray while you dip the remainder.

4 Lightly dust the tops with icing sugar then transfer the brioche slices back to the barbecue or grill rack. Grill for 1–2 minutes, or until the top is bubbling and the underneath is golden brown.

5 Transfer the hot brioche to serving plates and top with scoops of vanilla ice cream. Spoon the remaining syrup over them and serve immediately.

VARIATION
For a subtle difference in spiciness, substitute the same amount of ground cardamom for the cinnamon.

Energy 458kcal/1926kJ; Protein 9.1g; Carbohydrate 67.9g, of which sugars 45.8g; Fat 18.5g, of which saturates 10.2g; Cholesterol 1mg; Calcium 189mg; Fibre 1.8g; Sodium 253mg.

APPLE-STUFFED CRÊPES

WHILE THE COALS ARE STILL HOT AFTER THE BARBECUE YOU CAN HEAT UP TWO FRYING PANS AND COOK UP SOME LACE-THIN CRÊPES TO SERVE WITH GOLDEN FRIED APPLES. TOP THE CRÊPES WITH A DRIZZLE OF HONEY AND SOME CREAM AND THEY ARE SURE TO BE A POPULAR END TO THE MEAL.

SERVES FOUR

INGREDIENTS
115g/4oz/1 cup plain
  (all-purpose) flour
pinch of salt
2 large (US extra large) eggs
175ml/6fl oz/¾ cup milk
120ml/4fl oz/½ cup sweet cider
butter, for frying
4 eating apples
60ml/4 tbsp caster (superfine) sugar
120ml/4fl oz/½ cup clear honey, and
  150ml/¼ pint/⅔ cup double (heavy)
  cream, to serve

1 To make the batter, sift the flour and salt into a large bowl. Add the eggs and milk and beat until smooth. Stir in the cider. Leave to stand for 30 minutes. Prepare the barbecue. Position a grill rack over the hot coals.

2 Heat a small heavy frying pan or flat griddle on the grill rack. Add a knob (pat) of butter and enough batter to coat the pan thinly. Cook the crêpe for about 1 minute until it is golden underneath, then flip it over and cook the other side until golden. Slide the crêpe on to a plate, then repeat with the remaining batter to make seven more. Set the crêpes aside and keep warm.

3 Core the apples and cut them into thick slices. Heat 15g/½oz butter in a large frying pan. Add the apples to the pan and cook until golden on both sides. Transfer the slices to a bowl and sprinkle with sugar.

4 Fold each crêpe in half, then fold in half again to form a cone. Fill each with some of the fried apples. Place two filled crêpes on each dessert plate. Drizzle with a little honey and serve at once, accompanied by cream.

COOK'S TIP
For the best results, use full-fat (whole) milk in the batter.

Energy 524kcal/2200kJ; Protein 8.3g; Carbohydrate 71.1g, of which sugars 49.2g; Fat 24.1g, of which saturates 13.8g; Cholesterol 149mg; Calcium 140mg; Fibre 2.1g; Sodium 71mg.

FRESH FRUIT SALAD

AFTER A RICH MEAL, NOTHING QUITE HITS THE SPOT LIKE A CLEAR-TASTING SALAD OF FRESH FRUIT.
THIS SALAD HAS A PASSION FRUIT AND HONEY DRESSING THAT REALLY ACCENTUATES THE FLAVOUR OF
THE EXOTIC FRUIT USED. SERVE IT WITH SCOOPS OF COCONUT OR VANILLA ICE CREAM, IF YOU LIKE.

SERVES SIX

INGREDIENTS
   1 mango
   1 papaya
   2 kiwi fruit
   coconut or vanilla ice cream, to serve
For the dressing
   3 passion fruit
   thinly pared rind and juice of 1 lime
   5ml/1 tsp hazelnut or walnut oil
   15ml/1 tbsp clear honey

COOK'S TIP
A clear golden honey scented with
orange blossom or acacia blossom would
be perfect for the dressing.

1 Peel the mango, cut it into three
slices, then cut the flesh into chunks
and place it in a large bowl. Peel the
papaya and cut it in half. Scoop out the
seeds and discard, then chop the flesh
and put in the bowl with the mango.

2 Cut both ends off each kiwi fruit, then
stand them on a board. Using a small
sharp knife, cut off the skin from top to
bottom. Cut each kiwi fruit in half
lengthways, then cut into thick slices.
Combine all the fruit in a large bowl.

3 Make the dressing. Cut each passion
fruit in half and scoop the seeds out
into a sieve set over a small bowl. Press
the seeds well to extract all their juices.
Lightly whisk the remaining dressing
ingredients into the passion fruit juice,
then pour the dressing over the fruit.
Mix gently to combine. Leave to chill
for 1 hour before serving with scoops
of coconut or vanilla ice cream.

Energy 57kcal/240kJ; Protein 0.9g; Carbohydrate 12.4g, of which sugars 12.3g; Fat 0.7g, of which saturates 0.1g; Cholesterol 0mg; Calcium 21mg; Fibre 2.4g; Sodium 6mg.

LEMON SORBET

This smooth, tangy sorbet creates a light and refreshing dessert that can be served as it is or to accompany fresh fruit. If you have cooked a rich barbecue, this clean-tasting dessert might be just the right choice to end the meal.

SERVES SIX

INGREDIENTS
  200g/7oz/1 cup caster
    (superfine) sugar
  300ml/½ pint/1¼ cups water
  4 lemons
  1 large (US extra large) egg white
  a little sugar, for sprinkling

1 Put the caster sugar and measured water into a heavy pan and bring slowly to the boil, stirring occasionally, until the sugar has just dissolved.

2 Using a vegetable peeler, pare the rind thinly from two of the lemons directly into the pan. Simmer for about 2 minutes without stirring, then remove the pan from the heat. Leave the syrup to cool, then chill.

3 Squeeze the juice from all the lemons and carefully strain it into the syrup, making sure all the pips (seeds) are removed. Take the lemon rind out of the syrup and set it aside until you make the decoration.

4 If you have an ice cream maker, strain the syrup into the machine tub and churn for 10 minutes, or until thickening.

5 In a bowl, lightly whisk the egg white with a fork, then pour it into the tub. Continue to churn for 10–15 minutes, or until firm enough to scoop.

6 If working by hand, strain the syrup into a plastic tub or a similar shallow freezerproof container and freeze for 4 hours, or until the mixture is mushy.

7 Scoop the mushy mixture into a blender or food processor and process until smooth. Whisk the egg white with a fork until it is just frothy. Spoon the sorbet back into its container; beat in the egg white. Freeze for 1 hour.

8 To make the sugared rind decoration, use the blanched rind from step 2. Cut into very thin strips and sprinkle with granulated sugar on a plate. Scoop the sorbet into bowls or glasses and decorate with the sugared lemon rind.

VARIATIONS
Sorbet can be made from any citrus fruit. As a guide, you will need 300ml/½ pint/ 1¼ cups of fresh fruit juice and the pared rind of half the squeezed fruits. For example, use four oranges or two oranges and two lemons, or, to make a grapefruit sorbet, use the rind of one ruby grapefruit and the juice of two.

Energy 133kcal/569kJ; Protein 0.7g; Carbohydrate 34.8g, of which sugars 34.8g; Fat 0g, of which saturates 0g; Cholesterol 0mg; Calcium 18mg; Fibre 0g; Sodium 12mg.

CRANBERRY AND APPLE SPRITZER

DON'T FORGET TO LOOK AFTER THE NON-DRINKERS AT YOUR PARTY — ALL TOO OFTEN THEY'RE LEFT WITH JUST THE MIXERS, FIZZY DRINKS OR TAP WATER. THIS COLOURFUL, ZINGY COOLER COMBINES TANGY CRANBERRIES WITH FRESH JUICY APPLES AND A SUBTLE, FRAGRANT HINT OF VANILLA.

MAKES SIX TO EIGHT GLASSSES

INGREDIENTS
  6 red eating apples
  375g/13oz/3½ cups fresh or frozen
    cranberries, plus extra to decorate
  45ml/3 tbsp vanilla syrup
  ice cubes
  sparkling mineral water

COOK'S TIP
To make vanilla syrup, heat a vanilla pod (bean) with 50g/2oz/¼ cup sugar and 30ml/2fl oz water in a pan until the sugar dissolves. Simmer for 5 minutes then leave to cool.

1 Quarter and core the apples then cut the flesh into pieces small enough to fit through a juicer. Push the cranberries and apple chunks through the juicer. Add the vanilla syrup to the juice and chill until ready to serve.

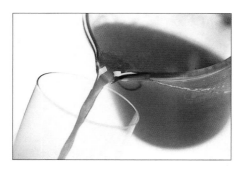

2 Pour the juice into glasses and add one or two ice cubes to each. Top up with sparkling mineral water and decorate with extra cranberries, threaded on to cocktail sticks (toothpicks). Serve immediately.

Energy 51kcal/218kJ; Protein 0.3g; Carbohydrate 13.1g, of which sugars 13.1g; Fat 0.1g, of which saturates 0g; Cholesterol 0mg; Calcium 5mg; Fibre 1.6g; Sodium 17mg.

GRAPEFRUIT AND RASPBERRY COOLER

MAKE PLENTY OF FRESHLY JUICED BLENDS LIKE THIS GORGEOUS COMBINATION AND YOUR GUESTS WILL KEEP COMING BACK FOR MORE. GRAPEFRUIT AND RASPBERRY JUICE MAKE A GREAT PARTNERSHIP, PARTICULARLY IF YOU ADD A LITTLE CINNAMON SYRUP TO COUNTERACT ANY TARTNESS IN THE FRUIT.

MAKES EIGHT TALL GLASSES

INGREDIENTS
  1 cinnamon stick
  50g/2oz/¼ cup caster
    (superfine) sugar
  4 pink grapefruits
  250g/9oz/1½ cups fresh or
    frozen raspberries
  wedge of watermelon
  crushed ice
  borage flowers, to decorate (optional)

COOK'S TIP
Make non-alcoholic drinks more interesting by dressing them up with extra fruits and decorations.

VARIATIONS
Serve other stirrers such as cinnamon sticks, or provide sugar stirrers so guests can sweeten their drinks to suit their own personal preference.

1 Put the cinnamon stick in a small pan with the sugar and 200ml/7fl oz/scant 1 cup water. Heat gently until the sugar has dissolved, then bring to the boil and boil for 1 minute. Reserve to cool.

2 Cut away the skins from the pink grapefruits. Cut the flesh into pieces small enough to fit through a juicer funnel. Juice the grapefruits and raspberries, and pour into a small glass jug (pitcher).

3 Remove the cinnamon from the syrup and add the syrup to the grapefruit and raspberry juice in the jug.

4 Carefully slice the watermelon into long thin wedges and place in eight tall glasses. Half-fill the glasses with the crushed ice and sprinkle with borage flowers, if you like. Pour over the pink fruit juice and serve immediately with plenty of napkins to allow your guests to eat the watermelon wedges.

Energy 57kcal/240kJ; Protein 1.1g; Carbohydrate 13.4g, of which sugars 13.4g; Fat 0.2g, of which saturates 0g; Cholesterol 0mg; Calcium 30mg; Fibre 1.8g; Sodium 4mg.

ALCOHOLIC FRUITY PUNCH

THE TERM "PUNCH" COMES FROM THE HINDU WORD PANCH (FIVE), RELATING TO THE FIVE INGREDIENTS TRADITIONALLY CONTAINED IN THE DRINK: ALCOHOL, CITRUS, TEA, SUGAR AND WATER. PUNCHES STILL COMBINE A MIXTURE OF SPIRITS, FLAVOURINGS AND A TOP-UP OF FIZZ OR JUICE.

MAKES ABOUT FIFTEEN GLASSES

INGREDIENTS
2 large papayas
4 passion fruit
300g/11oz lychees, peeled and pitted
300ml/½ pint/1¼ cups freshly
  squeezed orange juice
200ml/7fl oz/scant 1 cup
  Grand Marnier or other
  orange-flavoured liqueur
8 whole star anise
2 small oranges
ice cubes
1.5 litres/2½ pints/6¼ cups soda
  water (club soda)

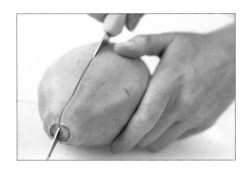

1 Halve the papayas using a sharp knife and discard the seeds. Halve the passion fruit and press the pulp through a sieve into a small punch bowl or a pretty serving bowl.

2 Push the papayas through a juicer, adding 105ml/7 tbsp water to help the pulp through. Juice the lychees. Add the juices to the bowl with the orange juice, liqueur and star anise. Thinly slice the oranges and add to the bowl. Chill for at least 1 hour, or until ready to serve.

3 Add plenty of ice cubes to the bowl and top up with soda water. Ladle into punch cups or small glasses to serve.

COOK'S TIP
This delightful punch also makes a fabulously alcoholic fruit syrup for a dessert of papaya halves stuffed with frozen yogurt or a fruit sorbet.

Energy 65kcal/274kJ; Protein 0.5g; Carbohydrate 11.6g, of which sugars 11.6g; Fat 0.1g, of which saturates 0g; Cholesterol 0mg; Calcium 10mg; Fibre 0.9g; Sodium 6mg.

APPLE-SPICED BEER

LIGHT BEER TAKES ON A WHOLE NEW DIMENSION IN THIS FUN AND FRUITY COOLER. DILUTED WITH FRESHLY JUICED APPLE AND FLAVOURED WITH GINGER AND STAR ANISE, IT'S A GREAT DRINK THAT IS REFRESHING AND LESS ALCOHOLIC THAN NORMAL BEER.

MAKES EIGHT TO TEN TALL GLASSES

INGREDIENTS
    8 eating apples
    25g/1oz fresh root ginger
    6 whole star anise
    800ml/1⅓ pints/3½ cups light beer
    crushed ice

1 Quarter and core the apples and, using a small, sharp knife, cut the flesh into pieces small enough to fit through a juicer. Roughly chop the ginger. Push half the apples through the juicer, then juice the ginger and the remaining apples.

2 Put 105ml/7 tbsp of the juice in a small pan with the star anise and heat gently until almost boiling. Add to the remaining juice in a large jug (pitcher) and chill for at least 1 hour.

3 Add the light beer to the juice and stir gently until the froth has dispersed a little. Pour the spiced beer over crushed ice in tall glasses, allow to settle again and serve immediately.

Energy 42kcal/178kJ; Protein 0.4g; Carbohydrate 4.8g, of which sugars 4.8g; Fat 0.1g, of which saturates 0g; Cholesterol 0mg; Calcium 6mg; Fibre 0.9g; Sodium 7mg.

ACCOMPANIMENTS

You have decided on your barbecue meal, but there are all kinds of accompaniments that will add to the satisfying selection of food you are going to cook on the grill. Nibbles will keep appetites going while the first course cooks, so try some of the super dips to serve with crudités or fingers of pitta bread. They also make good accompanying sauces to meat and vegetables, and for dressing salads. This chapter also includes home-made barbecue sauce, tomato ketchup and relishes that will really make the party go with a swing. There are also several suitable breads for outdoor eating. Pitta bread must be one of the favourites, because it is so useful as a holder for food, but tortillas, too, make good wraps. And then, of course, there is the good old burger bun — a slice of sesame-topped perfection for your sumptuous home-made burgers. There are also some delicious sweet sauces to transform simply grilled fruit or to top ice cream for a quick dessert. In short, there is everything you need to ensure a successful barbecue.

HUMMUS

THIS CLASSIC MIDDLE EASTERN DISH IS MADE FROM COOKED CHICKPEAS GROUND TO A PASTE AND FLAVOURED WITH GARLIC, LEMON JUICE, TAHINI, OLIVE OIL AND CUMIN. IT IS DELICIOUS SERVED WITH WEDGES OF TOASTED PITTA BREAD OR CRUDITÉS.

SERVES FOUR TO SIX

INGREDIENTS
   400g/14oz can chickpeas, drained
   60ml/4 tbsp tahini
   2–3 garlic cloves, chopped
   juice of ½–1 lemon
   cayenne pepper
   small pinch to 1.5ml/¼ tsp ground
     cumin, or more to taste
   salt and ground black pepper

VARIATION
Process 2 roasted red (bell) peppers with the chickpeas, then continue as above. Serve sprinkled with lightly toasted pine nuts and paprika mixed with olive oil.

1 Using a potato masher or food processor, coarsely mash the chickpeas. If you prefer a smoother purée, process them in a food processor or blender until smooth.

2 Mix the tahini into the chickpeas, then stir in the remaining ingredients, and salt and pepper to taste. If needed, add a little water. Serve at room temperature with grilled pittas.

Energy 144kcal/603kJ; Protein 7.2g; Carbohydrate 11.9g, of which sugars 0.4g; Fat 7.9g, of which saturates 1.1g; Cholesterol 0mg; Calcium 98mg; Fibre 3.8g; Sodium 149mg

GUACAMOLE

One of the best-loved Mexican salsas, this blend of creamy avocado, tomatoes, chillies, coriander and lime now appears on tables the world over. Serve with vegetable crudités, tortilla chips or breadsticks, or serve as a classic accompaniment to fajitas.

SERVES SIX TO EIGHT

INGREDIENTS
4 tomatoes
4 ripe avocados, preferably *fuerte*
freshly squeezed juice of 1 lime
½ small onion, finely chopped
2 garlic cloves, crushed
small bunch of fresh coriander
  (cilantro), chopped
3 fresh red fresno chillies
salt
tortilla chips or breadsticks, to serve

COOK'S TIP
Smooth-skinned *fuerte* avocados are native to Mexico, so would be ideal for this dip. If they are not available, use any avocados, but make sure that they are ripe. To test, gently press the top of the avocado; it should give a little.

1 Cut a cross in the base of each tomato. Place the tomatoes in a heatproof bowl and pour over boiling water to cover.

2 Leave the tomatoes in the water for 30 seconds, then lift them out using a slotted spoon and plunge them into a bowl of cold water. Drain. The skins will have begun to peel back from the crosses. Remove the skins completely. Cut the tomatoes in half, remove the seeds with a teaspoon, then chop the flesh roughly and set it aside.

3 Cut the avocados in half then remove the stones (pits). Scoop the flesh out of the shells and place it in a food processor or blender. Process the pulp until almost smooth, then scrape into a bowl and stir in the lime juice.

4 Add the onion and garlic to the avocado and mix well. Stir in the coriander until combined.

5 Remove the stalks from the chillies, slit them and scrape out the seeds with a small, sharp knife. Chop the chillies finely and add them to the avocado mixture, with the roughly chopped tomatoes. Mix well.

6 Taste the guacamole and add salt, if needed. Cover closely with clear film (plastic wrap) or a tight-fitting lid and chill for 1 hour before serving as a dip with tortilla chips or breadsticks. If it is well covered, guacamole will keep in the refrigerator for 2–3 days.

Energy 108kcal/449kJ; Protein 1.6g; Carbohydrate 3.3g, of which sugars 2.4g; Fat 9.9g, of which saturates 2.1g; Cholesterol 0mg; Calcium 23mg; Fibre 2.6g; Sodium 10mg.

BLUE CHEESE DIP

THIS DIP CAN BE MIXED UP IN NEXT TO NO TIME AND IS DELICIOUS SERVED WITH PEARS OR WITH FRESH VEGETABLE CRUDITÉS. THIS IS A VERY THICK DIP TO WHICH YOU CAN ADD A LITTLE MORE YOGURT FOR A SOFTER CONSISTENCY. ADD STILL MORE YOGURT TO MAKE A GREAT DRESSING.

SERVES FOUR

INGREDIENTS
  150g/5oz blue cheese, such as
    Stilton or Danish blue
  150g/5oz/²⁄₃ cup soft cheese
  75ml/5 tbsp Greek (US strained
    plain) yogurt
  salt and ground black pepper,
    plus extra to garnish

1 Crumble the blue cheese into a bowl. Using a wooden spoon, beat the cheese to soften it.

2 Add the soft cheese and beat well to blend the two cheeses together.

3 Gradually beat in the Greek yogurt, adding enough to give you the consistency you prefer.

4 Season with lots of black pepper and a little salt. Chill the dip until you are ready to serve it.

COOK'S TIP
If you like, add a handful of finely chopped walnuts to this dip, because they go wonderfully well with the cheese. It is advisable to grind the nuts in a food processor to avoid the dip being too chunky in texture.

Energy 206kcal/855kJ; Protein 12.1g; Carbohydrate 2.6g, of which sugars 2.6g; Fat 16.5g, of which saturates 10.7g; Cholesterol 44mg; Calcium 219mg; Fibre 0g; Sodium 473mg.

GARLIC DIP

TWO WHOLE HEADS OF GARLIC MAY SEEM LIKE A LOT, BUT ROASTING TRANSFORMS THE FLESH TO A TENDER, SWEET AND MELLOW PULP. SERVE WITH CRUNCHY BREADSTICKS AND CRISPS. FOR A LOW-FAT VERSION OF THIS DIP, USE REDUCED-FAT MAYONNAISE AND LOW-FAT NATURAL YOGURT.

SERVES FOUR

INGREDIENTS
    2 whole garlic heads
    15ml/1 tbsp olive oil
    60ml/4 tbsp mayonnaise
    75ml/5 tbsp Greek (US strained
      plain) yogurt
    5ml/1 tsp wholegrain mustard
    salt and ground black pepper

1 Preheat the oven to 200°C/400°F/ Gas 6. Separate the garlic cloves and place them in a small roasting pan.

2 Pour the olive oil over the garlic cloves and turn them with a spoon to coat them evenly. Roast them for 20–30 minutes, or until tender and softened. Leave to cool for 5 minutes.

3 Trim off the root end of each roasted garlic clove. Peel the cloves and discard the skins. Place the roasted garlic on a chopping board and sprinkle with salt. Mash with a fork until puréed.

4 Combine the garlic, mayonnaise, yogurt and mustard in a small bowl.

5 Check and adjust the seasoning, then spoon the dip into a bowl. Cover and chill until ready to serve. Garnish with extra black pepper before serving.

COOK'S TIP
If cooked on a barbecue, leave the garlic heads whole and cook until tender, turning occasionally. Peel and mash.

Energy 155kcal/640kJ; Protein 1.7g; Carbohydrate 0.8g, of which sugars 0.7g; Fat 16.4g, of which saturates 3.1g; Cholesterol 11mg; Calcium 34mg; Fibre 0.2g; Sodium 142mg.

THOUSAND ISLAND DIP

THIS VARIATION ON THE CLASSIC DRESSING IS FAR REMOVED FROM THE ORIGINAL VERSION BUT CAN BE SERVED IN THE SAME WAY — WITH GRILLED KING PRAWNS LACED ON TO BAMBOO SKEWERS FOR DIPPING OR WITH A SIMPLE MIXED SEAFOOD SALAD.

SERVES FOUR

INGREDIENTS

4 tomatoes
150g/5oz/²⁄₃ cup soft cheese
60ml/4 tbsp mayonnaise
30ml/2 tbsp tomato purée (paste)
30ml/2 tbsp chopped fresh parsley
4 sun-dried tomatoes in oil, drained
  and finely chopped
grated rind and juice of 1 lemon
red Tabasco sauce, to taste
5ml/1 tsp Worcestershire or soy sauce
salt and ground black pepper

1 Skewer each tomato in turn on a metal fork and hold in a gas flame for 1–2 minutes, or until the skin wrinkles and splits. Allow to cool, then slip off and discard the skins. Alternatively, plunge the tomatoes into boiling water for 30 seconds, then refresh in cold water. Peel away the skins. Halve the tomatoes and scoop out the seeds with a teaspoon. Finely chop the tomato flesh and set aside.

COOK'S TIP
Put together a colourful seafood medley – such as peeled prawns, calamari rings and mussels – to accompany this vibrant and popular party dip.

2 In a bowl, beat the soft cheese, then gradually beat in the mayonnaise and tomato purée to a smooth mixture.

3 Stir in the parsley and sun-dried tomatoes, then add the chopped tomatoes and their seeds, and mix well.

4 Add the lemon rind and juice, and Tabasco sauce to taste. Stir in the Worcestershire or soy sauce, and salt and pepper to taste.

5 Transfer the dip to a serving bowl, cover and chill until ready to serve.

Energy 194kcal/805kJ; Protein 4.7g; Carbohydrate 5.7g, of which sugars 5.6g; Fat 17.1g, of which saturates 5.2g; Cholesterol 27mg; Calcium 11mg; Fibre 1.2g; Sodium 184mg.

TZATZIKI

THIS CLASSIC GREEK DIP IS A COOLING MIX OF YOGURT, CUCUMBER AND MINT, PERFECT FOR A HOT SUMMER'S DAY. SERVE IT WITH STRIPS OF LIGHTLY TOASTED PITTA BREAD OR USE IT TO ACCOMPANY BARBECUED VEGETABLES. IT ALSO MAKES A TASTY ADDITION TO A SALAD SELECTION.

SERVES FOUR

INGREDIENTS
    1 mini cucumber
    4 spring onions (scallions)
    1 garlic clove
    200ml/7fl oz/scant 1 cup Greek
     (US strained plain) yogurt
    45ml/3 tbsp chopped fresh mint
    salt and ground black pepper
    fresh mint sprig, to garnish (optional)

1 Trim the ends from the cucumber, then cut it into 5mm/¼in dice. Set aside.

2 Trim the spring onions and garlic, then chop both very finely.

COOK'S TIP
• Use Greek (US strained plain) yogurt for this dip – it has a higher fat content than most yogurts, but this gives it a deliciously rich, creamy texture.
• Mint or coriander (cilantro) leaves will make a suitable garnish for this recipe.

3 Beat the yogurt until smooth, if necessary, then gently stir in the cucumber, onions, garlic and mint.

4 Season to taste, then transfer the mixture to a serving bowl. Chill until ready to serve with pitta breads.

Energy 62kcal/258kJ; Protein 3.6g; Carbohydrate 1.7g, of which sugars 1.6g; Fat 5.2g, of which saturates 2.6g; Cholesterol 0mg; Calcium 84mg; Fibre 0.3g; Sodium 37mg.

CHILLI RELISH

BURGERS OR BARBECUED SAUSAGES TASTE GREAT WITH A SPICY RELISH, AND A HOME-MADE ONE IS SO MUCH NICER THAN ONE FROM A JAR. THIS CHILLI RELISH WILL LAST FOR AT LEAST A WEEK STORED IN A REFRIGERATOR, SO YOU COULD MAKE IT A FEW DAYS IN ADVANCE OF YOUR BARBECUE.

2 Heat the olive oil in a pan. Add the onion, red pepper and garlic to the pan.

3 Cook the vegetables gently for 5–8 minutes, or until the pepper is softened. Add the chopped tomatoes, cover and cook for 5 minutes, until the tomatoes release their juices.

4 Stir in the remaining ingredients except for the basil. Bring gently to the boil, stirring, until the sugar dissolves.

5 Simmer, uncovered, for 20 minutes, or until the mixture is pulpy. Stir in the basil leaves and check the seasoning.

6 Allow to cool completely, then transfer to a glass jar or a plastic container with a tightly fitting lid. Store, covered, in the refrigerator.

SERVES EIGHT

INGREDIENTS
  6 tomatoes
  30ml/2 tbsp olive oil
  1 onion, roughly chopped
  1 red (bell) pepper, seeded
    and chopped
  2 garlic cloves, chopped
  5ml/1 tsp ground cinnamon
  5ml/1 tsp chilli flakes
  5ml/1 tsp ground ginger
  5ml/1 tsp salt
  2.5ml/½ tsp ground black pepper
  75g/3oz/⅓ cup light muscovado
    (brown) sugar
  75ml/5 tbsp cider vinegar
  handful of fresh basil leaves, chopped

1 Skewer each tomato on a metal fork and hold in a gas flame for 1–2 minutes, turning, until the skin splits and wrinkles. Alternatively, plunge the tomatoes into boiling water for 30 seconds, then refresh in cold water. Peel away the skins and roughly chop the flesh.

COOK'S TIP
This relish thickens slightly on cooling so do not worry if the mixture seems a little wet at the end of step 6.

Energy 84kcal/355kJ; Protein 0.9g; Carbohydrate 14.1g, of which sugars 13.9g; Fat 3.1g, of which saturates 0.5g; Cholesterol 0mg; Calcium 14mg; Fibre 1.2g; Sodium 8mg.

CORN RELISH

HERE IS A LOVELY INDIAN-INSPIRED RELISH TO PERK UP ALL KINDS OF BARBECUED DISHES. SERVE WITH BAKED OR ROASTED VEGETABLES, PLAIN GRILLED MEATS OR FISH, OR WITH PITTA BREAD OR VEGETABLE FINGERS FOR DIPPING AS A NIBBLE WHILE THE FOOD COOKS ON THE GRILL.

SERVES FOUR

INGREDIENTS

   30ml/2 tbsp vegetable oil
   1 large onion, chopped
   1 red chilli, seeded and chopped
   2 garlic cloves, chopped
   5ml/1 tsp black mustard seeds
   10ml/2 tsp hot curry powder
   320g/11¼oz can corn, drained
   grated rind and juice of 1 lime
   45ml/3 tbsp chopped fresh
    coriander (cilantro)
   salt and ground black pepper

4 Add the drained corn to the bowl containing the onion mixture and stir to mix.

5 Add the lime rind and juice, coriander and seasoning. Mix well, then cover and serve at room temperature.

COOK'S TIP
If you like, use frozen corn in this recipe. Defrost quickly by rinsing in boiling water.

1 Heat the oil in a large frying pan and cook the onion, chilli and garlic over a high heat for 5 minutes, or until the onions are just beginning to brown.

2 Stir in the mustard seeds and curry powder, then cook for 2 minutes more, stirring, until the seeds start to splutter and the onions are browned.

3 Remove the fried onion and spice mixture from the heat and allow to cool completely. Transfer the mixture to a glass bowl.

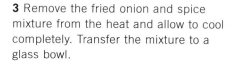

Energy 169kcal/708kJ; Protein 3.2g; Carbohydrate 25.5g, of which sugars 10.7g; Fat 6.7g, of which saturates 0.8g; Cholesterol 0mg; Calcium 36mg; Fibre 2.3g; Sodium 221mg.

QUICK SATAY SAUCE

THERE ARE MANY VERSIONS OF THIS TASTY PEANUT SAUCE. THIS ONE IS VERY SPEEDY AND IT TASTES DELICIOUS DRIZZLED OVER BARBECUED SKEWERS OF CHICKEN. FOR PARTIES, SPEAR CHUNKS OF CHICKEN WITH COCKTAIL STICKS AND ARRANGE AROUND A BOWL OF WARM SAUCE.

SERVES FOUR

INGREDIENTS
200ml/7fl oz/scant 1 cup coconut
cream
60ml/4 tbsp crunchy peanut butter
5ml/1 tsp Worcestershire sauce
Tabasco sauce, to taste
fresh coconut, to garnish (optional)

COOK'S TIP
Thick coconut milk can be substituted
for coconut cream, but take care to buy
an unsweetened variety for this recipe.

1 Pour the coconut cream into a small pan and heat it gently over a low heat for about 2 minutes.

2 Add the peanut butter and stir vigorously until it is blended into the coconut cream. Continue to heat until the mixture is warm but not boiling hot.

3 Add the Worcestershire sauce and a dash of Tabasco to taste. Pour into a serving bowl.

4 Use a potato peeler to shave thin curls from a piece of fresh coconut, if using. Scatter the coconut over the dish of your choice and serve immediately with the sauce.

Energy 108kcal/451kJ; Protein 3.6g; Carbohydrate 5.8g, of which sugars 4.9g; Fat 8g, of which saturates 2.1g; Cholesterol 0mg; Calcium 30mg; Fibre 0.8g; Sodium 150mg.

TOMATO KETCHUP

Sweet, tangy, spicy tomato ketchup is perfect for serving with barbecued or grilled burgers and sausages. This home-made variety is so much better than store-bought tomato ketchup, and the recipe will be enough to serve about 15 people.

MAKES ABOUT 1.3KG/3LB

INGREDIENTS
- 2.25kg/5lb very ripe tomatoes
- 1 onion
- 6 cloves
- 4 allspice berries
- 6 black peppercorns
- 1 fresh rosemary sprig
- 25g/1oz fresh root ginger, sliced
- 1 celery heart and leaves, chopped
- 30ml/2 tbsp soft light brown sugar
- 65ml/4½ tbsp raspberry vinegar
- 3 garlic cloves, peeled
- 15ml/1 tbsp salt

1 Skewer each tomato on a metal fork and hold in a gas flame for 1–2 minutes, turning, until the skin splits and wrinkles. Alternatively, plunge the tomatoes into boiling water for 30 seconds, then refresh in cold water. Peel away the skins and remove the seeds then chop and place in a large pan. Peel the onion, leaving the tip and root intact and stud it with the cloves

2 Tie the onion in a double layer of muslin (cheesecloth) with the allspice, peppercorns, rosemary and ginger and add to the pan. Add the celery to the pan with the remaining ingredients.

3 Bring the mixture to the boil over a fairly high heat, stirring occasionally. Once it is beginning to bubble, reduce the heat and simmer for 1½–2 hours, stirring regularly, until the liquid has reduced by around half.

4 Purée the mixture in a food processor, then return to the pan, bring to the boil and simmer for 15 minutes. Bottle in clean, sterilized jars and store in the refrigerator. Use within 2 weeks.

Energy 586kcal/2509kJ; Protein 19.9g; Carbohydrate 116.3g, of which sugars 114.9g; Fat 8.2g, of which saturates 2.5g; Cholesterol 0mg; Calcium 329mg; Fibre 29.1g; Sodium 409mg.

BARBECUE SAUCE

THIS TRADITIONAL SAUCE CAN BE PREPARED IN ADVANCE, BOTTLED AND USED WHENEVER YOU FEEL LIKE HOLDING A BARBECUE, AS IT WILL LAST FOR SEVERAL MONTHS IN A REFRIGERATOR. SERVE IT WITH YOUR FAVOURITE BURGERS, SAUSAGES, GRILLED CHICKEN AND BARBECUED VEGETABLES.

MAKES ABOUT 900ML/1½ PINTS/3¾ CUPS

INGREDIENTS

   30ml/2 tbsp olive oil
   1 large onion, chopped
   1 garlic clove, crushed
   1 fresh red chilli, seeded and sliced
   2 celery sticks, sliced
   1 large carrot, sliced
   1 medium cooking apple, quartered,
     cored, peeled and chopped
   450g/1lb ripe tomatoes, quartered
   2.5ml/½ tsp ground ginger
   150ml/¼ pint/⅔ cup malt vinegar
   1 bay leaf
   4 cloves
   4 black peppercorns
   50g/2oz/¼ cup soft light brown sugar
   10ml/2 tsp English mustard
   2.5ml/½ tsp salt

1 Heat the oil in a large heavy pan. Add the onion and cook over a low heat for 5 minutes.

2 Stir the garlic, chilli, celery and carrot into the onions and cook for 5 minutes, stirring frequently, until the onion just begins to colour.

3 Add the apple, tomatoes, ground ginger and malt vinegar to the pan and stir to combine.

COOK'S TIP

Just add a little yogurt to the barbecue sauce to make a quick and easy dip.

4 Put the bay leaf, cloves and peppercorns on to a square of muslin (cheesecloth) and tie into a bag with fine string. Add to the pan and bring to the boil. Reduce the heat, cover and simmer for about 45 minutes, stirring the mixture occasionally.

5 Add the sugar, mustard and salt to the pan and stir until the sugar dissolves. Simmer for 5 minutes. Leave to cool for 10 minutes, then remove the bag and discard.

6 Press the mixture through a sieve and return to the cleaned pan. Simmer for 10 minutes, or until thickened. Adjust the seasoning.

7 Pour the sauce into hot sterilized bottles or jars, then seal. Store in a cool, dark place and use within 6 months. Once opened, store in the refrigerator and use within 2 months.

VARIATION

For Quick Barbecue Sauce, heat 20ml/ 2 tbsp oil in a pan and fry 1 finely chopped onion and 2 crushed garlic cloves until soft. Add a 200g/7oz can of chopped tomatoes, 30ml/2 tbsp tomato purée (paste), 15ml/1 tbsp soft light brown sugar, 15ml/1 tbsp Worcestershire sauce, a dash of Tabasco sauce, 30ml/2 tbsp vinegar and 15ml/ 1 tbsp English mustard. Simmer for 10 minutes and serve hot or cold.

Energy 723kcal/3036kJ; Protein 12.2g; Carbohydrate 114.3g, of which sugars 102.5g; Fat 29.1g, of which saturates 3.8g; Cholesterol 0mg; Calcium 243mg; Fibre 14.2g; Sodium 118mg.

SPICED TAMARIND MUSTARD

TAMARIND HAS A DISTINCTIVE SWEET AND SOUR FLAVOUR, A DARK BROWN COLOUR AND STICKY TEXTURE. COMBINED WITH SPICES AND GROUND MUSTARD SEEDS, IT MAKES A WONDERFUL CONDIMENT. SERVE WITH STEAKS AND GRILLED MEATS.

MAKES ABOUT 200G/7OZ

INGREDIENTS
    115g/4oz tamarind block
    150ml/¼ pint/⅔ cup warm water
    50g/2oz/¼ cup yellow mustard seeds
    25ml/1½ tbsp black or brown
      mustard seeds
    10ml/2 tsp clear honey
    pinch of ground cardamom
    pinch of salt

COOK'S TIP
The mustard will be ready to eat in 3–4 days. It should be stored in a cool, dark place and used within 4 months.

1 Put the tamarind in a small bowl and pour over the water. Leave to soak for 30 minutes. Mash to a pulp with a fork, then strain through a fine sieve into a bowl.

2 Grind the mustard seeds in a spice mill or coffee grinder and add to the tamarind with the remaining ingredients. Spoon into sterilized jars, cover and seal.

Energy 262kcal/1095kJ; Protein 15g; Carbohydrate 18.9g, of which sugars 8.5g; Fat 22.8g, of which saturates 0.8g; Cholesterol 2mg; Calcium 207mg; Fibre 1.1g; Sodium 64mg.

HOT FUDGE SAUCE

IF YOU'RE LOOKING FOR A QUICK AND EASY BARBECUE DESSERT, MAKE UP SOME OF THIS WICKED SAUCE TO ACCOMPANY ICE CREAM OR BARBECUED FRUIT, AND SIMPLY REHEAT IT IN A SMALL PAN ON THE GRILL RACK. IT ALSO MAKES A LUSCIOUS SUNDAE WITH BANANAS, CREAM, ICE CREAM AND ALMONDS.

SERVES FOUR

INGREDIENTS
   60ml/4 tbsp light muscovado
      (brown) sugar
   115g/4oz/⅓ cup golden (light
      corn) syrup
   45ml/3 tbsp strong black coffee
   5ml/1 tsp ground cinnamon
   150g/5oz dark (bittersweet)
      chocolate, broken up
   75ml/5 tbsp whipping cream
   45ml/3 tbsp coffee liqueur (optional)
To serve
   600ml/1 pint/2½ cups vanilla
      ice cream
   600ml/1 pint/2½ cups coffee
      ice cream
   2 large ripe bananas
   whipped cream and toasted sliced
      almonds, to top

1 Combine the sugar, golden syrup, coffee and cinnamon in a heavy pan. Bring to the boil. Boil the mixture, stirring constantly, for about 5 minutes.

COOK'S TIP
Use a good quality, dark (bittersweet) chocolate with at least 70% cocoa solids for a richer sauce.

2 Remove from the heat and stir in the chocolate. When melted and smooth, stir in the cream and liqueur, if using. Let the sauce cool just to lukewarm, or, if made ahead, reheat gently while assembling the sundaes.

3 To serve as an ice cream sundae, using an ice-cream scoop, fill four sundae dishes with 1 scoop each of vanilla and coffee ice cream.

4 Slice the bananas on top of each dish. Pour the warm sauce over the bananas.

5 Add a generous rosette of whipped cream over the bananas, and top with the toasted almonds.

Energy 986kcal/4137kJ; Protein 13.8g; Carbohydrate 133.7g, of which sugars 128.9g; Fat 44g, of which saturates 29.4g; Cholesterol 95mg; Calcium 339mg; Fibre 1.5g; Sodium 266mg.

SABAYON SAUCE

THIS FROTHY SAUCE IS VERY VERSATILE AND CAN BE SERVED ALONE WITH DESSERT BISCUITS OR HOT OVER CAKE, FRUIT OR ICE CREAM. IT IS GOOD SERVED COLD WITH BARBECUED DESSERTS, BECAUSE YOU CAN PREPARE IT EARLIER IN THE DAY, BUT NEVER LET IT STAND BEFORE SERVING AS IT WILL COLLAPSE.

SERVES FOUR TO SIX

INGREDIENTS

1 egg
2 egg yolks
75g/3oz/scant ½ cup caster sugar
150ml/¼ pint/⅔ cup Marsala or
   other sweet white wine
finely grated rind and juice of
   1 lemon
dessert biscuits, to serve

1 Put the egg, yolks and sugar into a medium bowl and whisk until they are pale and thick.

2 Stand the bowl over a pan of hot, but not boiling, water. Gradually add the Marsala or sweet white wine and lemon juice, a little at a time, whisking vigorously all the time.

3 Continue whisking until it is thick enough to leave a trail. If serving hot, serve immediately.

4 To serve the sabayon cold, place it over a bowl of iced water and continue whisking until chilled. Add the finely grated lemon rind and stir in. Pour into small glasses and serve at once, with the dessert biscuits.

COOK'S TIP
A generous pinch of arrowroot whisked together with the egg yolks and sugar will prevent the sauce collapsing too quickly.

Energy 105kcal/444kJ; Protein 2.1g; Carbohydrate 14.5g, of which sugars 14.5g; Fat 2.8g, of which saturates 0.8g; Cholesterol 99mg; Calcium 23mg; Fibre 0g; Sodium 19mg.

PAPAYA DIP

SWEET AND SMOOTH PAPAYA TEAMS UP WELL WITH CRÈME FRAÎCHE TO MAKE A LUSCIOUS, TROPICAL SWEET DIP WHICH IS VERY GOOD FOR DIPPING WITH SWEET BISCUITS OR FRESH FRUIT. IF FRESH COCONUT IS NOT AVAILABLE, BUY COCONUT STRANDS AND LIGHTLY TOAST IN A HOT OVEN UNTIL GOLDEN.

SERVES SIX

INGREDIENTS
   2 ripe papayas
   200ml/7fl oz/scant 1 cup
     crème fraîche
   1 piece of preserved stem ginger
   fresh coconut, to decorate
   papaya or other fresh fruit, to serve

1 Halve the papayas lengthways, but do not peel them. Scoop out the insides and discard the seeds.

2 Separate the seeds from the flesh and process the latter until smooth, using a food processor or blender.

3 Stir in the crème fraîche and process until well blended. Finely chop the stem ginger and stir it in, then chill until ready to serve.

4 Pierce a hole in the "eye" of the coconut and drain off the liquid. Put the coconut in a polythene bag. Hold it securely in one hand and hit it sharply with a hammer.

5 Remove the shell from a piece of coconut, then snap the nut into pieces no wider than 2.5cm/1in. Use a swivel-bladed vegetable peeler to shave off 2cm/¾in lengths of coconut. Scatter these over the dip. Serve with pieces of extra papaya or other fresh fruit.

Energy 156kcal/646kJ; Protein 1.2g; Carbohydrate 8.1g, of which sugars 8g; Fat 13.4g, of which saturates 9g; Cholesterol 38mg; Calcium 39mg; Fibre 1.8g; Sodium 12mg.

STRAWBERRY AND PASSION FRUIT COULIS

A FRESH FRUIT COULIS TASTES HEAVENLY WITH ALL KINDS OF DESSERTS AND IT TRANSFORMS ICE CREAM, CRÈME FRAÎCHE OR YOGURT INTO SOMETHING SPECIAL. THE SWEET AND DELECTABLE FLAVOURS OF STRAWBERRY AND PASSION FRUIT MAKE A PERFECT SAUCE FOR A SUNDAE OF FROZEN YOGURT.

SERVES FOUR

INGREDIENTS

- 175g/6oz/1½ cups strawberries, hulled and halved
- 1 passion fruit
- 10ml/2 tsp icing (confectioners') sugar (optional)

To serve

- 175g/6oz/1½ cups strawberries, hulled and halved
- 2 ripe peaches, stoned (pitted) and chopped
- 8 scoops (about 350g/12oz) vanilla or strawberry frozen yogurt

1 Purée the strawberries in a food processor. Scoop out the passion fruit pulp and add it to the coulis. Sweeten with icing sugar, if necessary.

2 Spoon half the strawberries and half the chopped peaches into four tall sundae glasses.

3 Add a scoop of frozen yogurt. Set aside a few choice pieces of fruit for decoration, and use the rest to make a further layer on the top of each sundae. Top each with a final scoop of frozen yogurt.

4 Pour the strawberry and passion fruit coulis over, and decorate the sundaes with the reserved strawberries and pieces of peach. Serve immediately.

VARIATION
You can make a coulis with any berry fruit with or without the passion fruit. Raspberries are particularly fine because they have a delicate and sweet flavour.

COOK'S TIP
Fresh summer strawberries are unlikely to need sweetening, but some varieties may need a little sugar. Taste the coulis before adding the icing sugar.

Energy 126kcal/534kJ; Protein 4.8g; Carbohydrate 26.6g, of which sugars 26.6g; Fat 0.8g, of which saturates 0.4g; Cholesterol 4mg; Calcium 150mg; Fibre 1.7g; Sodium 63mg.

SAFFRON BREAD SKEWERS

THIS ANTIPODEAN'S FIRESIDE FAVOURITE, CALLED DAMPER, IS ALSO A BIT OF A GIRL GUIDE
TRADITION. IT'S A FUN THING FOR A LONG, LAZY BEACH BARBECUE. IT IS USUAL TO COOK DAMPER
IN THE EMBERS OF THE FIRE, BUT ROSEMARY SKEWERS ARE A STYLISH ALTERNATIVE.

SERVES EIGHT

INGREDIENTS
  24 rosemary spikes or wooden
    skewers (or 12 of each)
  500g/1¼lb/5 cups plain
    (all-purpose) flour
  25ml/1½ tbsp baking powder
  250g/9oz/generous 1 cup plus
    30ml/2 tbsp butter
  30ml/2 tbsp chopped fresh rosemary,
    plus 1 sprig
  1 large pinch of saffron threads
    mixed with 15ml/1 tbsp
    boiling water
  175ml/6fl oz/¾ cup milk
  salt

1 Soak the rosemary spikes or wooden skewers in cold water for 30 minutes. Sift the flour, baking powder and salt into a large bowl. Rub in 200g/7oz/ scant 1 cup of the butter until the mixture looks like fine breadcrumbs, then add the chopped rosemary.

2 Strain the saffron water into the milk and add to the flour mixture all in one go. Mix to a paste with your hands and knead until the dough is smooth and elastic. Melt the remaining butter and stir it with the rosemary sprig to infuse it with the flavour.

3 Prepare the barbecue. Drain the skewers or rosemary spikes. Divide the dough into 24 equal pieces and twist one piece around each skewer or spike.

4 Position a lightly oiled grill rack over the hot coals. Grill the spiked dough over medium-high heat for 5 minutes, turning often, until cooked and golden. Brush occasionally with the rosemary dipped in butter and serve the saffron bread hot.

COOK'S TIP
If you're cooking a pan of soup *al fresco*, these breads taste terrific dipped in the soup.

Energy 456kcal/1905kJ; Protein 6.8g; Carbohydrate 49.8g, of which sugars 2.2g; Fat 26.9g, of which saturates 16.6g; Cholesterol 68mg; Calcium 119mg; Fibre 1.9g; Sodium 201mg.

SESAME BURGER BUNS

PUT YOUR HOME-MADE BURGERS INSIDE A TRADITIONAL SOFT BURGER BUN WITH A SESAME SEED TOPPING. TRADITIONALLY, SOFT BUNS WORK BEST WITH MEAT OR VEGETARIAN BURGERS AND ARE EASIER TO HOLD AND TO EAT THAN A CRUSTY ROLL. JUST ADD RELISH!

<u>MAKES SIX</u>

INGREDIENTS
   500g/1¼lb/5 cups strong white
      bread flour
   7.5ml/1½ tsp salt
   25g/1oz butter, softened
   5ml/1 tsp easy-blend (rapid-rise)
      dried yeast
   15ml/1 tbsp sugar
   150ml/¼ pint/⅔ cup lukewarm milk
   about 150ml/¼ pint/⅔ cup
      lukewarm water
   10ml/2 tsp sesame seeds

1 Sift the flour and salt into a bowl and rub in the butter with your fingertips. Add the yeast and sugar. Mix well. Make a well in the centre and pour in the milk and the water. Stir the liquid into the flour from the centre outwards to make a soft dough.

2 Knead the dough on a lightly floured surface for 10 minutes then return to the cleaned bowl and cover with lightly oiled clear film (plastic wrap). Leave in a warm place until doubled in size (about 1 hour).

3 Knock back (punch down) the dough then divide into six equal pieces. Form into rounds and place on a greased baking sheet. Cover with lightly oiled clear film and leave to rise for 1 hour or until doubled in size.

4 Meanwhile, preheat the oven to 220°C/425°F/Gas 7. Brush the buns with a little milk and sprinkle with sesame seeds. Cook the buns for 15–20 minutes, or until golden brown. Cool on a wire rack.

VARIATION
To use a bread machine, substitute the milk and water quantities with 300ml/½ pint/1¼ cups water and include 30ml/2 tbsp milk powder to the above ingredients. Put the ingredients in the bread machine in the order specified in the manufacturer's instructions. Set to a basic dough setting and then shape into buns and proceed as above.

Energy 352kcal/1488kJ; Protein 9.2g; Carbohydrate 68.6g, of which sugars 5.1g; Fat 6.4g, of which saturates 2.8g; Cholesterol 10mg; Calcium 166mg; Fibre 2.8g; Sodium 39mg.

CORN TORTILLAS

THESE DELICIOUS AND VERSATILE MEXICAN SPECIALITIES COOK VERY QUICKLY. GRIDDLE THEM OVER THE BARBECUE AND HAVE A CLEAN DISH TOWEL ON HAND TO KEEP THE HOT STACKS WARM.

MAKES ABOUT FOURTEEN

INGREDIENTS
275g/10oz/2½ cups masa harina
250–350ml/8–12fl oz/
  1–1½ cups water

COOK'S TIPS
• When making tortillas, it is important to get the dough texture right. If it is too dry and crumbly, add a little water; if it is too wet, add more masa harina. If you do not manage to flatten the ball of dough into a neat circle the first time, just re-roll it and try again.
• These tortillas can also be cooked in the oven at 150°C/300°F/Gas 2.

1 Prepare the barbecue. Put the masa harina into a bowl and stir in 250ml/8fl oz/1 cup of the measured water, mixing it to a soft dough that just holds together. If it is too dry, add a little more water. Cover the bowl with a cloth and set aside for 15 minutes.

2 Knead the dough lightly, divide into 14 pieces, and shape into balls.

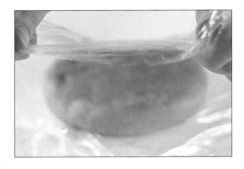

3 Using a rolling pin, roll out each ball between sheets of clear plastic film until you have a thin round of dough measuring about 15cm/6in in diameter.

4 Put a griddle over the hot coals and griddle the first tortilla for 1 minute. Turn it over and cook for a minute more. Wrap in a clean dish towel and keep warm. Repeat for the other tortillas.

COOK'S TIP
An alternative to rolling out rounds of tortilla dough with a rolling pin is to use a tortilla press. Open the press and line both sides with sheets of clear plastic film. Shape the tortilla dough into balls, put one ball on the press and bring the top down firmly to flatten it into a neat round. Open the press, peel off the top layer of plastic and, using the bottom layer, lift the tortilla out of the press. Peel off this layer of plastic and repeat the process with the other dough balls.

Energy 72kcal/303kJ; Protein 1.9g; Carbohydrate 14.4g, of which sugars 0g; Fat 0.7g, of which saturates 0g; Cholesterol 0mg; Calcium 1mg; Fibre 0.4g; Sodium 0mg.

FLOUR TORTILLAS

HOME-MADE TORTILLAS TASTE SO GOOD FILLED WITH BARBECUED VEGETABLES AND THINLY SLICED CHICKEN OR MEAT. YOU CAN MAKE THEM IN ADVANCE AND THEN REHEAT THEM TO SERVE.

MAKES ABOUT FOURTEEN

INGREDIENTS
225g/8oz/2 cups plain
   (all-purpose) flour
5ml/1 tsp salt
15ml/1 tbsp lard or white cooking fat
120ml/4fl oz/½ cup water

1 Sift the flour and salt into a large mixing bowl. Gradually rub in the lard or white cooking fat using your fingertips until the mixture resembles coarse breadcrumbs.

2 Gradually add the water and mix to a soft dough. Knead lightly, form into a ball, cover with a cloth and leave to rest for 15 minutes. Prepare the barbecue.

COOK'S TIPS
• Make flour tortillas whenever masa harina is difficult to find. To keep them soft and pliable, make sure they are kept warm until ready to serve, and eat as soon as possible.
• These flour tortillas can also be cooked in the oven at 150°C/300°F/Gas 2.

3 Carefully divide the dough into about 14 portions and form these portions into small balls. One by one, roll out each ball of dough on a lightly floured wooden board to a round measuring about 15cm/6in. Trim the rounds if necessary.

4 Heat an ungreased flat griddle or frying pan over a medium heat. Cook the tortillas for about 1½–2 minutes on each side. Turn over with a palette knife or metal spatula when the bottom begins to brown. Wrap in a clean dish towel to keep warm until ready to serve.

Energy 64kcal/272kJ; Protein 1.5g; Carbohydrate 12.5g, of which sugars 0.2g; Fat 1.3g, of which saturates 0.5g; Cholesterol 1mg; Calcium 23mg; Fibre 0.5g; Sodium 141mg.

PITTA BREAD

FOR A RELAXED BARBECUE WHERE FINGERS ARE KEPT FAIRLY CLEAN, YOU CAN'T BEAT SERVING TASTY SLICES OR CHUNKS OF FOOD IN PITTA BREAD POCKETS. YOU CAN MAKE THE DOUGH EARLIER AND THEN COOK IT IN A HEAVY FRYING PAN ON THE BARBECUE.

5 Prepare the barbecue. Heat a large, heavy frying pan over a medium-high heat. When it is smoking hot, gently lay one piece of flattened dough in the pan and cook for 15–20 seconds. Carefully turn it over and cook the second side for about 1 minute.

6 When large bubbles start to form on the bread, turn it over again. It should puff up. Using a clean dish towel, gently press on the bread where the bubbles have formed. Cook for a total of 3 minutes, then remove the pitta from the pan. Repeat with the remaining dough until all the breads have been cooked.

7 Wrap the pitta breads in a clean dish towel, stacking them as each one is cooked. Serve the pitta breads hot while they are soft and moist.

MAKES TWELVE

INGREDIENTS
   500g/1¼lb/4½ cups strong white
     bread flour, or half white and
     half wholemeal (whole-wheat)
   7g/¼oz packet easy-blend
     (rapid-rise) dried yeast
   15ml/1 tbsp salt
   15ml/1 tbsp olive oil
   250ml/8fl oz/1 cup water

1 Combine the flour, yeast and salt. In a large bowl, mix together the oil and water, then stir in half of the flour mixture, stirring in the same direction, until the dough is stiff. Knead in the remaining flour.

2 Place the dough in a clean bowl, cover with a clean dish towel and leave in a warm place for at least 30 minutes and up to 2 hours.

3 Knead the dough for 10 minutes, or until smooth. Lightly oil the bowl, place the dough in it, cover again and leave to rise in a warm place for about 1 hour, or until doubled in size.

4 Divide the dough into 12 equal-size pieces. With lightly floured hands, flatten each piece, then roll out into a round about 20cm/8in in diameter and about 5mm–1cm/¼–½in thick. Keep the rolled breads covered with a clean dish towel while you make the remaining breads.

VARIATION
To cook the breads in the oven, preheat the oven to 220°C/425°F/Gas 7. Fill an unglazed or partially glazed dish with hot water and place in the bottom of the oven. Alternatively, arrange a handful of unglazed tiles in the bottom of the oven. Use either a non-stick baking sheet or a lightly oiled ordinary baking sheet and heat in the oven for a few minutes. Place two or three pieces of flattened dough on to the hot baking sheet and place in the hottest part of the oven. Bake for 2–3 minutes. They should puff up. Repeat with the remaining dough until all the pittas have been cooked.

Energy 150kcal/638kJ; Protein 3.9g; Carbohydrate 32.4g, of which sugars 0.6g; Fat 1.5g, of which saturates 0.2g; Cholesterol 0mg; Calcium 59mg; Fibre 1.3g; Sodium 493mg.

CIABATTA

THE VERY WET DOUGH USED TO MAKE CIABATTA BREAD RESULTS IN A LIGHT AND AIRY CRUMB. CIABATTA IS ONE OF THE MOST POPULAR BREADS AND TASTES WONDERFUL WHEN HOME-MADE. IT CAN BE USED AS AN ACCOMPANIMENT TO BARBECUED FOOD OR SLICED, TOPPED WITH DELICIOUS MORSELS AND GRILLED.

MAKES THREE LOAVES

INGREDIENTS
For the starter
   7g/¼oz fresh yeast
   175–200ml/6–7fl oz/¾–scant 1 cup
     lukewarm water
   350g/12oz/3 cups unbleached strong
     white bread flour, plus extra
     for dusting
For the dough
   15g/½oz fresh yeast
   400ml/14fl oz/1⅔ cups
     lukewarm water
   60ml/4 tbsp lukewarm milk
   500g/1¼lb/5 cups unbleached strong
     white bread flour
   10ml/2 tsp salt
   45ml/3 tbsp extra virgin olive oil

1 For the starter, cream the yeast with a little of the measured water. Sift the flour into a large bowl. Gradually mix in the yeast mixture and sufficient of the remaining water to form a firm dough.

2 Turn out the starter dough on to a lightly floured surface and knead for about 5 minutes until smooth and elastic. Return the dough to the bowl, cover with lightly oiled clear film (plastic wrap) and leave in a warm place for 12–15 hours, or until the dough has risen and is starting to collapse.

3 Sprinkle three baking sheets with flour. Mix the yeast for the dough with a little of the measured water until creamy, then mix in the remainder. Add the yeast mixture to the starter and gradually mix in.

4 Mix in the milk, beating thoroughly with a wooden spoon. Using your hand, gradually incorporate the flour, lifting the dough as you mix. Mixing the dough will take 15 minutes or more and it forms a very wet mix, which is impossible to knead on a work surface.

5 Beat in the salt and olive oil. Cover with lightly oiled clear film and leave to rise, in a warm place, for 1½–2 hours, or until doubled in bulk.

6 With a spoon, carefully tip one-third of the dough at a time on to the baking sheets without knocking back (punching down) the dough in the process.

7 Using floured hands, shape into rough oblong loaf shapes, about 2.5cm/1in thick. Flatten slightly with splayed fingers. Sprinkle with flour and leave to rise in a warm place for 30 minutes.

8 Meanwhile, preheat the oven to 220°C/425°F/Gas 7. Bake for 25–30 minutes, or until golden brown and sounding hollow when tapped on the base. Transfer to a wire rack to cool.

Energy 1074kcal/4554kJ; Protein 27.3g; Carbohydrate 221.1g, of which sugars 5.2g; Fat 15g, of which saturates 2.4g; Cholesterol 1mg; Calcium 421mg; Fibre 8.8g; Sodium 1327mg.

GARLIC AND HERB BREAD

THIS IRRESISTIBLE GARLIC BREAD INCLUDES PLENTY OF FRESH MIXED HERBS. YOU CAN VARY THE OVERALL FLAVOUR BY USING DIFFERENT HERBS. PREPARE IT EARLIER AND HEAT IT IN THE OVEN WHEN YOU NEED IT, OR WARM IT UP ON THE GRILL RACK.

SERVES THREE TO FOUR

INGREDIENTS
1 baguette or bloomer loaf
For the garlic and herb butter
115g/4oz/½ cup unsalted (sweet) butter, softened
5–6 large garlic cloves, finely chopped or crushed
30–45ml/2–3 tbsp chopped fresh herbs (such as parsley, chervil and a little tarragon)
15ml/1 tbsp chopped fresh chives
coarse salt and ground black pepper

1 Preheat the oven to 200°C/400°F/ Gas 6. Make the garlic and herb butter by beating the butter with the garlic, herbs, chives and seasoning.

VARIATIONS
• Use 105ml/7 tbsp extra virgin olive oil instead of the butter.
• Flavour the butter with garlic, a little chopped fresh chilli, grated (shredded) lime rind and chopped fresh coriander (cilantro).
• Add chopped, pitted black olives or sun-dried tomatoes to the butter with a little grated lemon rind.

2 Cut the bread into 1cm/½in thick diagonal slices, but be sure to leave them attached at the base so that the loaf stays intact.

3 Spread the garlic and herb butter between the slices evenly, being careful not to detach them, and then spread any remaining butter over the top of the loaf.

4 Wrap the loaf in foil and bake in the preheated oven for 20–25 minutes, or until the butter is melted and the crust is golden and crisp. Cut the loaf into slices to serve.

COOK'S TIP
This loaf makes an excellent addition to a barbecue. If space permits, place the foil-wrapped loaf on top of the barbecue and cook for about the same length of time as for oven baking. Turn the foil parcel over several times to ensure it cooks evenly.

Energy 920kcal/3877kJ; Protein 22.1g; Carbohydrate 135.1g, of which sugars 7.2g; Fat 36.2g, of which saturates 20.8g; Cholesterol 82mg; Calcium 317mg; Fibre 6.3g; Sodium 1714mg.

RED ONION AND ROSEMARY FOCACCIA

MAKE THIS RICH AND TASTY ITALIAN BREAD WITH ITS TOPPING OF ROSEMARY AND RED ONION TO SERVE WITH YOUR BARBECUE FEAST. YOU COULD SERVE IT WITH A TOMATO, BASIL AND MOZZARELLA SALAD FOR A QUICK AND EASY FIRST COURSE WHILE YOU WAIT FOR THE COALS TO HEAT UP FOR BARBECUING.

2 Set the yeast aside in a warm, but not hot, place for 10 minutes, until it has turned frothy.

3 Add the yeast, the remaining water, 15ml/1 tbsp of the oil and the chopped rosemary to the flour. Mix all the ingredients together to form a dough, then gather the dough into a ball and knead on a floured work surface for about 5 minutes, until smooth and elastic. You may need to add a little extra flour if the dough is very sticky.

4 Place the dough in a lightly oiled bowl and slip it into a polythene bag or cover with oiled clear film (plastic wrap) and leave to rise. The length of time you leave it for depends on the temperature: leave it all day in a cool place, overnight in the refrigerator, or for 1–2 hours in a warm, but not hot, place.

5 Lightly oil a baking sheet. Knead the dough to form a flat loaf that is about 30cm/12in round or square. Place on the baking sheet, cover with oiled polythene or clear film and leave to rise again in a warm place for a further 40–60 minutes.

6 Preheat the oven to 220°C/425°F/ Gas 7. Press indentations into the dough with your fingers Toss the onion in 15ml/1 tbsp of the oil and scatter over the loaf with the rosemary sprigs and some coarse salt. Bake for 15–20 minutes until golden brown. Serve the bread freshly baked or leave to cool on the baking sheet and serve warm.

SERVES FOUR TO FIVE

INGREDIENTS
   450g/1lb/4 cups strong white bread
     flour, plus extra for dusting
   5ml/1 tsp salt
   7g/¼oz fresh yeast or generous 5ml/
     1 tsp dried yeast
   2.5ml/½ tsp light muscovado
     (brown) sugar
   250ml/8fl oz/1 cup lukewarm water
   60ml/4 tbsp extra virgin olive oil,
     plus extra for greasing
   5ml/1 tsp very finely chopped fresh
     rosemary, plus 6–8 small sprigs
   1 red onion, thinly sliced
   coarse salt

1 Sift the flour and salt into a bowl. Set aside. Cream the fresh yeast with the sugar, and gradually stir in half the water. If using dried yeast, stir the sugar into the water and sprinkle the dried yeast over the surface.

Energy 496kcal/2094kJ; Protein 11g; Carbohydrate 90.4g, of which sugars 3.8g; Fat 12.5g, of which saturates 1.8g; Cholesterol 000mg; Calcium 167mg; Fibre 4g; Sodium 496mg.

INDEX

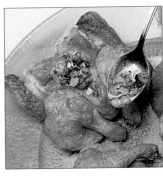